UNLEASHING GREATNESS
A STRATEGY FOR SCHOOL IMPROVEMENT

DAVID HOPKINS

Orders: please contact Hachette UK Distribution, Hely Hutchinson Centre, Milton Road, Didcot, Oxfordshire, OX11 7HH. Telephone: +44 (0)1235 827827. Email education@hachette.co.uk. Lines are open from 9 a.m. to 5 p.m., Monday to Friday.

ISBN: 9781398389090

© David Hopkins 2024

First published in 2024 by
John Catt from Hodder Education,
An Hachette UK Company
15 Riduna Park, Station Road,
Melton, Woodbridge IP12 1QT
Telephone: +44 (0) 1394 389850

4500 140th Ave North,
Suite 101, Clearwater,
FL 33762-3848, US
Telephone: +1 561 448 1987

www.johncatt.com

This book is dedicated to:
Trish,
the love of my life.

And my children:
Jeroen, Jessica Cariad and Dylan,
in whom I am inordinately proud.

CONTENTS

Part 2: All the moving parts

Chapter 3: The story is always about moral purpose

Part 3: Moving to scale

ACKNOWLEDGEMENTS

I have been blessed throughout my educational career by having wonderful colleagues who have sustained, educated, and cared for me both personally and professionally. As that career has progressed, I am humbled to realise that the list continues to grow. The generosity of colleagues and friends who are driven by a moral purpose is the striking characteristic of those working in our field. They are the gift that keeps on giving.

Principally, I owe an enormous great debt of gratitude to my old teachers and mentors – Michael Fullan, Maurice Gibbons, David Hargreaves, Bruce Joyce, Tony McKay, Roger Putnam and Marv Wideen – without them none of this would have happened.

There is a wider group of colleagues from the visible and invisible global college with whom I have collaborated and learned from over the years and for whom I have enormous respect and feel privileged to have worked with. Among them are the late Ray Bolam, Sir Michael Barber, Emily Calhoun, Chris Chapman, Chris Day, Brent Davies, David Egan, the late Richard Elmore, Graham Handscomb, Andy Hargreaves, Alma Harris, John Hattie, Rob Higham, Ken Leithwood, the late Peter Matthews, the late Matthew Miles, John Munro, Peter Norman. Dave Reynolds, the late Jean Rudduck, Pasi Sahlberg, Pam Sammons, Richard Schmuck, and the late Sam Stringfield.

In relation to the ideas and strategies of this book, there are those colleagues with whom I developed the school improvement programmes described on these pages: Improving the Quality of Education for All – Mel Ainscow and Mel West, during our Cambridge days; Curiosity and

Powerful Learning – Wayne Craig, Victoria and Brad Russell, New South Wales; *Unleashing Greatness* and the University of Bolton *Laboratory School Network* – Vice Chancellor George Holmes, Mohammed Abdel-Haq and Geoff Baker. Colleagues at ACEL (Australian Council for Educational Leadership) and MCREL (Denver Colorado) have been enormously supportive in disseminating and publishing the Curiosity and Powerful Learning programme and manuals.

Members of the Curiosity and Powerful Learning programme in New South Wales and the University of Bolton's Laboratory School Network have contributed cameos and case studies to the book. Many thanks to Stacey Exner and Julie Kennedy, Chris Bingley, Helen Phillips and Nic Brindle, and Stacey Postle, who wrote the case studies and to Helen Bradford-Keegan, Jo Lindon, Simon Oldfield and Stacey Postle who contributed the cameos. Thanks also to John Catt Educational who sourced the cover for the book – *The Great Wave off Kanagawa* by Hokusai. Although there are various interpretations of that evocative image, it captures for me the essence of *Unleashing Greatness*.

I remain indebted and in awe of the work of those thousands of heads, principals, and teachers with whom I have been privileged to work with in recent years. You are too many to name, but your work has inspired me and is reflected in the pages that follow. I must however mention Geoff Ashton, Tom Clark, Chris Cotton, Karen Endicott, Andrew Fell, Sir Paul Grant, Sir Dexter Hutt, David Jackson, Oli Knight, Jo Lindon, Sir Alasdair Macdonald, Kevan Naughton, Stacey Postle, Marcia Puckey, John Perry, Joe Spence and Sir Mike Wilkins.

Finally, I would never have got to the starting point of this book, nor many other things if it had not been for the personal and professional love and support of Trish Franey. An outstanding educator and leader in her own right, she has provided an exemplary example of how the 'committed individual' lives a personal and professional life to the benefit of both and all those around her.

PREFACE

I have been fortunate enough to have written many books on education over the past forty years. So why is there a need for one more? For most of that time I have self-consciously striven to locate my professional practice in the middle of that triangle bounded by the vertices of practice, research and policy. In recent years, as part of that commitment, I have written a range of practical manuals for middle tier professionals, school leaders, improvement teams and teachers. On reflection, I feel that these manuals have been too 'free floating' and that there is a need for a book that provides a rationale, conceptual framework and scaffolding for their use.

In choosing a title for the book, I owe a debt of gratitude to my friend and colleague Sir Michael Barber (2009), who once memorably pointed out that, ' … one can mandate the move from poor to adequate and fair to good, but that as one progresses, one needs to unleash greatness'. I can think of no more apposite title for this book.

The purpose of this book therefore is to outline a school improvement strategy that assists in Unleashing Greatness. As such it inevitably builds on our proven school improvement programmes and manuals: Improving the Quality of Education for All (IQEA) and Curiosity and Powerful Learning (C&PL).[1] In particular, the practical manuals developed as part

---

1   For further details see:
    Hopkins, D. (2002) *Improving the Quality of Education for All* (Second Edition). London: Fulton.
    Hopkins, D. and Craig, W. (2015/18a) *The System and Powerful Learning*. Melbourne: McREL International [Kindle Edition 2018 available from Amazon and www.profdavidhopkins.com].

of the C&PL programme are referred to frequently in what follows as they provide strategies and tools for delivering and embedding improvement at the school level. They should be regarded as essential companions to this current volume.

The book also draws on the evidence base and reviews of practice described and analysed in my school improvement trilogy: *School Improvement for Real* (2001), *Every School a Great School* (2007), and *Exploding the Myths of School Reform* (2013).

- In *School Improvement for Real* (2001), I attempted to summarise the knowledge base on school improvement as it then existed some twenty-five years ago.

- In *Every School a Great School* (2007), I explored how previously, as a senior civil servant and chief adviser to the secretary of state on school standards in a reforming government and working with ministers such as Estelle Morris and David Miliband, we not only raised standards but also introduced personalised learning and its implications into the system.

- In *Exploding the Myths of School Reform* (2013), I used the artifice of the 'myth' to illustrate principles for school and system improvement using the evidence from the emerging knowledge base on global system change.

In writing this book I inevitably draw on much of that material, but in a way that is intended to reformulate and add value. This, I believe, is a justifiable and mature way of conducting action research and contributing to practical improvement. In the introduction to *Exploding the Myths*, I mentioned David Hockney's Bigger Picture exhibition that we visited during the writing of that book and reflected on his technique of 'layering'. Martin Gayford (2011), in his book *A Bigger Message: Conversations with David Hockney*, described the approach like this:

> ... *I began to grasp the point of Hockney's insistence on that word 'layers'. A painter is not simply adding more and more paint to a canvas or piece of paper; fresh thoughts and observations are going on, each adjusting the one that came before. The process of writing – reflecting on the subject, editing and adding to what we have written before –*

is essentially similar. Much human experience, when one comes to think about it, is a matter of layering. We understand the present by comparing it with the past – layer on layer – then we think about it afterwards, adding more and more layers. As we do, our angle of vision changes.

As it so happens, in the preparation of this book we visited Hockney's audacious and stupendous *Bigger and Closer* exhibition at the Lightroom, Kings Cross. In the exhibition guide (Lightroom 2023). Hockney says:

I like looking at things and there's a lot of ways to look at things. ... With photography, you're not really looking. But when you are drawing one blade of grass, you're looking and then you see the other blades of grass and you're always seeing more. ... I've painted for 60 years now. I'm still painting. And I'm still enjoying it enormously. Yes.

Without wishing to strain the analogy too much, one can equate photography with top-down instrumental change: in Michael Barber's words *mandating the move from poor to adequate and fair to good.* Painting is more akin to the fine-grained contextual analysis and planning one engages in as part of authentic school improvement; it is about *Unleashing Greatness.*

Let me give an example of what I mean from a primary school who belongs to the University of Bolton Laboratory School network where I recently led an instructional round.

Early in the round I went into a Year 5 classroom – it was quiet, there was no sound, all the students were working individually completing some form of test. As I looked over one student's shoulder, let us call him Louis, I saw that he was fully engaged in circling modal verbs, underlining relative clauses, identifying relative pronouns and so on. We smiled, I introduced myself and asked him how he was doing. 'Fine', he said and returned to his task.

Later in the round, I entered a different classroom, but surprisingly it contained the same group of students that I had observed earlier. Louis recognised me and called me over to join the group that he was working with. He explained to me the task that they were engaged in and demonstrated how everyone on the table was contributing to solving the problem. As I was about to move on and join another group Louis stopped me. I guess by then he knew that I was interested in how students learned and he said: 'Do you know what is so good about being in Year 5?'

I intimated that I did not, so he told me: 'Well in Year 4 when I had a problem and asked the teacher, she told me the answer. But in Year 5 when I have a problem and ask the teacher, she explains how I can solve the problem myself. That is great and I learn much more that way.'

Having explained the secrets of the universe to me, Louis smiled and happily returned to his group. For me in cameo that is the difference between mandating the move from adequate to good and Unleashing Greatness.

My intent is to use this preface to explain the genesis and rationale for the book, particularly the way in which it draws on previous work and the values underpinning the *Unleashing Greatness* framework. So, before I launch into the main narrative, I would like to share with the reader a couple of quotations from Jerome Bruner and Lawrence Stenhouse that I have found inspirational, sustaining and keep ringing in my ears as I write. They have also helped me define my approach to *Unleashing Greatness*, personalisation and the achievement of both equity and excellence.

First, Jerome Bruner (1966:21), the distinguished American psychologist. This is a quotation from *Towards a Theory of Instruction*, which I read early in my teaching career:

> *I suspect that much of growth starts out by our turning around on our own traces and recoding in new forms, with the aid of adult tutors, what we have been doing or seeing, then going on to new modes of organisation with the new products that have been formed by these recodings. We say, 'I see what I'm doing now.' 'So that's what the thing is.' The new models are formed in increasingly powerful representational systems. It is this that leads me to think that the heart of the educational process consists of providing aids and dialogues for translating experience into more powerful systems of notation and ordering. And it is for this reason that I think a theory of development must be linked both to a theory of knowledge and to a theory of instruction, **or be doomed to triviality**.*

Bruner would argue that we should introduce pupils to the process of knowledge. In his own words, 'Knowledge is a process not a product'. He further argues that 'any body of knowledge can be presented in a form simple enough so that any particular learner can understand it in a recognisable form'. The implication of this is that the skills of disciplinary enquiry can and should be introduced in the primary school. These ideas and processes are then refined and become more sophisticated as one goes through the school, hence his notion of the spiral curriculum.

I owe a great deal to Lawrence Stenhouse both his work and him personally. He led the teacher research movement and reconceptualisation of curriculum development in the UK in the 1970s and beyond. As a young teacher his seminal book *An Introduction to Curriculum Research and Development* (Stenhouse 1975) influenced me enormously and helped shape my thinking both at that time and in the long term. My doctoral students tell me that it is still as fresh and relevant today as it was almost fifty years ago. We became professional friends as I continued to learn from him. Following his premature death, Jean Ruddock, his personal and professional partner and I collected together and edited his papers to form a book length argument on the theme that he is best known for – *Research as a Basis for Teaching* (Rudduck and Hopkins 1985).

Stenhouse fervently believed that 'only teachers can create good teaching', and thus it is imperative that they occupy a central role in developing the instructional core and that they develop with it. In concluding the preface, consider this quotation from *Research as a Basis for Teaching* (Rudduck and Hopkins 1985:68–9):

> No curriculum development without teacher development', reads one of the poker-work mottoes we hung on our wall during the Humanities Project and haven't taken down. But that does not mean, as it often seems to be interpreted to mean, that we must train teachers in order to produce a world fit for curricula to live in. It means that by virtue of their meaningfulness, curricula are not simply instructional means to improve teaching but are expressions of ideas to improve teachers. Of course, they have a day-to-day instructional utility: cathedrals must keep the rain out. But the students benefit from curricula not so much because they change day-to-day instruction as because they improve teachers.

We must be dedicated to the improvement of schooling. The improvement of schooling is bound to be experimental: it cannot be dogmatic. The experiment depends on the exercise of the art of teaching and improves that art. The substantive content of the arts of teaching and learning is curriculum.

So, it is with *Unleashing Greatness*. We turn to a fuller discussion of these themes in the chapters that follow.

David Hopkins

Hope Valley, Peak District and Argentière, Mont Blanc, October 2023

INTRODUCTION

There is a paradox at the heart of contemporary system change in education. On the one hand, there is the unequivocal conclusion from the accumulation of PISA evidence that both excellence and equity are possible at the school and system level (Schleicher 2018). Yet on the other hand there are overwhelming examples from most educational jurisdictions expressing concern over poor standards. As a recent World Bank report (2018) succinctly put it, 'While countries have significantly increased access to education, being in school isn't the same thing as learning'. Why is it that, despite the phenomenal increase in our knowledge about what works in schooling in recent years, standards lag behind expectations and school level performance is far too unpredictable? As Ernest Becker (1985:xix) put it in a slightly different context: '... either we get some kind of grip on the accumulation of thought or we continue to wallow helplessly, to starve amidst plenty'.

Put another way, there is no doubt that the world's education systems have made significant progress over recent decades. It is also indubitably true that we have generated substantial practical knowledge over the past twenty years or so about how to improve both schools and education systems. Yet debates still rage at the policy, practitioner and academic levels over which policy levers and strategies actually make the difference. Sadly, the most significant consequence of this 'debate' has been to slow the progress of student achievement at the system level.

This has been the case for some time and even three years ago it presented a daunting challenge for those committed to educational improvement, but the situation is considerably more serious now. The advent of the coronavirus pandemic has almost instantaneously changed life for just about everyone globally. In most countries of the world, economic discipline was abandoned, businesses closed, staff furloughed, or asked to work from home, and so on. So, for example, the government in England, through lockdown, imposed restrictions on how long citizens can leave their home, if at all. In terms of education, in March 2020, the secretary of state closed all schools and colleges until further notice. Similarly, universities made decisions that have led to the closure of their campuses. Although at the time of writing, this situation has thankfully resolved itself somewhat, the challenge remains dramatically the same.

The question for educational leaders is how to respond to such a cataclysmic event in a morally purposeful, authentic and principled way. Here, I stand full square with McKinsey (2020) when they argue that 'issues regarding equity – that is, ensuring that the needs of the most vulnerable are met – should be front and centre, both during the closure and after students return to school'. Further, McKinsey set out five steps – resolve, resilience, return, re-imagine, and reform – to move through and beyond the coronavirus pandemic. The last two of these steps provide a focus for much that follows in this book:

- **Re-imagine**: leaders think about what the 'next normal' could be like, and how education systems could re-invent themselves.
- **Reform**: educators reconsider education priorities in light of lessons learned.

It is now crystal clear that conventional strategies are unable to meet the post-coronavirus challenge and that it is foolish in the extreme to even contemplate their use. Ironically, the coronavirus hiatus allows us to create an educational future that delivers on the moral purpose most teachers and leaders have for their students. Pasi Sahlberg (2022) graphically expressed the challenge in figure 1.

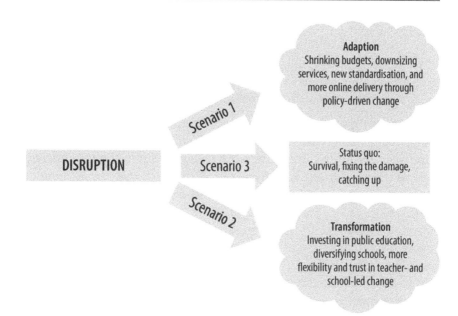

Figure 1 The coronavirus disruption (from Pasi Sahlberg)

The disruption, of course, is the coronavirus pandemic. That is the given, but the question is how do we respond? Unfortunately, as I survey the world's education systems they seem to be responding by either downsizing and reducing budgets (scenario 1), or by trying to maintain the status quo (scenario 3). I am with Pasi Sahlberg, we should be courageous by using this unprecedented event to make a paradigm change that embraces diversity and achieves equity through excellence (scenario 2).

Michael Fullan (2021) makes a similar argument in 'The Right Drivers For Whole System Success'. To summarise, Fullan proposes:

- Above all, we recommend avoiding a 'loss of learning' mindset that would take us back to traditional learning – to a system that we know was not working for the vast majority of students.

- In short, this prolonged ambiguity [the coronavirus pandemic] creates a tangible opportunity to make positive change happen.

- One might conclude that, over the past 40 years, the problem is not an absence of change but rather the presence of too many ad hoc, uncoordinated, ephemeral, piecemeal policies, programmes, and leaders that come and go.

- There is little credibility in the stance that we need not change the system. We have such a chance now – a once-in-a-generation opportunity that we dare not miss or bungle.

Fullan (2021) goes on to argue for a 'paradigm shift' drawing on Thomas Kuhn's (1962) seminal work, *The Structure of Scientific Revolutions*. I too will use Kuhn's insight in what follows but in a slightly different way. We know all too well from our daily work that the ubiquitous 'top-down' and 'outside–in' approaches to educational change produce structures, policy options, and ways of working that are instrumental and regress performance to the mean. They generate bureaucratic forms of organisation that although efficient and probably necessary, certainly in the early phases of the evolution of a system, also have a dark side. Max Weber (see Hopkins 2013, pg. 279), whose classic studies on bureaucracy are still insightful, warns that they pose a threat to individual freedoms and that ongoing bureaucratisation leads to a 'polar night of icy darkness' in which increasing rationalisation of human life traps individuals in the 'iron cage' of bureaucratic, rule-based, rational control. So dominant have been bureaucratic forms of administration in our public services – and notably in education – that they now appear to be the norm and consequently, they place a ceiling on the move of a system from good to great. As we move forward, we need to eschew these practices.

There are two insights in the polemic of the previous paragraph that are critical to the mission of this book. The first is the ubiquity of top-down change and consequently in many situations, the utilisation of the wrong policy levers for schooling; the second is that a school or educational system inevitably passes through a series of qualitatively different yet predictable phases on their journeys towards excellence. So important are these ideas to the development of the argument that follows that it is important initially to briefly define them particularly as they are interrelated and at times reinforcing. They are, however, described more fully in the chapter that follows.

The first theme is the ubiquity of top-down change. To change it, it is first necessary to understand why it is so prevalent. I draw on the seminal work of Jurgen Habermas (1972), particularly *Knowledge and Human Interests* to explain why we are where we currently are. For Habermas, knowledge is the outcome of human activity that is motivated by natural needs and interests. These interests guide and shape the way knowledge is constituted in different human activities. He describes the three ways or paradigms in which humans know and construe the world. These, he terms, 'technical', 'practical' and 'critical'. The *technical* orientation relates to positivism; the *practical* orientation to the interpretative or subjective paradigm; and the *critical* to emancipation and transformation.

It is the technical or top-down paradigm that is dominant. The type of human interest that it represents is prediction and control; the kind of knowledge that it values is instrumental, i.e., causal explanation and empirical knowing. Inevitably then the school improvement focus is short term and utilises bureaucratic policy options and narrow outcome measures. It is because of the dominance or even hegemony of the technical paradigm that we are where we are. This book argues that if we are to fulfil the aspirations of school improvement then we need to embrace other paradigms and human interests. Inevitably this has social as well as political implications.

The second theme is that if a school or educational system is to improve, then, as it progresses, it will inevitably pass through a fairly predictable series of phases. As we will see in the following chapters, this observation is now well-established and evidenced. The key point, however, is that different strategies are required to move from one phase to another. It is now clear that in the initial phase of improvement moving, from say poor to fair performance, then top-down or prescriptive change is often the most effective strategy. Yet because it is appropriate at one phase of development, it does not necessarily mean that it is equally effective across all other phases. Indeed, as intimated, the opposite is almost always the case. This is the reason why in systems that continue to use top-down strategies, either because of ignorance or a predilection for control, performance inevitably stagnates. This is why we place so much emphasis in our work on differentiated strategies for school improvement.

Unleashing Greatness proposes a simple and practical approach to school improvement designed for schools that are currently overwhelmed by a myriad of often incompatible demands from governments, community, and professional associations. Many schools find themselves besieged and bogged down by competing policy initiatives and external accountabilities yet wish to chart their own distinctive way that serves to enhance the learning journeys of all their students.

The eight steps link together (as seen in figure 1.2) and the key evidence behind each of them is:

1. **Clarify moral purpose** – Ensure that the achievement and learning of students expressed as moral purpose is at the centre of everything that the school and teachers do.

2. **Focus on classroom practice and the instructional core** – The quality of a school or system cannot exceed the quality of its teachers: it is axiomatic, therefore, that the focus of school improvement is on the practice of teaching.

3. **Decide on the non-negotiables** – These are the key improvement objectives that the school focuses on unrelentingly in the short/medium term that are underpinned by a 'development' (as compared with a 'maintenance') structure that ensures that adequate resources are made available for improvement work.

4. **Articulate the narrative** – Moral purpose may be at the heart of successful school and system improvement, but we will not realise this purpose without powerful and increasingly specified strategies and protocols embraced in a narrative that both energises and provides direction for our colleagues, students and communities.

5. **Utilise instructional rounds & theories of action** – These are the key strategies for diagnosing and articulating effective teaching practice through non-judgmental observation and the development of protocols to ensure consistency and precision.

6. **Embrace peer coaching and triads** – Provide the infrastructure for professional development in the school and the means for putting the theories of action into practice.

7. **Practice instructional leadership** – The leadership strategy most closely associated with increased levels of student achievement through the employment of four key behaviours: setting vision;

managing teaching and learning; developing people and organisation re-design.

8. **Exploit networking** – The most effective schools network with each other in order to learn from their best, collaborate purposefully, and share outstanding practices.

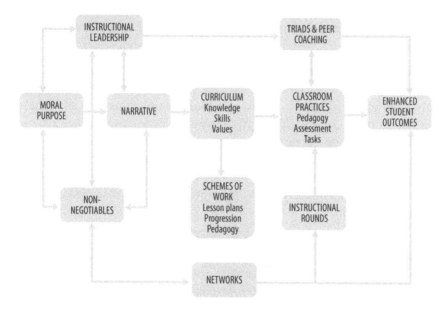

Figure 2 The Unleashing Greatness Framework

Unleashing Greatness provides a guide to action for implementing the eight steps described. The book is divided into three sections:

Part one contains two chapters that first reviews the global evidence on school reform and then, secondly, outlines the eight steps for unleashing greatness.

Part two describes in four chapters the essential ingredients of a school-level infrastructure for delivering both excellence and equity in terms of student performance. Each chapter provides evidence-based strategies, examples of practice, frameworks for action and advice on future-proofing. The focus is initially on pedagogy, both teaching effects and models of teaching, followed by accessible guidance on personalised learning. These chapters contain the essence of professional practice and are subsequently supported by advice on the necessary infrastructure for implementation – staff development and peer coaching.

Part three broadens the landscape with two further chapters on leadership and systemic reform that contain the potential to lead to large-scale system reform impact. These chapters are similarly practical and action-oriented and are of relevance for school networks and multi-academy trusts.

Each chapter, apart from the first that sets the scene, reflects a particular step in the *Unleashing Greatness* process. In turn, each chapter, following an overview introduction, focuses on four specific aspects of that phase in the strategy. So, the book can be read cover to cover to get a sense of the overarching narrative, or more pragmatically to gain advice and direction on a specific aspect of the process. Each chapter concludes with a coda that posits diagnostic questions for that particular phase of the school improvement journey and provides a couple of case studies of the process in action.

In concluding the introduction to this book, let me be a little more personal and reflective in attempting to summarise the values and aspirations that inform the approach described on the following pages. In the late 1980s, when we were developing the *Improving the Quality of Education for All (IQEA)* school improvement programme (Hopkins 2002), we used the metaphor of the 'journey' to describe our overall approach. During an early workshop, the head of a large catholic school in the North of England commented that he liked the metaphor but counselled us 'to journey as pilgrims rather than nomads'. By this, he meant that our school improvement journey should be driven by a moral purpose, rather than travelling around in circles following this or that latest educational fad.

Some of you will know that I have been most fortunate to have had a second career as an international mountain guide. Consequently, I value and see much virtue in mountaineering images and traditions. I have recently enjoyed reading Alex Buisse's (2022) beautiful and profusely illustrated book, *Mont Blanc Lines*. In the introduction he states that the book 'is at the crossroads between guidebook and landscape photography'. This is most certainly the case as the book is too large and precious to be put into a rucksack! He continues:

> *To a mountaineer or skier, drawing lines is a way of combining their personal vision with the natural form of the mountain, of forever leaving their mark on a summit without touching it other than with a crampon or ski edge, erased by the next storm. The most aesthetic of these lines follow a logical path and immediately become all too obvious. ... Together, all these lines sketch the contours of each mountain, almost allowing them to be recomposed on a blank page.*

Without wishing to strain the analogy, I see some connection between Buisse's concept of a line on a mountain and this attempt to describe the journey of school improvement. This is not a dictum or advice to be followed slavishly, rather it provides tools and strategies that teachers and leaders can utilise and enhance their capacity and abilities as change agents in their own settings.

It is that *thought* that distinguishes the approach taken in this book from the more formulaic approaches to school improvement determined by instrumental ends and bureaucratic means. This is the argument that will be developed at length in the chapters that follow and that has already been presaged in this introduction. It is the 'good society' that critical theory, emancipation and the principles of authentic school improvement eventually and ineluctably lead us towards. It is this that informs Unleashing Greatness and the journey of school improvement.

HOW TO USE THIS BOOK

I hope this book will distinctively present new ideas and ever-widening concepts on school reform, rooted in the current evidence base, and informed by the benefit of reflection and analysis of the lived experience of those actively involved in school improvement efforts. It is written for all those involved in school development and leadership roles and those in the wider community who are interested in finding ways to meet the current challenges of school and system reform. It has four principal audiences in mind:

1. **Education professionals** such as teachers, principals, network leaders and regional directors who are looking for an action framework to guide their work. The book contains a strategic framework for in-school and system reform based on an interpretation of the best research and thinking, but framed in a way that leads directly to intelligent and informed action. This knowledge will be equally helpful for both school improvement teams working directly within schools and system leaders who work both within and between schools in order to build local capacity.

2. **Students and researchers**, particularly masters and professional doctorate candidates, who require a comprehensive review of current research and thinking about school improvement and practical examples of educational reform within an action-oriented framework.

3. **Policy-makers** who are seeking a sustained argument for an approach to policy-making based on improved attainment and learning for all students, irrespective of their socioeconomic backgrounds. This embraces values such as social equity and a commitment to creating the conditions whereby all students can reach their potential; strategies that enhance the quality of teaching and leadership; and an approach that integrates all levels within the system. My recent productive collaboration with FED [Foundation for Education Development] and the important work that they are doing in re-imagining the future education policy agenda suggests that these ideas can profitably contribute to their and others policy proposals.

4. **Parents and members of the wider community** may also find the book useful. Particularly those who are interested in the key features of an effective school and who wish to understand it better, either to support their own children, or to support the education system more generally.

As seen in the introduction, the book is essentially structured around the eight key steps of the *Unleashing Greatness* framework with the first and last chapters taking a broader systemic focus. Each chapter contains summaries of the relevant knowledge base and outlines strategies for practical action related to each step in the framework. Every chapter concludes with a discussion of the key questions related to each phase in the framework together with brief case studies of how primary, secondary and special schools have responded to the challenge of moving through the process.

SCHOOL IMPROVEMENT MATERIALS AND TOOLS

This book is intended to be conceptual, strategic and practical – all at the same time! Besides giving an overview of the field of school improvement and educational reform, it also provides a strategy, as well as guidance as to what to do. Although the conceptual frameworks and strategies are described in the pages that follow, the bulk of the detail of the actual practical advice and tools are to be found in the three Curiosity and Powerful Learning manuals:

* The System and Powerful Learning
* Curiosity and Powerful Learning
* Leadership for Powerful Learning

These manuals are available from Amazon and my website – www.profdavidhopkins.com. In addition, the specific materials and tools referred to in each of the chapter can be downloaded *gratis* from my website.

Chapter two

* The three Curiosity and Powerful Learning Manuals
* Unleashing Greatness original article
* Unleashing Greatness questions

Chapter three

* School improvement pathway

Chapter four

* Fertile questions
* Being a learner framework

Chapters five and six

* Curiosity and Powerful Learning Manual – see the 10 protocols

- Models of Practice Vol 1:

  - 1. Cooperative Group Work Model – see the Peer Coaching Guides

  - 2. Synectics Model – see the Peer Coaching Guides

- Models of Practice Vol 2:

  - 3. Whole Class Teaching Model – see the Peer Coaching Guides

  - 4. Concept Attainment Model – see the Peer Coaching Guides

- Models of Practice Vol 3:

  - 5. Inductive Teaching Model – see the Peer Coaching Guides

  - 6. Mnemonics Model – see the Peer Coaching Guides

Chapter seven

- Leadership for Powerful Learning Manual

PART 1:

THE SCHOOL IMPROVEMENT IMPERATIVE

CHAPTER 1:
WHY SCHOOL IMPROVEMENT?

A PERSONAL INTRODUCTION

In the summer of 1979, I read a book that changed my professional life. It seems inconceivable now that, until that point in time, the conventional wisdom was that schools per se had little effect on the progress of students. Rather the belief was that that academic achievement was related to race, class, gender or genetics. This fallacy was laid bare in *Fifteen Thousand Hours* by Michael Rutter and his colleagues (1979). Their book was one of the first major studies to demonstrate unequivocally that schools do make a difference; the school a child goes to and the classroom they join has a significant positive impact on their academic progress and subsequent life chances. Rutter and his colleagues compared the 'effectiveness' of ten secondary schools in south London on a range of student outcome measures and found that despite similarities in intake and socio-economic context, some schools performed better and were more effective than others. The identification of the factors associated with the effective school soon led to my involvement in the nascent school improvement movement where we used this research to begin to develop strategies and policies for making the school and later school systems more effective. The rest, as they say, is history.

School improvement as a field of action and research has now come of age. In their recent review of sixty years of research on educational administration, Hallinger and Kovačević (2019) identify school improvement as one of the key areas of research and development to have emerged during that period. They maintain that the field is not only well specified but also contributes to enhanced practice. This chapter traces my own over forty-year involvement in the evolution of school improvement and so provides a personal perspective on the development of the field. The narrative:

- begins with outlining a brief history of educational change, then the emerging focus on equity and excellence and a review of the evolution of school improvement as a series of phases.

- considers some of the most relevant critiques of policy and practice before summarising the current knowledge base as a series of 'myths' with associated theories of action for implementation.

- distinguishes between prescription and professionalism in school reform and introduces the concept of differential school (and system) improvement.

- Finally, in the coda, we return to a further consideration of Habermas's tri-paradigmatic framework and argues for critical theory as being the most suitable paradigm for authentic school improvement.

A BRIEF HISTORY OF EDUCATIONAL CHANGE AND SCHOOL IMPROVEMENT

It is surprising to realise, as Fullan (2015) has pointed out, how short the history of serious investigation into the change process in schools actually is. It is also quite remarkable to appreciate that this recent history stems from a specific event on a particular day. This was the launch of Sputnik on the 4th October 1957. The launch of Sputnik created a crisis of confidence in the USA; the nation was chagrined to find that the Russians had beaten them in this first major round of the space race. As a response, the decision was taken to invest heavily in education to increase the knowledge, problem-solving ability, and productivity of the next generation of Americans, to ensure that this would never ever happen again.

This led to the first phase of educational change that dates from the early-1960s, which had an emphasis on the *adoption of curriculum materials*. During this phase, educational change strategies were conceived of within a top-down or 'centre-periphery' model. The curriculum reform movement was intended to have major impact on student achievement through the production and dissemination of exemplary curriculum materials. The belief being that if the materials were of sufficiently high quality, they would disseminate and be adopted almost automatically. This was a flawed assumption and although the materials were often excellent, in the main they failed to have an impact. Teachers proved resilient to the adoption of these materials and educational archaeologists are still finding the partly rifled packages of original materials where teachers had taken relevant worksheets and activities and incorporated them into their existing lesson plans! This meant that the metacognitive and epistemological content and quality of the curricula were completely squandered. Although this analysis applies more to North America than to the UK or Australia, the materials emanating from the Schools Council in England in the late 1960s (see Stenhouse 1980 for a comprehensive account of these projects) cannot escape censure. The failure of the curriculum reform movement to impact on student learning was predicated on the fact that curriculum do not disseminate just by themselves and that there needs to be a strong connection between teaching style and curriculum development.

As a consequence of this failure, there was a subsequent emphasis, covering most of the 1970s, on understanding the process of implementation. A more adaptive style of educational change strategies was assumed during this period, as it became increasingly apparent that top-down models of change do not work by themselves. It was now acknowledged that implementation does not occur spontaneously as a result of legislative fiat, and that teachers require in-service training to acquire new knowledge and skills. It became clear that implementation is an extremely complex and lengthy process that requires a sensitive combination of strategic planning, individual learning and commitment to succeed. The contribution of Michael Fullan during this phase, in particular his *New Meaning of Educational Change* (2015) was pivotal.

The popularisation of concepts such as the 'implementation dip', the emphasis on teacher in-service development and the identification of change agent skills, all stem from this period (for more detail see Hopkins 2001).

The next significant event in the history of educational change came in the summer of 1979 with the publication of Fifteen Thousand Hours by Michael Rutter and his colleagues (1979). This research was referred to in the introduction and many regard it as laying the basis for the effective schools movement. The 'effective schools' described in *Fifteen Thousand Hours*, were characterised by factors 'as varied as the degree of academic emphasis, teacher actions in lessons, the availability of incentives and rewards, good conditions for pupils, and the extent to which children are able to take responsibility' (Rutter et al 1979:178). It was this constellation of factors that Rutter and his colleagues later referred to as the school's 'ethos'. They further claimed (Rutter et al 1979:179) that the:

> *... cumulative effect of these various social factors was considerably greater than the effect of any of the individual factors on their own. The implication is that the individual actions or measures may combine to create a particular ethos, or set of values, attitudes and behaviours which will become characteristic of the school as a whole.*

The identification of the factors associated with the effective school soon led to a complementary emphasis on school improvement – strategies for making the school more effective.

The genesis of the school improvement movement was both accelerated and given definition by the OECD's International School Improvement Project (ISIP) (Hopkins 1987). ISIP was a major project involving some 150 people in 14 countries. The project work was carried out by cross-national groups that focused on one of six aspects of school improvement: school-based review, leadership, external support, research and evaluation, the role of local authorities, and conceptual mapping of school improvement. In addition to Hopkins' (1987) comprehensive overview, ISIP also produced a significant range of published outcomes that focused on both practical strategies and policy advice. With the benefit of hindsight, Hopkins and Reynolds (2001:12) later commented that this phase of school improvement tended to be 'loosely conceptualised and under-theorised. It did not represent a systematic, programmatic and coherent approach to school change'.

Be that as it may, ISIP did put school improvement on the map and influenced a wide range of school improvement interventions that were based on tested practices. Programmes such as *Improving Quality of Education for All* (Hopkins 2002) and *High Reliability Schools* (HRS) (Stringfield, Reynolds and Schaffer 2008; 2010) in England, the *Improving School Effectiveness Project* in Scotland (MacBeath and Mortimore 2001), the *Manitoba School Improvement Project* in Canada (Earl et al 2003), and the *Dutch National School Improvement Project* (see van Velzen et al 1985) were all examples of well-researched school improvement programmes that were productive in terms of student achievement. All these interventions took advantage of a key finding from Nunnery (1998), that, in general, schools are more likely to achieve measurable improvements in student performance if they are connected to an external reform-assistance team than if they try to go it alone.

A second-related development was the growth, especially in the United States, of comprehensive models of school reform that could be adopted by individual schools. These include approaches such as the Comer School Development Model (1992), Glickman's *Renewing America's Schools* (1993), Levin's Accelerated Schools (2005), Sizer's Coalition of Essential Schools (1989), Bob and Nancy Slavin's *Success For All* (Slavin 1996; Slavin et al 1996; Slavin and Madden 2010), and the *New American Schools Designs* (Stringfield, Ross and Smith 1996).

As this emphasis on school improvement deepened, so did the interest in large-scale system reform intensify. In his chapter in *Change Wars*, Sir Michael Barber (2009) explains the progression in this way by reminding us that it was the school effectiveness research in the 1980s that gave us increasingly well-defined portraits of the effective school that led in the 1990s to increasing knowledge of school improvement, i.e. how to achieve effectiveness. In the same way, we have in the last decade begun to learn far more about the features of an effective educational system but are now only beginning to understand the dynamics of improvement at system level.

It is PISA that has given us these 'increasingly well-defined portraits' of the effective school system. They are described as:

[Pisa is] *the OECD's Programme for International Student Assessment. Since 2000, PISA has involved more than 90 countries and economies and around 3,000,000 students worldwide. PISA 2021 is the eighth cycle of the programme. Every three years, PISA tests what 15-year-olds can do in reading, mathematics and science. The tests are designed to capture how students master certain skills such as reading strategies, problem solving in mathematics and critical reading in science, skills that are important beyond the classroom. PISA therefore focuses not on knowledge acquisition and retention, but rather on the application of knowledge in applied situations* (Oxford University 2021).

Despite some recent critiques, it is important to emphasise the contribution made by PISA to our understanding of the dynamics of educational improvement at scale (Schleicher 2018). In assessing PISA's contribution, we need to remind ourselves of key three issues.

The first is that as PISA has now been administered on eight occasions (the eighth PISA round was administered in 2021 and at time of writing is still to report) we have significant real-time information as to how national performance changes (or not) over time. As is intimated in figure 1.1, the performance of some countries has remained stable: Finland, for example, has consistently scored very well. The trajectories of others have moved both up and down as they have tried to secure their position on the 'stairway to heaven'. What explains the dramatic movement of Poland say, from the bottom right-hand segment to the top-left in a little over six years, or the equally dramatic fall of my own country of Wales from the top-left segment to the ignominy of the bottom-right? There are good explanatory reasons for both movements related to the policy choices made by respective national governments. The details need not concern us here, the point is that we are getting to a stage where we can predict cause and effect in system change related to the policy levers that governments, for whatever reasons, choose to select.

The second issue is also illustrated in figure 1.1. Here the OECD compares national performance against two criteria (OECD 2018). The first is 'excellence' represented on the vertical axis by mean performance on PISA mathematics and science cores in 2015; the second is 'equity' represented by the strength of the relationship between achievement and family background. When the OECD average for both dimensions is inserted, it enables a two-by-two matrix to be constructed. So, in the high excellence/high equity segment is Finland and now Canada, with both Australia and England remaining in the high excellence/low equity segment. The advantage of this analysis is that it gives an indication not only of academic performance, but also of how far aims of social justice and moral purpose have been achieved.

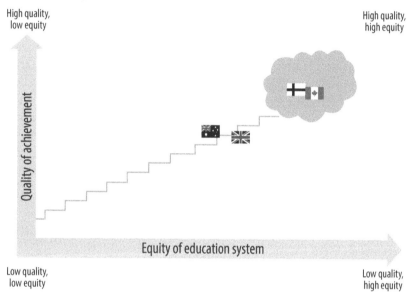

Figure 1.1 Excellence and equity as defined by PISA (OECD 2018)

The third and crucial issue is that there is no doubt that the knowledge base on educational effectiveness at the school and system level has expanded exponentially over recent decades. However, it is still open to debate whether this research and policy evidence has resulted in consistent increases in student learning and performance. Too many political and policy debates focus on standardised testing as a measure of educational excellence. This is problematic for at least two reasons. First, there is convincing international evidence that too strong a focus on externally determined and narrow academic learning outcomes is associated with deteriorating student performance. Second, there can be no national educational excellence without stronger equity of outcomes – equity and excellence are inseparable. Indeed, equity is the surest path to excellence in education (Sahlberg 2020). This is a continuing theme of this chapter and the book itself.

THE FIVE PHASES OF SCHOOL REFORM

For the moment, let us summarise more formally how over the last five decades or so, the school effectiveness and school improvement research bases have gained prominence and recognition on the international stage. As has just been illustrated, in both a theoretical and empirical sense they have matured through a wide range of well-documented research projects, interventions and innovations across a range of countries. This work in general has described how efforts to help schools become increasingly effective learning environments for the full range of their students have been more or less successful. In our comprehensive review, 'School and system improvement: A narrative state of the art review', (Hopkins et al 2014) we presented and described evidence of the effects of reform efforts at the school and system levels, through articulating five phases of development, as seen in table 1.1.

These phases are not mutually exclusive; they overlap and flow into one another, but they do represent a natural progression. The more that we learn about them the quicker we can progress through them.

- **Phase 1** provided a foundation with its emphasis on how organisations can improve through specific interventions and the highlighting of the importance of culture in any change process.
- **Phase 2** focused on teacher action research, school self-review, and concern for meeting the needs of disadvantaged students. It began to lay out the distinctive educational values and strategies that define the school improvement field.
- **Phase 3** built on the emerging school effectiveness knowledge base and brought to the surface the idea of the school as the unit of change. This phase included the greater attention to the importance of staff development integrated into replicable comprehensive school reform approaches that addressed both organisational and classroom improvement.

- **Phase 4** emphasised the ability to scale up reforms to produce valued outcomes across a number of schools, and the recognition of the vital role that districts and local education authorities have to play in school improvement. Phase 4 also included an increasing focus on the importance of school leadership as a means of enhancing the learning and achievement of all students.

- **Phase 5** continues evolving. We are seeing the spread of the knowledge base globally and at the same learning more about achieving school improvement at scale – systemic reform. There is also a frustration by many at the uneven pace of change, which is leading to a clamour for 'transformation' (Salzburg Global Seminar 2022). It will be suggested however that a more productive way forward lies in the application of critical theory to school improvement policy and practice.

Phase of school and system improvement	Key features of each phase
Phase 1: Understanding the organisational culture of the school	• The legacy of the organisational development research • 'The cultures of the schools and the challenges inherent in change'
Phase 2: Action research and research initiatives at the school level	• Teacher research and school review • Research programmes such as the Rand Study, DESSI, Special Strategies and the OECD International School Improvement project
Phase 3: Managing change and comprehensive approaches to school reform	• Managing centralised policy change • 'Comprehensive' approaches to school reform, such as: Success for All, New American Schools, High Reliability Schools and IQEA
Phase 4: Building capacity for student learning at the local level and the continuing emphasis on leadership	• Professional learning communities and networks • Recognising the continuing importance and impact of leadership

Phase 5: Towards systemic improvement	• The influence of the knowledge base and the impact of national and international benchmarking studies • Differentiated approaches to school and system reform, transformation and critical theory

Table 1.1 Five phases of research on school and system improvement (Hopkins et al 2014)

The narrative portrayed here is of journey and it is in the nature of the journey that it progresses. As the gains in knowledge and practice in each phase are consolidated, we understand more about the one we are currently inhabiting. This reflection also helps us think about the future and consider the challenges that will confront us as we continue to make progress. This is where the chronological nature of a review like this has its downside. Writing in this way gives the impression that school and system reform is an iterative and logical process – sadly, this is far from the truth. Before we segue too glibly into describing an overarching framework for school improvement, we need to consider more thoroughly the contemporary critiques of educational change and the fault lines that engender them.

So, in the following two sections of this chapter, we engage with this reality by first considering some of the most relevant critiques of policy and practice, and then portraying the current knowledge base as a series of 'myths' with associated theories of action.

YET DEBATES STILL RAGE

The accumulation of research evidence and practical wisdom outlined in the previous section has potentially a powerful impact on student performance. Despite this, debates still rage over which policy levers and strategies actually make the difference. This is the issue that I addressed directly in *Exploding the Myths of School Reform* (Hopkins 2013) by arguing that the failure of so many educational reform efforts to impact on the learning and performance of students is due to misguided action based on a few myths.

The discussion of the myths, which are outlined in the following section, stems from a deep frustration that despite what we collectively know about school and system reform, the potential contained in this knowledge is not systematically realised. This is because as Fullan (2011) says 'the wrong drivers are chosen' and often occurs because of ineptness, misunderstanding, or cultural and bureaucratic hegemony. This is a theme that has been taken up and pursued with much passion and intellectual vigour by several of the most influential opinion leaders in our field. Three are reviewed here.

Michael Fullan's (2011; 2021) papers address this issue face on. In these papers, Fullan describes how certain popular policy options are implemented but without any serious consideration of context. The following quotes give a flavour of the argument (Fullan 2011):

> A 'wrong driver' is a deliberate policy force that has little chance of achieving the desired result, while a 'right driver' is one that ends up achieving better measurable results for students. (p. 3)

> The glue that binds the effective drivers together is the underlying attitude, philosophy, and theory of action. The mindset that works for whole system reform is the one that inevitably generates individual and collective motivation and corresponding skills to transform the system. (p. 5)

Fullan's drivers, as he admits, may be wrong for one of two reasons, or both. They may be wrong because they are wrong, or wrong because they are inappropriate to the stage that the school or system is currently at. As Fullan (2011:5) comments:

> In the rush to move forward, leaders, especially from countries that have not been progressing, tend to choose the wrong drivers. Such ineffective drivers fundamentally miss the target. There are four main 'wrong driver' culprits:
>
> 1. Accountability: using test results and teacher appraisal to reward or punish teachers and schools vs capacity building;
> 2. Individual teacher and leadership quality: promoting individual vs group solutions;

3. *Technology: investing in and assuming that the wonders of the digital world will carry the day vs instruction;*

4. *Fragmented strategies vs integrated or systemic strategies.*

In reflecting on this issue, it is worth quoting David Hargreaves (2012:25) and note his quite appropriate emphasis on the contextualisation of any change to context.

There may be real gains from looking around the world for some educational policies and practices that might benefit our schools. But a transformation of schooling that is self-generating and sustainable requires that attention be paid to the deep cultural capital that underpins the life of individual schools, of partnerships and alliances, and of the school system as a whole. This is the key lesson we learn from China and East Asia, one by which we can develop our version, based on our own well-established native roots of extended moral purpose and distributed system leadership.

So, the key point being advanced here by both Fullan and Hargreaves is the danger of promiscuous policy borrowing; a contention that one finds enthusiastically endorsed in the recent writings of Pasi Sahlberg.

Pasi Sahlberg (2021) in his bestselling book *Finnish Lessons 3.0*, explains the success of the Finnish educational system, not in terms of the adoption of a range of external strategies and policies, but more in terms of carefully reflective, customised and culturally relevant approaches. Listen to him speak and he talks about the Finnish paradox that 'less is more' with the following implications: teach less, learn more; test less, learn more; and ensure more equity through growing diversity. This is not a universal panacea, and it certainly does not apply to all systems, but it is an intelligent response to the cultural context of Finland. The Finns themselves sensibly prefer to combine knowledge of what works, together with a view as to how the Finnish system itself will continue to evolve.

In an earlier blog, *Global Reform Movement is Here!* Sahlberg (2012) argues that the main strategies for developing an equitable, high-performing education system are similar to those underlying the social and economic transformation of Finland into a welfare state and a competitive knowledge society. He continues to say that because of the professional strength and moral health of Finnish schools, their system has remained virtually free of the viruses associated with the Global Educational Reform Movement [GERM]. These are the collection of ubiquitous policy agendas critiqued by myself, Fullan and Hargreaves. The main components of GERM are:

- Standardisation
- Focus on core subjects
- Search for low risk ways to reach learning goals
- Use of corporate management models
- Test-based accountability policies

By contrast, he argues that the typical features of teaching and learning in Finland are:

- great confidence in teachers and principals as high-performing professionals;
- encouraging teachers and students to try new ideas and approaches, in other words, to put curiosity, imagination and creativity at the heart of learning; and,
- seeing the purpose of teaching and learning as pursuing the happiness of learning and cultivating the development of the whole child.

He concludes that:

> The best way to avoid infections of GERM is to prepare teachers and leaders well.

And

> Lessons from Finland will help you kill 99.9% of GERMs!

The conclusion to be drawn from the critiques of the current policy reform reviewed is that the potential impact of the knowledge bases on student achievement and the practical strategies derived from them noted earlier has not been realised. The ubiquity of the 'wrong drivers' and 'GERM' approaches to school reform have placed a ceiling on student performance in those jurisdictions that follow the paucity of that orthodoxy. Space precludes a detailed analysis of this proposition, but the contention is widely accepted by informed opinion; see for example, Harris and Jones 2017a, Hargreaves and Shirley 2009, as well as those quoted earlier. The question remains, how can the school improvement knowledge base be re-formulated so that it can have a consistent and positive impact on student performance? My attempt at doing this is summarised in the following section.

ON CONSIDERING MYTHS AND PROPOSING THEORIES OF ACTION

The failure of so many educational reform efforts to impact on the learning and performance of students is due to misguided action based on a number of myths associated with school reform that remain prevalent in education to the present day (Hopkins 2013). It is instructive here to be reminded of the danger of living by myths, as Jonathan Powell (2010:5) does in this quotation from Machiavelli's *The Prince* that he cited in his book, *The New Machiavelli*: 'But since it is my object to write what shall be useful to whosoever understands it, it seems to me better to follow the real truth of things than an imaginary view of them. For many republics and princedoms have been imagined that were never known to exist in reality.'

Powell's point is that too often in politics a conventional wisdom emerges that satisfies a particular group's version of the truth and quite rapidly enters the zeitgeist but, at best, it is a myth, a parody of the truth. If the myths are then acted on, the subsequent actions will fail. Sadly, myths abound in education. Think, for example, of contemporary debates around class size, teaching quality and the influence of external accountability.

In *Exploding the Myths of School Reform,* an alternative approach was taken to reviewing the evolution of the knowledge base on schools and system reform (Hopkins 2013). The use of the 'myth' as a narrative artifice provided a structure for the critique of contemporary school and system research, policy and practice. By identifying the ten myths and then 'exploding' them, this enabled a realistic and increasingly precise and aligned approach to school and system reform to be presented.

The overarching narrative went something like this:

- We know increasing amounts about school and system reform.
- Unfortunately, this knowledge is often misused and an illusion or myth is generated that leads in unproductive directions and consequently has little impact on the learning and achievement of students.
- In order to fulfil our moral purpose we must correct the myths and present 'the real truth of things'.
- The knowledge then needs to be couched as theories of action that guide implementation within an overall strategy for school and system reform.

In this section, it may be helpful to signpost the future direction of the field in an action-oriented way, by both reflecting on the phases outlined and being mindful of the myths that are increasingly accreting our work. The following eight proposals for implementation are, as has just been suggested, couched as theories of action within an overall strategy for school and system reform. The overall strategy and the Unleashing Greatness framework are described in the following chapter.

1. All successful schools and systems have developed a robust narrative related to the achievement and learning of students expressed as moral purpose that is predicated on an unrelenting commitment to ensure that all learners will reach their potential wherever that may lead.

   When schools and systems are driven by a narrative grounded in moral purpose related to student achievement and learning, then all students are more likely to fulfil their potential.

   Key questions: What is the nature of successful narrative related to student achievement and learning in school and system reform? How and by whom are they constructed?

2. There is an obstinate myth that poverty is a determinant of student and school performance. This is an important myth to explode for both social justice and strategic reasons. Not only is it morally wrong that poverty is a determinant of educational achievement, but it is also important to remind ourselves that those 'effective schools' and systems that do break the association between poverty and achievement share similar characteristics.

When schools and teachers are of high quality, poverty is no longer a determinant of educational success.

Key questions: What are those transferable practices of schools and systems that comprise that 'high quality' and deny the association between poverty and performance? How is the necessary 'will' generated within schools, their communities and the system to ensure that these practices are adopted in a sustainable way?

3. It is the enhancement of the quality of teaching, rather than structural change that needs to be the central theme of any improvement strategy. The quality of teaching is necessarily related to system goals and targeted support that are likely to have a heavy emphasis in the first instance on the teaching of literacy and numeracy and the development of curiosity.

When the focus of policy is on the quality of teaching rather than structural change, then student achievement will increase.

Key questions: How can the research knowledge on effective teaching be best translated into specifications of practice for teachers and who is best suited to do it? What are the most effective recruitment strategies and forms of professional development opportunities that develop a common 'practice' of teaching and learning through blending theory, evidence and action through collaborative forms of enquiry?

4. The development of this professional practice occurs within a system context where there is increasing clarity on the standards implied by the goals set, and the generation of the most appropriate curriculum, teaching and above all learning strategies necessary to achieve those standards. These goals will necessarily relate to learning skills, dispositions and citizenship practices as well as the more usual narrow definitions of achievement.

When the focus is on 'powerful learning', then students will both attain more and develop their cognitive and social skills.

Key questions: What in operational and implementable terms are those learning skills and values needed to create the increasingly technological citizen of the future? How can such richer and more profound societal goals be developed and put into practice?

5. To enable this, procedures are needed to provide formative, ongoing and transparent data (both assessment data and inspection evidence) on the performance of the student, school and system that facilitate improvements in learning and teaching. There needs to be a shift from external to internal forms of accountability over time as the school and system makes progress.

When data is used to monitor, feedback and enhance student performance on a range learning goals, then students' progress will more quickly accelerate.

Key questions: What are the most appropriate accountability and assessment structures for schools and systems at the various stages of their development? What are the most effective metrics for assessing students' achievement learning and progress at the various stages of their development?

6. Student and school performance is enhanced by teachers and leaders 'going deeper' and intervening early. This follows diagnosis that reflects a range of differential strategies based on performance, with targets being set that are related to implementation. In most schools and systems, the focus has been on initiation rather than implementation, and yet without deep implementation, student achievement and learning can never be transformed.

When teachers and schools go deeper in their search for improvement (rather than adopting fads) then the student learning experience also deepens and outcomes improve.

Key questions: How can the educational culture be shifted more towards an implementation focus rather than an initiation focus that responds reactively to the latest trend? What are the most effective leadership and monitoring practices that lead to deep implementation?

7. The development of professional practice, utilisation of data and early intervention using differential strategies takes place in schools where the leadership has:

- very high levels of expectation for both teachers and students;
- an unrelenting focus on the quality of learning and teaching;

- created management structures that ensure an orderly learning environment;
- empowered and generated professional responsibility and accountability;
- developed a work culture that takes pride in sharing excellence;
- a high degree of trust and reciprocity; and,
- supported leadership development across a locality.

When leadership is instructionally focused, widely distributed, within a systems context, then both teachers and students can fully capitalise on their capacity to learn and achieve.

Key questions: What are the most effective leadership development programmes that can ensure the acquisition of such comprehensive leadership practices? How is leadership expertise best deployed within a school and system to ensure sustained success for all?

8. Finally, system level structures need to be established that reflect the processes just described, linking together the various levels of the system through to the school and classroom, developing capacity by balancing professional autonomy and accountability, and promoting disciplined innovation as a consequence of networking. These activities combine to produce a work culture that has at its core strong pressure to improve, takes seriously its responsibility to act on and change context, and that embodies a commitment to focus, flexibility and collaboration.

When the system as a whole takes student learning seriously then moral purpose is achieved.

Key questions: What are the most effective school and system strategies at each stage of development and how are they best sequenced over time? How is a 'guiding coalition' developed at all levels of the system to ensure the generation, implementation and sustainability of an educational narrative driven by moral purpose?

As will be seen in the following sections of the chapter, these propositions and theories of action underpin the Unleashing Greatness approach to school and system improvement and provide an antidote to the 'wrong drivers' and 'GERM' critiques.

BUILDING CAPACITY FOR THE
NEXT STAGE OF REFORM

I have argued for some time that the key to managing system reform is by strategically re-balancing 'top-down' and 'bottom-up' change over time (Hopkins 2007). The argument goes something like this:

- Most agree that when standards are too low and too varied that some form of direct state/outside intervention is necessary. Typically, the resultant 'national prescription' proves very successful in raising standards in the short term.

- But progress soon tends to plateau and whilst a bit more improvement could be squeezed out especially in underperforming schools, one must question whether prescription still offers the recipe for sustained large scale reform into the medium/long term.

- There is a growing recognition that schools need to lead the next phase of reform. But, if the hypothesis is correct, it must categorically not be a naïve return to the not so halcyon days when a thousand flowers bloomed and the educational life chances of too many of our children wilted.

- The implication is that we need a transition from an era of prescription to an era of professionalism – in which the balance between national prescription and schools leading reform will change.

However, achieving this re-balancing is not straightforward. As Michael Fullan (2003) once commented, it takes capacity to build capacity, and if there is insufficient capacity to begin with, it is folly to announce that a move to 'professionalism' provides the basis of a new approach. The key question is 'how do we get there?' because we cannot simply move from one era to the other without self-consciously building professional capacity throughout the system. Building professional capacity implies the adoption of authentic school improvement principles and strategies that raise standards and emancipate at the same time.

It is this progression that is illustrated in figure 1.2 and discussed at length in *Every School a Great School* (Hopkins 2007). This insight seems by now to have achieved widespread support. Barber (2009) stressed the need for system leadership along with capacity building. Hargreaves and Shirley (2009) argued for a 'Fourth Way of Change' that consisted of combining top-down 'national vision, government steering and support with "professional involvement" and "public engagement" all for the purpose of promoting "learning and results".' It is this general approach that seems to feed current debates of transformation change in education (e.g. Salzburg Global Seminar 2022).

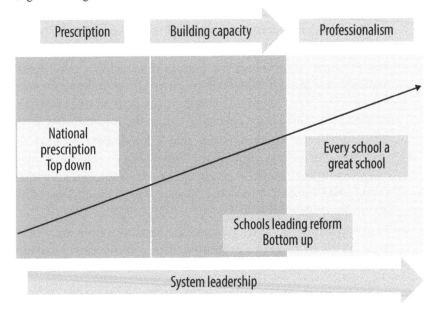

Figure 1.2 Towards system wide sustainable reform

It is worth taking a little time to unpack the thinking underlying the diagram – four points in particular need to be made:

- The first is to emphasise that neither top-down nor bottom-up change work when conducted in isolation; they must be in balance, in a creative tension. At any one time, the balance between the two will, of course, depend on context.
- Secondly, at the early stages of a reform programme when the system is in a relatively poor performing state then more central direction is needed. This reflects the initial emphasis on national

prescription as seen in the left-hand segment of the diagram. Over time, as competence and confidence increases, the policy agenda and school practice moves towards the right-hand side of the diagram.

- Thirdly, it should be no surprise to realise that the right-hand segment is relatively unknown territory. It implies horizontal and lateral ways of working with assumptions and governance arrangements very different from what is conventionally known. The main difficulty in imagining this landscape is that the thinking of most people is constrained by their experiences within the power structure and norms of the left-hand segment of the diagram, and the binary distinction between top-down and bottom-up.

- Finally, it needs to be reiterated that the transition from prescription to professionalism implied by the diagram is not easy to achieve. To move from one to the other, strategies are required that not only continue to raise standards, but also build capacity within the system through an emancipatory process.

It needs to be emphasised that successful school improvement is neither singularly system-led nor led by individual schools – it is best achieved by one supporting the other in an actively interdependent, mutually beneficial relationship. This is why system leadership as the main driver of such an approach is so important. As will be seen in chapter 7, system leaders care about and work for the success of other schools as well as their own. They measure their success in terms of improving student learning and increasing achievement and strive to both raise the bar and narrow the gap(s). Crucially they are willing to shoulder system leadership roles in the belief that to change the larger system you must engage with it in a meaningful way' (Hopkins 2009; Higham, Hopkins and Matthews 2009).

Returning to the strategic dimension of figure 1.2, as has already been intimated, the transition from 'prescription' to 'professionalism' requires strategies that not only continue to raise standards but also build capacity and realise emancipation within the system. This point is key, one cannot just drive to continue to raise standards in an instrumental way, and one also needs to develop social, intellectual and organisational capital. Building capacity demands, as is argued in chapter 8, that we replace numerous central initiatives with a national consensus on a limited number of educational trends. For the moment, it is vital to stress that each of the phases identified in figure 1.2, imply a different set of complementary strategies that propel the school progressively from one phase of development to the next.

There are two relatively new features to the analysis so far. The first is the emphasis on narrative and its impact on both on strategy and culture. As is seen in chapter 3, it is the nature of narrative that makes it integrative and cumulative, presenting a series of complex and interacting initiatives within a unifying story around the image of a journey. This is 'strategic' insofar as it integrates a wide variety of initiatives and projects with a forward-looking perspective and is 'cultural' insofar as it speaks both to the individual and collective contribution. The second feature is the emphasis on 'systems, structures and scaffolding' and the transferability and sustainability of best practice. School improvement and system reform depends, not just on correlating growth state and improvement strategy, but critically on excellent practice being developed, shared, demonstrated, and adopted across and between systems as well as schools. We will see a variety of examples of this in the following pages.

CODA: TRANSFORMATION AND PARADIGM SHIFTS

The argument made in the introduction about the inadequacy of 'top-down' or instrumental policies in dealing with the accumulation of challenges facing many educational systems is consistent with a range of other educational exhortations that are currently calling for transformation rather than reform. The Salzburg Statement for Education Transformation (2022) argues that reform which results in a better version of existing systems improvement can only be incremental. Whereas transformation begins with values and mindsets and through that changes the purpose of the system. Similarly, both WISE (2022) and Mckinsey (2020) as we have seen, call for 're-imagination' in terms of educational leadership and teaching and learning.

Similarly, the Foundation for Education Development (2022:5):

- *Flag that one of the biggest challenges to education in England is its historically short-termist approach to policymaking.*

- *Highlights the need for a new approach to empower politicians and education stakeholders to find solutions to long-term problems.*

Many agree on the problem and share my unease, the question is what is the most productive way forward?

In the introduction, I connected the call for transformation with Jurgen Habermas's articulation of three contrasting paradigms. Fullan (2021:36) in *The Right Drivers for Whole System Success* contends that if you want system change, you must change the system or at least the way in which you think about the system and the values that underpin it in radical ways. He reminds us of Thomas Kuhn's (1962) *The Structure of Scientific Revolutions*. In that seminal work, Kuhn argued that 'paradigm shifts' (alterations in the principles that govern models of thinking and action) occur under two conditions. One requirement is that the current model is patently no longer working; the second is the presence of a viable alternative.

That the first condition is met is palpably true if the argument of this book is accepted. It is with the second condition that I deviate a little from Fullan; he argues that his 'right drivers' constitute the components of the new paradigm. There is no doubt that they are consistent with the analysis conducted here, but before adopting such a strategic solution, I would like us to consider in a little more depth the nature of paradigms. In a slightly different context, Paulo Freire once memorably remarked that, '[...] methodological confusion can always be related to ideological error' (Hopkins 2001:19). This is also the case with school and system improvement!

We have already noted that the tension in contemporary school improvement and system reform efforts is commonly related to a tension between 'top down' and 'bottom up'. One can characterise these two opposing forces like this:

Top down = Outside in = Positivism

Positivism in terms of school improvement, as with GERM, is related to top-down initiatives designed to result in short-term, measurable gains against largely politically defined criteria.

Bottom up = Inside out = Interpretive approach

The interpretive approach acknowledges that reality is constructed through the meanings and actions of individuals.

The tension felt by many of the educational leaders that I work with around the world is explained by the fact that they are on the one hand the victims of GERM and are subjected to top-down policy forces; and on the other, they wish to create a school culture that is driven by moral purpose and that serves the best purposes of their students (and teachers). They are caught between the proverbial rock and a hard place and there seems to be no escape.

Neither of these two broad approaches provides an entirely satisfactory basis for authentic school improvement as I define it in *School Improvement for Real* (Hopkins 2001) and again here. Yet advocates of both the positive and the interpretative perspective assume (Carr and Kemmis 1986:105): '... that the two positions they represent more or less exhaust the range of possible options available for educational research to adopt.'

Yet, as Carr and Kemmis (1986:129–130) continue, there are major objections to both approaches:

... the positivist idea that knowledge has a purely instrumental value in solving educational problems and the consequent tendency to see all educational issues as technical in character needs to be firmly resisted. ... However, the recognition that educational theory must be grounded in the interpretations of teachers (or leaders), is not in itself sufficient.

Fortunately, there is a third approach or paradigm – 'critical theory' – that addresses both weaknesses. This approach originated with the 'Frankfurt School' of philosophy; a community of scholars based in Frankfurt. The overriding concern of the Frankfurt School was (Carr and Kemmis 1986:130):

... to articulate a view of theory that has the central task of emancipating people from the positivist 'domination of thought' through their own understandings and actions.

In *Knowledge and Human Interests*, Jurgen Habermas (1972), the favourite son of the Frankfurt School, describes the three ways in which humans know and construe the world. These, he terms, technical, practical and emancipatory. For Habermas, knowledge is the outcome of human activity that is motivated by natural needs and interests. These interests guide and shape the way knowledge is constituted in different human activities. The *technical* orientation relates to positivism, the practical orientation to the interpretative paradigm, and the *critical* to emancipation and transformation.

Table 1.2 summarises Habermas's tri-paradigmatic framework by relating the three types of human interest to the kind of knowledge it generates and its school improvement focus. Ted Aoki (Pinar and Irwin 2004) in particular, has applied these orientations to education in terms of curriculum inquiry research with insight and wisdom.

It is critical theory then that offers us a way out of the binary dichotomy of top-down and bottom-up and provides the opportunity for our hard-working heads and principals to maximise the benefit of their vision and endeavor. Critical theory provides the basis for a third way towards school and system improvement in line with the argument of this book. Critical theory provides the architecture for the paradigm that school improvement activists need to inhabit. We return to this theme, in a little more detail, in the epilogue at the end of the book.

Type of human interest	Kind of knowledge	School improvement focus
Technical – top down - Prediction and control	**Instrumental** - Causal explanation and empirical knowing	… is **short term**, using bureaucratic policy options and narrow outcome measures.
Practical – bottom up - Interpretation and understanding	**Practical** - Understanding and giving meaning	… is on **process and culture** and on creating a harmonious school environment.
Critical – transformation - Critique and liberation	**Emancipatory** - Critical knowing that combines reflection and action	… is **authentic**, with an emphasis on student learning, intervention and empowerment

Table 1.2 Habermas's tri-paradigmatic framework

Yes, of course, our educational systems need 'transformation' (Salzburg Global Seminar 2022). This is not achieved however by just adopting *The Next Big Thing in School Improvement* as Allen (2021) and her colleagues so clearly argue. Rather, we realise this by abandoning the current dominant paradigm that is based on 'technical – top-down' instrumental approaches focused on prediction and control. We need instead to embrace the critical paradigm that values critique, liberation and emancipation. It is the critical paradigm that underpins authentic school improvement (Hopkins 2001) and provides the action framework for Unleashing Greatness.

In concluding, it is important to remember that the challenge of school and system reform has great moral depth to it. This is because it directly addresses the learning needs of our students, the professional growth of teachers and the enhancement of the role of the school as an agent of social change. The Unleashing Greatness framework described in the following chapter presents a simple and practical approach to school improvement Hopkins (2020). It is based on the principles discussed in this chapter and designed for schools who are driven by a moral purpose and are committed to developing the capacity that will enable their students to achieve excellence wherever their potential leads them (Hopkins 2022a).

CHAPTER 2:
THE UNLEASHING GREATNESS FRAMEWORK

INTRODUCTION: EDMONDS'S DICTUM

In the mid-1970s, at the very start of the effective school's movement in the USA, the renowned black educator Ron Edmonds (1979) posed the following challenge by way of three declarative statements:

1. We can, whenever and wherever we choose, successfully teach all children whose schooling is of interest to us.
2. We already know more than we need to do that.
3. Whether or not we do it must finally depend on how we feel about the fact that we haven't so far.

Although these declarations are now more than 40 years old, in several respects Edmonds' assertions still ring true today. His aspiration echoes that of this book in underlining the belief that student achievement can be realised at scale, but only if it is underpinned by a strong sense of moral purpose linked to strategic acumen.

The purpose of this chapter is to outline a school improvement strategy that assists in 'unleashing greatness' and delivers on Ron Edmond's aspiration. The Unleashing Greatness framework proposes a simple and practical approach to school improvement designed for schools who are currently overwhelmed by a myriad of often incompatible demands from governments, community and professional associations. Many schools find themselves besieged and bogged down by competing policy initiatives and external accountabilities yet wish to chart their own distinctive way that serves to enhance the learning journeys of all their students. In the face of such innovation overload, I am reminded of the wise advice that Michael Fullan (2016) gave to our schools some years ago – just do one or two things as well as you possibly can, and then do everything else as well as you would have done anyway!

In outlining the Unleashing Greatness framework, in this chapter:

- I begin by locating the framework within the tradition of whole school improvement strategies and the practice of our proven school improvement programmes.
- Then, outline the Unleashing Greatness framework and describe the first four of the eight steps as the planning phase.
- Followed by steps 5 to 8 as the action phase.
- We then pose the question, 'Where do we start?'
- In the coda, we review the series of questions that can aid the implementation of the framework and provide some case studies of how schools begun their journeys of school improvement.

A GENERIC MODEL FOR SCHOOL IMPROVEMENT

In the previous chapter, reference was made to the growth of comprehensive models of school reform that could be adopted by individual schools. These 'whole school designs' combined elements from the school effectiveness and school improvement research bases to focus upon curriculum and instruction, as well as management and organisational variables (Stringfield and Nunnery 2010). Some of these approaches were designed to meet particular curriculum needs in literacy such as 'Success for All' (Slavin and Madden 2013), while others such as the 'High Reliability Schools' (Reynolds et al 2006) tended to reflect a broad set of principles for organisational change and development and were not targeted at any specific curriculum or subject area.

The framework for school improvement utilised by Unleashing Greatness follows in this tradition. The approach eschews both top-down and à la carte approaches, in favour of a whole school improvement strategy designed to address the learning needs of all students in a particular school (Hopkins 2013). Consistency and high expectations are the lubricants for such integrated whole school strategies. Some thought also needs to be given to how the school organises itself to become what is commonly called 'a professional learning community' (Harris and Jones 2017b). This, as we will see, involves teachers not only planning together but also observing each other and gathering formative data on the impact of the various strategies on student learning. School improvement from the inside out, as we term it, occurs where individual programme elements combine to create a comprehensive strategy that is both systemic and purposeful. The basic generic or default approach described here is amenable to adaptation to context, as well as laying the basis for differential approaches to school improvement.

The generic school improvement strategy that follows was initially developed as part of the *Improving the Quality of Education for All* programme (Hopkins 2002). The model not only focuses on improving student behaviour, learning and attainment, but also pays attention to teacher and school development. The approach has been refined over time and adapted to changing circumstances, particularly in relation to *Curiosity and Powerful Learning* (Hopkins and Craig 2018a). It is based on a belief that to advance achievement for all students, it is necessary to address not only the learning of individual teachers but also the organisational capacity of the school. In other words, without an emphasis on capacity building, a school will be unable to sustain continuous improvement efforts that result in student attainment. As shown in figure 2.1, the approach has two major components: the capacity building dimension and the strategic dimension.

The capacity building dimension relates to the conditions at both school and classroom levels. Through sustained work on the conditions for development, the school enhances its capacity for managing change. The strategic dimension reflects the ability of the school to plan sensibly for development. Most schools are by now familiar with the need to establish a clear and practical focus for their improvement efforts. In this sense, the choice about priorities for development represents the school's interpretation of the current reform agenda. The final element in the framework is school culture. A key assumption is that school improvement strategies will lead to cultural change in schools through modifications to their internal conditions. It is this cultural change that supports innovations in teaching and learning processes, which leads to enhanced outcomes for students.

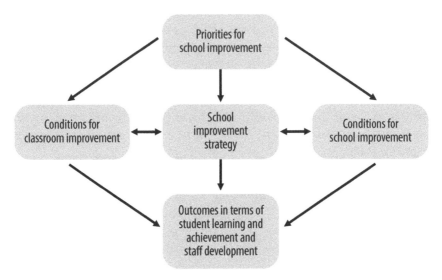

Figure 2.1 A strategic school improvement framework

It is in these ways that the most successful schools pursue their improvement efforts. While focusing on the learning needs of students in the context of systemic and environmental demands, they also recognise that school structures must reflect both these demands, as well as offering a suitable vehicle for the future development of the school. In this sense, the structure of the school provides the skeleton that supports cultural growth, rather than the framework that constrains it. This three-stage school improvement process has an unrelenting focus on learning and attainment at its core. Given this central focus, the school improvement strategy encompasses classroom practice, particularly the expansion of teachers' pedagogic repertoire, and the building of capacity at the school level especially the redesign of staff development. While this is not a 'quick fix' approach, many of the activities involved will bring short as well as medium-term gains.

The three stages are: establishing the process, going whole school, and sustaining momentum.

Stage 1: Establishing the process

This stage involves:

- Commitment to the school improvement approach
- Selection of a school improvement team
- Enquiring into the strengths and weaknesses of the school
- Designing the whole school program
- Seeding the whole school approach

Stage 2: Going whole school

This cycle of activity usually lasts between two terms and up to a year. The activities in this phase are:

- Initial whole school training day(s)
- Establishing the curriculum and teaching focus through instructional rounds, or other forms of non-judgmental observation
- Establishing learning teams
- Initial cycle of enquiry
- Sharing initial success and impact on student learning from the 'curriculum tour'

Stage 3: Sustaining momentum

It is in this phase that the capacity for change at school and classroom level becomes more secure. Learning teams become an established way of working and there is an expansion of the range of teaching strategies used throughout the curriculum. This activity includes:

- Establishing further cycles of enquiry
- Building teacher learning into the process
- Sharpening the focus on student learning
- Finding ways of sharing success and building networks
- Reflecting on the culture of the school and department

When these ways of working are embedded, then not only will student attainment have risen, but also the school will have established itself as an effective learning organisation.

This potential is best realised and learning capability enhanced through the range of theories of action and teaching and learning models (see chapter 5) that teachers use with their students. The teaching and learning strategies are not 'free floating', but embedded in the schemes of work and curriculum content that teachers use to structure the learning in their lessons. These schemes of work also have the potential to be shared between schools and be available for wider dissemination.

Finally, this way of working assumes a whole school dimension through the establishment of a staff development infrastructure, an emphasis on high expectations and the careful attention to the consistency of teaching and the discussion of pedagogy that pervades the cultures of these schools through the exercise of instructional leadership (see chapter 7). It is this generic model that provides a context for discussing the eight steps of the Unleashing Greatness framework in the rest of this chapter.

THE UNLEASHING GREATNESS FRAMEWORK

Although the eight steps of the Unleashing Greatness framework are described sequentially starting below, they are essentially interactive. As it will become evident further into the book, schools can actually start anywhere in the process. The eight steps are also just a starting point, school improvement is more complex than this. They do, however, provide a way in and summarise many of the key ideas in school improvement research, policy and practice, many of which are reviewed in *Exploding the Myths of School Reform* (Hopkins 2013). The eight steps and the key evidence behind each of them are:

1. **Clarify moral purpose**: Ensure that the achievement and learning of students expressed as moral purpose is at the centre of everything that the school and teachers do.

2. **Focus on classroom practice**: The quality of a school or system cannot exceed the quality of its teachers: it is axiomatic therefore that the focus of school improvement is on the practice of teaching.

3. **Decide on the non-negotiables**: These are the key improvement objectives that the school focuses on unrelentingly in the short/medium term that are underpinned by a 'development' (as compared with a 'maintenance') structure that ensures that adequate resources are made available for improvement work.

4. **Articulate the narrative**: Moral purpose may be at the heart of successful school and system improvement, but we will not realise this purpose without powerful and increasingly specified strategies and protocols embraced in a narrative that both energises and provides direction for our colleagues, students and communities.

5. **Utilise instructional rounds and theories of action**: These are the key strategies for diagnosing and articulating effective teaching practice through non-judgmental observation and the development of protocols to ensure consistency and precision.

6. **Embrace peer coaching and triads:** Provide the infrastructure for professional development in the school and the means for putting the theories of action into practice.

7. **Practice instructional leadership**: Is the leadership strategy most closely associated with increased levels of student achievement through the employment of four key behaviours: setting vision; managing teaching and learning; developing people and organisation re-design.

8. **Exploit networking**: The most effective schools network with each other in order to learn from their best, collaborate purposefully, and to share outstanding practice.

The eight steps fall into two phases: the planning phase (steps 1–4) and the action phase (steps 5–8).

THE PLANNING PHASE

CLARIFY MORAL PURPOSE

Moral purpose is not to be confused or equated with some form of romantic sentimentalism. It is clear from the global evidence of school performance that the most successful schools ensure that the achievement and learning of students expressed as moral purpose is at the centre of all that teachers and leaders do. Aspiration such as 'enabling every student to realise their potential' is fine as far as it goes, but we then have to define in more concrete and contextual terms what that means for our students. This requires a focus on those strategies that have a track record of accelerating student achievement such as building student learning capability, personalising learning and the curriculum, assessment for learning and giving students a voice in their own learning.

The importance of moral purpose (as we shall revisit in chapter 6) is underscored by Daniel Pink (2011) in his book, *Drive*. In it he outlines the three key components of intrinsic motivation: autonomy, mastery and purpose. He argues that people, teachers, may become disengaged and demotivated at work if they don't understand, or can't invest in, the 'bigger picture'. But those who believe that they are working toward something larger and more important than themselves are often the most hard-working, productive and engaged. So, encouraging teachers to find moral purpose in their work – for instance, by focusing on enhancing the life scripts of students through using increasingly powerful forms of curriculum that integrate content, learning and values – can win not only their minds, but also their hearts. Thus, moral purpose in the gift that keeps on giving, it not only ensures better outcomes for students but also deepens the work culture of the school as well as the commitment of teachers.

Moral purpose may be at the heart of successful school and system improvement, but we will not be able to realise this purpose without powerful and increasingly specified strategies and tools to allow us to deal with the increasingly turbulent and complex communities and contexts we serve. The key is that moral purpose and strategic action are opposite sides of the same coin.

KEY QUESTIONS

- Does your school's version of moral purpose link aspiration to action?
- Does your school's version of moral purpose reflect the values of students, parents and the community?
- Is your school's version of moral purpose widely accepted by the whole school staff?

FOCUS ON CLASSROOM PRACTICE

Barber and Mourshed's (2007:40) widely referenced international study based on the PISA research referred to earlier concluded that:

- the quality of an education system cannot exceed the quality of its teachers.
- the only way to improve outcomes is to improve instruction.
- this means taking professional development into the classroom and making it routine (e.g., through peer observation, lesson study, demonstration lessons).

The global evidence is clear – it is improving the quality of classroom practice rather than structural reform that has the most powerful effect in terms of raising student outcomes. It is axiomatic that the focus of school improvement, the non-negotiables described, need to be on teaching.

It is the lack of such a focus that has inhibited recent reform efforts from enhancing the potential of our students. We need to reach down into the classroom and deepen reform efforts by moving beyond superficial curriculum change to a more profound understanding of how teacher behaviour connects to learning. It requires a direct and unrelenting focus on what many are now calling the 'instructional core' (City et al 2009). As seen in figure 2.2, and, in its simplest terms, 'the instructional core is composed of the teacher and the student in the presence of content' (City et al 2009).

We discuss the instructional core further in chapter 4, but there are two features associated with it that require emphasising at the outset:

- The first feature is that one element of the instructional core cannot be changed without impacting directly on the others.
- The second feature is the appreciation that the 'instructional task' is at the centre of the instructional core. The instructional task is the actual work that students do as part of classroom practice. It is the tasks that students undertake and complete that predict their performance. This is particularly the case when the task is firmly located within the student's 'zone of proximal development'.

Although each of the three elements of the instructional core are equally important, in the early stages of our school improvement work we focus primarily on the quality and consistency of teaching. This is not necessarily in precedence to the curriculum, but more as a means of delivering it. Enhancing the quality of teaching practice will have the most immediate and sustained impact on student performance. The truth of this contention has been evidenced over the past ten years through the work of John Hattie (2009; 2023), particularly his books *Visible Learning* and *Visible Learning: The Sequel.* In both books, he analyses many hundreds of research studies on how different teacher practices influence student learning. We discuss his work further in chapter 5 particularly his summary (in table 5.1) of those practices with low impact on student outcomes as compared with those with high levels of impact. What is interesting is that many popular policy initiatives and structural changes have low impact as compared with the more precise teaching strategies that focus directly on student learning. We obviously try to focus our school improvement efforts on those teacher behaviours in the right column of his diagram!

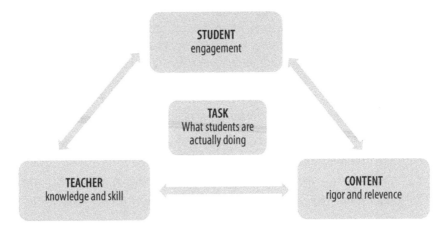

Figure 2.2 The instructional core (modified from City et al 2019)

KEY QUESTIONS

- Does your school staff understand the importance of the instructional core both strategically and operationally?
- How confident are you that all the tasks that your student's undertake are located within their zones of proximal development?

- Are the teaching practices employed in the school well specified, consistently applied, and directly applicable to the learning needs of your students?

DECIDE ON THE NON-NEGOTIABLES

We noted earlier the common experience of many schools who are overloaded by the pressure for change and the overload of policy initiatives. So much so that many schools and their leaders feel virtually paralysed by them. With the best of intentions, they try and do everything and then end up by doing nothing well. We also noted Michael Fullan's advice to just do one or two things as well as you possibly can, and then do everything else as well as you would have done anyway. There is now global evidence to support this common sense guidance (Mourshead et al 2010). Those successful leaders who do this tend to follow a common 'playbook' of practices:

- Decide on what is 'non-negotiable'.
- Install capable and like-minded people in the most critical positions.
- Engage with stakeholders.
- Secure the resources for non-negotiables.
- Get 'early wins' on the board quickly.

The non-negotiables become the key development objectives that the school focuses on unrelentingly in the short/medium term. They are underpinned by a 'development' (as compared with a 'maintenance') structure that ensures that adequate resources are made available for improvement work, in particular the identification of a school improvement team and peer coaching. This last sentence is crucial but needs a little unpacking.

Part of the overload problem is related to the school's inability to distinguish between 'maintenance' and 'development' (Hopkins 2013). Schools obviously need to be able to maintain their existing organisational functions to a high level, but also at the same time to have the capacity to develop and change. The **maintenance structure** is concerned with relatively permanent systems and processes that are necessary for the school to get its work done as efficiently as possible. The **development**

structure is there to adopt new ways of working – the non-negotiables – that over time add value to the school as new practices become common practice and the 'way we do things around here'. What usually happens though is that schools tend to overburden their maintenance system by asking it to take on development roles for which it was never designed. The separation of maintenance activities from development work is essential for the continuous improvement of a school and both need their separate infrastructures as shown in figure 2.3.

The three key elements of the schools development structure are: the establishing of a school improvement team, peer coaching, and teacher collaboration. All three components are described later, but a brief word here about school improvement teams.

Typically, the school improvement team is cross-hierarchical and could be as few as three or four in comparatively small schools, to between six and eight in large schools. Though one of the team is likely to be the head or principal, it is important to establish groups that are genuinely representative of the range of perspectives and ideas available in the school. The school improvement group is responsible for managing school improvement efforts, the non-negotiables, on a day-to-day basis within the school. They are supported through a core training program, through networking with school improvement teams from other schools, by external consultancy support and facilitation, and a limited amount of allocated time to do their work.

KEY QUESTIONS

- Is the whole staff clear about what the non-negotiables are in your school and are actively working on them?
- Is there a distinction between the maintenance and development functions in your school, particularly the purposes, funding and responsibilities involved?
- Is there a school improvement team in your school and how do they operate?

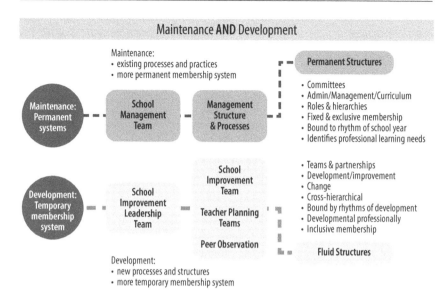

Figure 2.3 Maintenance and development structures

ARTICULATE THE NARRATIVE

Stories help us make sense of where we are and to remember where we are headed. Moral purpose may be at the heart of successful school and system improvement, but we will not realise this purpose without powerful and increasingly specified strategies and protocols embraced in a narrative to take the school forward. It is this that both energises and provides direction for our colleagues, students and communities. Steering a school improvement strategy is easier when everyone who must contribute to it – leaders, teachers, support staff, our students, and the wider school community – shares a common story about:

- where our school is now (and what will happen if we stay on the same course).
- where our school is headed as we take the course mapped out in our school improvement strategy.
- why we should commit to the new direction.

Another way of thinking about these points is offered by Chip and Dan Heath (2011) in *Switch: How to change things when change is hard.*

The Switch idea	The school improvement perspective
A credible idea makes people believe	Our theories of action
An emotional idea makes people care	Our moral purpose
The right story makes people act	Our collaborative action influences every classroom, the whole school, the system

Deep in our minds, we give stories a privileged place. They are a currency for conversation, for exchanging ideas. A story is a medium for understanding in concrete ways how things are and how we can improve them.

Next time you are in an audience listening to a speech larded with statistics and facts, try to recall them afterwards. One or two may stick, but most are lost to us. Yet when speakers tell us stories, we are more likely to remember the story and the speaker. As Mark Turner (1998) once presciently wrote in *The Literary Mind*:

> *Story, projection and parable do work for us; they make everyday life possible; they are the root of human thought; they are not primarily – or even importantly – entertainment.*

A story is a flight simulator for the mind – we can chart a new direction and vividly see where it takes us. It's this vividness that schools and system leaders can summon through stories. It is a vividness about both seeing the path ahead, and about taking that path – it is about acting with clarity. Good stories follow a familiar narrative arc as seen in figure 2.4.

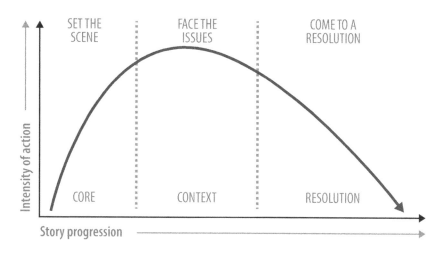

We draw on the narrative arc to construct our school improvement story.

Core	Context	Response
The core story describes: - the direction - what success will look like (desired state)	The context details: - challenges - opportunities	The response describes what we intend to do about the context factors: - how we will manage the challenges - how we will grasp the opportunities

Figure 2.4 The narrative arc

Good school improvement stories have the following characteristics (Hopkins and Craig 2018c:10); they:

- are **urgent** and translate the vision of curiosity, of a focus on inquiry, into clear principles for action.

- offer a **motivating** image of the future we are creating for our school and our students.

- link **moral purpose** to action in practical and concrete ways – our values are the constant companions of our actions.

- make **tangible connections** between teaching and learning. These connections sustain a teaching and learning culture that produces and maintains high standards and student empowerment.
- are **inclusive**, and **oriented to action** in every classroom and across the whole school.
- are **shared and understood** by staff, students and the school community.

We have found it very helpful if not essential to, at some point, translate the narrative into a two/three-year school improvement planning framework that steers implementation of the non-negotiables and monitors their impact (Hopkins and Craig 2018c:12). This framework provides both guidance and evidence for:

- building the narrative.
- ensuring priorities are selected that produce short-term gains.
- laying the foundations for the next phase of the school improvement journey.

The school improvement team is responsible for implementing the school improvement framework. Further guidance for developing the narrative is found at the start of the following chapter.

KEY QUESTIONS

Does your school's narrative link moral purpose to action?

Does the core story describe the direction the school is moving in and what success will look like – the desired state?

Is your narrative understood and owned by all sections of the school community – students, staff, parents and governors?

THE ACTION PHASE

INSTRUCTIONAL ROUNDS AND THEORIES OF ACTION

Viewing classroom practice in terms of the instructional core described earlier, offers us the potential of establishing a professional practice in the school that can create a new culture of teaching and learning. The question is, how do we actually create this new culture of teaching and learning that embraces the instructional core?

One answer is to establish an instructional rounds process to generate a shared understanding and common language around effective teaching practices (City et al 2009). In our school improvement work, the outcome of the process is the identification of a set of theories of action for the school and network that can be used as a basis for further professional development and school improvement.

A theory of action connects the actions of teachers with the consequences of their actions – the learning and achievement of their students. A theory of action is a link between cause and effect: if we take a particular action, *then* we expect that action to have specific effects. Together, these theories of action provide the basis of the protocols we have developed that ensure precision, consistency and engagement in the classrooms of our schools

The process works like this:

- The network convenes in the host school for an instructional round visit. The purpose of the instructional round is to generate a series of theories of action that present a positive picture of the pedagogic practice of the school. The emphasis is solely on description, not evaluation or judgment.
- After completing the round of classroom observations, the entire group assembles in a common location to work through the process of description, analysis and prediction.
- Participants then develop a series of 'theory of action' principles from the analysis of the observations and discusses the next level of work for the school and network to assist them on their school improvement journeys.

As our experience with instructional rounds has continued to deepen through experience in schools in the UK, Australia, Sweden and elsewhere, we have learned that despite the phase or context of schooling, the theories of action generated by each school were in most cases very similar. They are (see chapter 5):

- harnessing learning intentions, narrative and pace.
- setting challenging learning tasks.

- framing higher order questions.
- connecting feedback and data.
- committing to assessment for learning.
- implementing cooperative group structures.

It is important to note that all of these theories of action are characterised by an approach to teaching that has enquiry and personalised learning at its centre. They also have a high level of empirical support in the educational research literature (see Hattie 2009) and are consistent with most policy and accountability prescriptions related to effective teaching. The six theories of action for comprise the content of our Curiosity and Powerful Learning manual (Hopkins and Craig 2018b). The manual contains a description of the individual theory of action as well as a protocol or rubric. Each rubric provides a precise description of the habits, behaviours and ways of doing that characterise teacher practice at four phases of a professional development continuum: commencing, intermediate, accomplished and expert. The teacher protocols provide a common reference point, specification and language for teachers to use for professional learning and development through for peer coaching as seen in the section on the following page. We discuss the theories of action that we have developed as part of our ongoing school improvement programmes in chapter 5.

KEY QUESTIONS

Does your school staff regularly engage in instructional rounds and appreciate that the focus of the observations is on description not evaluation or judgment?

How far do the six theories of action reflect common consistent and widespread practice in your school?

Does your school's school improvement team contextualise and provide examples of the theories of action related to the specific context of teaching and learning in the school?

PEER COACHING AND TRIADS

The potential contained in the theories of action described is to create a new culture of teaching within the school that promotes both enquiry and achievement. This requires adopting staff development strategies that have the ability to build a common language of instructional practice within and across schools.

The strategy most suited to the acquisition of the theories of action is the now established approach to 'peer coaching' process developed by Bruce Joyce and his colleagues (Joyce and Showers 1995; Joyce and Calhoun 2010). Their research on staff development has identified a number of key training components which, when used in combination, have much greater power than when they are used alone. The major components of training are:

1. Presentation of theory or description of skill or strategy.
2. Modelling or demonstration of skills or models of teaching.
3. Practise in simulated and classroom settings.
4. Structured and open-ended feedback (provision of information about performance).
5. Peer coaching for application (hands-on, in-classroom assistance with the transfer of skills and strategies to the classroom).

It is also helpful to distinguish between the locations in which these various forms of staff development are best located – either in the 'workshop' or the 'workplace'. The workshop, which is equivalent to the best practice on the traditional professional development course, is where teachers gain understanding, see demonstrations of the teaching strategy they may wish to acquire, and have the opportunity to practise them in a non-threatening environment. This is steps 1–4 above. If the aim, however, is to transfer those skills back into the workplace – the classroom and school – then merely attending the workshop is insufficient. This implies changes to the workplace and the way in which staff development is organised. In particular, this means the opportunity for immediate and sustained practice, collaboration and peer coaching, within triads or small groups of staff – step 5.

Ideally every adult working with students in the school will be in a triad or peer coaching group. It is common practice for the composition of peer coaching groups to be in mixed ability, cross – curricula or cross year groups. Different combinations obviously have different advantages – friendship groups for example may be preferred initially if staff are not experienced with, or are fearful of, observation. Most schools have a member of the school improvement team as a member of or linked to each group.

Peer observation within triads needs to be scheduled on a regular basis and built into the timetable. This however need not be time consuming: fifteen to twenty minutes observation when using the protocol is usually sufficient. This though needs to be followed as soon as possible by a debrief discussion using the data gathered from the protocol. This can be during coffee breaks or over lunch. Ideally peer coaching member A observes peer coaching member B in week one; then peer coaching member B observes peer coaching member C in week two, and so on. The triad should meet once every half term as a group of three to record progress and plan the next half terms observations. Using these reports, the school improvement team then reviews progress overall.

KEY QUESTIONS

Does every member of your school staff part belong to a peer coaching group?

Do the peer coaching groups meet regularly as part of timetabled staff development activity?

How far do the outcomes of these peer observations contribute to higher standards of learning and teaching in the school?

INSTRUCTIONAL LEADERSHIP

Instructional leadership is the leadership approach most closely associated with increased levels of student achievement. It is a function that is a) pervasive in the school/network/trust rather than being located in a single role; b) generates a culture of high expectations and collaborative working; and, c) has moral purpose and the enhancement of student learning at its core.

Our recent work on instructional leadership has been widely cited (Leithwood, Harris and Hopkins 2019). Our seven strong claims are listed in table 2.1.

1	School leadership is second only to classroom instruction as an influence on student learning.
2	Almost all successful leaders draw on the same repertoire of basic leadership practices.
3	It is the enactment of these basic leadership practices – not the practices themselves – that is responsive to the context.
4	School leaders improve pupil learning indirectly through their influence on staff motivation and working conditions.
5	School leadership has a greater influence on schools and pupils when it is widely distributed.
6	Some patterns of leadership distribution are much more effective than others.
7	A small handful of personal 'traits' (such as being open minded, flexible, persistent and optimistic) explain a high proportion of the variation in leader effectiveness.

Table 2.1 Seven strong claims about successful school leadership

In the paper we describe the four central domains of instructional leadership: setting direction, managing teaching and learning, developing people and developing the organisation. Table 2.2 sets out these practices (Leithwood, Harris and Hopkins 2019). This analysis reinforces the argument that enhancing learning and teaching is the key priority for school leadership.

Core practices	Key instructional leadership behaviours
Setting direction	Ensuring that the school's vision sees every learner reaching their potential.
	Translating this vision into a whole school curriculum and high expectations.
Managing teaching and learning	Ensuring a high degree of consistency by planning, implementing and using specifications of practice.
	Supporting innovation in teaching practices that enable personalised learning for all students.
	Expanding the repertoire of teaching practice to include high leverage practices that influence the learning of all students.

Developing people	Enabling students to become active learners. Creating a school that operates as a professional learning community for teachers.
Developing the organisation	Creating an evidence-based school and an effective organisation. Participating in collaborative networks that build curriculum diversity, professional support, and extended services.

Table 2.2 Key capabilities of instructional leaders

Although the impact of leadership on student achievement and school effectiveness has been acknowledged for some time, it is only recently that we have begun to understand more fully the fine-grained nature of instructional leadership. We explore this further in chapter 7.

KEY QUESTIONS

How far are the seven strong claims from table 2.1 evident in the leadership behaviours in your school?

What proportion of their working time are the senior leaders in your school focusing on the four key behaviours? If it is not 75% or above, why not?

Is there a development or implementation plan in your school that leads coherently and strategically in identifiable phases from narrative to eventual culture change?

NETWORKING

So far, the discussion has focused on the individual school however, no school is an island and will always be part of a 'system' of one sort or another. If a school's improvement journey is to be sustained over the long term, the developments must be integrated into the very fabric of the system pedagogy. McKinsey (Mourshed, Chijioke and Barber 2010) identified three ways that improving systems do this:

- by establishing collaborative practices,
- by developing a mediating layer between the schools and the centre; and
- by architecting tomorrow's leadership.

We have already discussed collaboration and leadership, so it is important to stress here the need for some 'mediating level' within the system to connect the centre to schools and schools to each other. The most effective networks have assumed this role and developed productive ways of learning from their best, for collaborating purposefully and the sharing of outstanding practice.

In England currently, the most common middle tier organisation is the multi-academy trust (MAT) (Hopkins 2016). In outstanding MATs, capacity is built at the local level to ensure that all those in the trust's family of schools progress as rapidly as possible towards excellence. There is a fuller discussion on how to build capacity in MATs through networking in chapter 6.

In our experience, the three key components of this strategy – school improvement teams, staff development processes and networking – should provide the focus for much of the training for executive principals or equivalent within the MAT, as they play their critical role in systemic improvement. In moving to scale, it is clear from international bench marking studies of school performance that (Hopkins 2013):

- Decentralisation by itself increases variation and reduces overall system performance. There is a consequent need for some 'mediating level' within the system to connect the centre to schools and schools to each other – *academy chains and MATs can provide this function.*

- Leadership is the crucial factor both in school transformation and system renewal, so investment particularly in head/principal and leadership training is essential – *hence the use of frameworks such as these eight steps and the school improvement pathway (see chapter 3) to guide action.*

- The quality of teaching is the best determinant of student performance, so that any reform framework must address the professional repertoires of teachers and other adults in the classroom – *thus the focus in high performing trusts on the progress of learners and the development of teachers.*

- Outstanding educational systems find ways of learning from its best and strategically uses the diversity within the system to good advantage – *this is why capacity needs to be built not only within trusts but also between them at the system level.*

KEY QUESTIONS

Is your school a member of an established network or MAT?

If so, does the network or MAT have a coherent and systematic approach to capacity building?

Do you feel that as part of being a member of your network or MAT that best practice is shared and that the whole 'system' is on an improvement trajectory?

WHERE TO START?

For ease of exposition, it is inevitable that chapters such as this tend to follow a linear logic. This has both strengths and weaknesses. A strength is that there is clarity and strategic rationality in the way the phases or steps are described and build on each other. A weakness would be that this approach does not accommodate the contextual realities that schools regularly face. In contemplating where to start there are a number of considerations to take into account.

First, in the introduction, I somewhat arbitrarily divided the eight steps of the Unleashing Greatness framework into a *planning phase* and an *action phase*, which reflects the linear logic noted. Although it is not essential to follow this sequence, it does make sense to plan before moving into action, but as in the tradition of action research, one reflects on the impact of that action and then plans again and moves into another cycle of action research (Hopkins 2014). The structure of this book reflects this way of thinking and acting. As seen in figure 2.5, the following chapters map onto the Unleashing Greatness interactive framework in a way that advice is provided at each step in the process. Consequently, it is hoped that the book will support leaders and school improvement teams at each phase of their school improvement journeys.

Second, as intimated in the previous paragraph, it is not mandatory to follow each step slavishly and that schools may choose to enter at different points in the sequence. For example, one of the schools that we have recently begun to work with had just started an episode of curriculum innovation and did not wish for a variety of reasons to delay implementation. Our advice was that they continue with the curriculum innovation and then backward map to the non-negotiables, which would be related to the curriculum, and establish the narrative around those changes. They would then plan forward to embed curriculum implementation within a more comprehensive process. Other points of entry are, of course, possible.

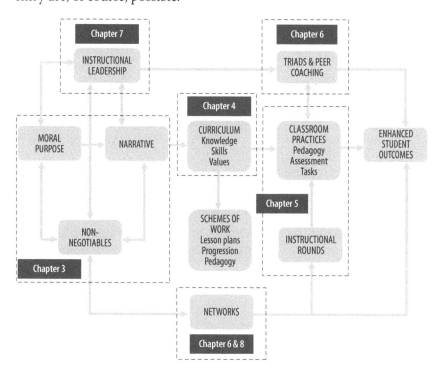

Figure 2.5 Unleashing Greatness chapter structure

Third, as has already been seen in this chapter, we have generated a set of questions related to implementation at the end of each step of the process. The questions are designed to help schools focus on the key actions they need to take for Unleashing Greatness. Many schools that we work with use the questions as a self-evaluation tool before they embark on their school improvement journeys. The full set of questions in a single document can be downloaded from my website (www.profdavidhopkins. com). Each of the following chapters has a coda in which a selection of relevant questions are presented together with some brief illustrative cameos from schools that we work with.

Fourth, the steps in the Unleashing Greatness process should now be clear. In presenting the strategy to colleagues, leaders and school improvement teams, the approach should communicate the strategy in the most effective way possible in order to generate action. Some years ago, Matthew Miles set out some of those conditions under which knowledge is best acted on and then added some comments on the process (cited in Hopkins 2013):

- **Clarity**: The knowledge must be understood clearly, not be fuzzy, vague or confusing.
- **Relevance**: The knowledge is seen as meaningful, as connected to one's normal life and concerns, not irrelevant, inapplicable or impractical.
- **Action images**: The knowledge is or can become exemplified in specific actions, clearly visualised. Without such images, knowledge-based action is unlikely.
- **Will**: There must be motivation, interest, action orientation, a will to do something with the knowledge.
- **Skill**: There must be actual behavioural ability to do the action envisioned. Without skill, the action will be either be aborted or done incongruently with the knowledge undergirding it.

Miles continues this analysis by commenting that although there is a rough sequence from clarity to skill, the conditions are interactive. For example, seeing clear action images may result in an increased relevance, or added skill may increase will, since a good outcome is expected. In line with a theme emphasised throughout this book, Miles adds a further reflection. He remarks that it is sad but true that plenty of school improvers think that skill can be developed through reading, lectures, or watching videotapes. It can't.

Improving skill requires doing, practice, getting feedback, reshaping the doing until the doing makes sense, is smooth and gets you where you want. We know this about skiing, tennis and golf, but not quite it seems about those behaviours in educational change (cited in Hopkins 2013).

We pursue this latter comment in some detail in chapter 6.

CODA: BEGINNING THE JOURNEY

We have already seen the series of questions related to each phase of the *Unleashing Greatness* process at various points in this chapter. There is no point in rehearsing them again here. What we have included, as in the following chapters are two cameos from schools who are members of the University of Bolton Laboratory School network. Here, Beaumont Primary School, Bolton and Northgate High School, Norfolk illustrate how they began their journey of Unleashing Greatness.

ESTABLISHING THE TEACHING AND LEARNING POLICY

BEAUMONT PRIMARY SCHOOL, BOLTON

The school website declares that the 'Beaumont family endeavours to create a love of lifelong learning, grow healthy resilient minds, and develop aspirational future citizens'. Beaumont is a laboratory school linked to the University of Bolton University and the International Centre for Educational Leadership. The International Centre is committed to building capacity for school and system improvement and driven by a moral purpose informed by personalisation, social mobility and globalisation. Within this mission are like-minded professionals who have a shared moral purpose, collaborate and drive school improvement together. Beaumont has been fortunate enough to have been a part of this network since 2020.

Senior leaders began the process of creating a pedagogy at Beaumont that suited its context and students. Beaumont's teaching and learning policy was updated to reflect the Unleashing Greatness strategy. We followed the Unleashing Greatness proposition that: 'Lifting student learning is a collaborative enterprise. It relies on students, teachers, and school leaders working together. Lifting student learning does not happen serendipitously. It cannot happen if we keep doing what we are already doing and wait for change to occur.'

A range of collaborative staff development meetings were conducted at which Beaumont's teaching model was devised (see case study in chapter 8). Governors, teachers, staff and students were involved in the development of this fundamental document. It was crucial that the teaching and learning model and policy reflected the school as we wanted it to be. Figure 2.6 indicates the aspects of Beaumont's school development plan that were actioned to ensure the school had begun implementing the instructional core as the foundation for development.

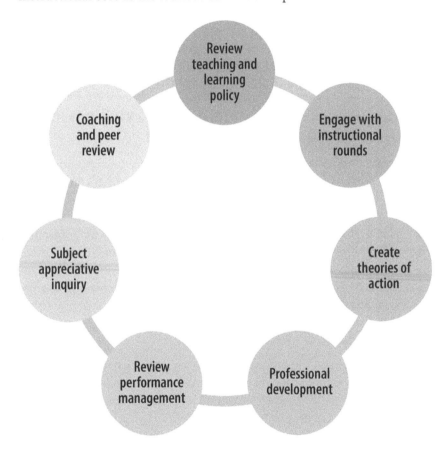

Figure 2.6 Beaumont School's development plan

CREATING THE LEARNING CYCLE
NORTHGATE HIGH SCHOOL, DEREHAM, NORFOLK

Northgate High School converted to academy status in September 2014. It is a co-educational comprehensive school for ages 11–18 and is one of two high schools in the town of Dereham, Norfolk. Due to the commitment of some existing staff members, there was already a culture of research-based practice and research-lead CPD within the school. The leadership within the school had also established informal and formal connections to networks of like-minded schools both nationally and internationally. This meant that we were well placed to enter the orbit of the laboratory school concept and strategy.

At the start of the laboratory school process, we invested time into conducting whole school surveys for staff, parent and carers, as well as students. The results of these led to a clear understanding of where the school was at, enabling a plan to be put in place that addressed real rather than felt needs. Colleagues had previously researched cognitive load theory that led to the creation of our learning cycle (see figure 2.7). The learning cycle informed our laboratory school instructional round process which, in turn, led to our theories of action being developed that allowed us to work with the laboratory school/school improvement team to be clear about the non-negotiable elements of classroom practice through the creation of a series of protocols. This enabled classroom teachers to consider, through staff survey, where the focus of the instructional core needed to place. The protocols were central to developing and shaping high impact teaching and learning.

Our most recent Ofsted inspection in May 2023 commented: 'The curriculum enables pupils to achieve well. This is a result of the ambition of leaders for all pupils to succeed'.

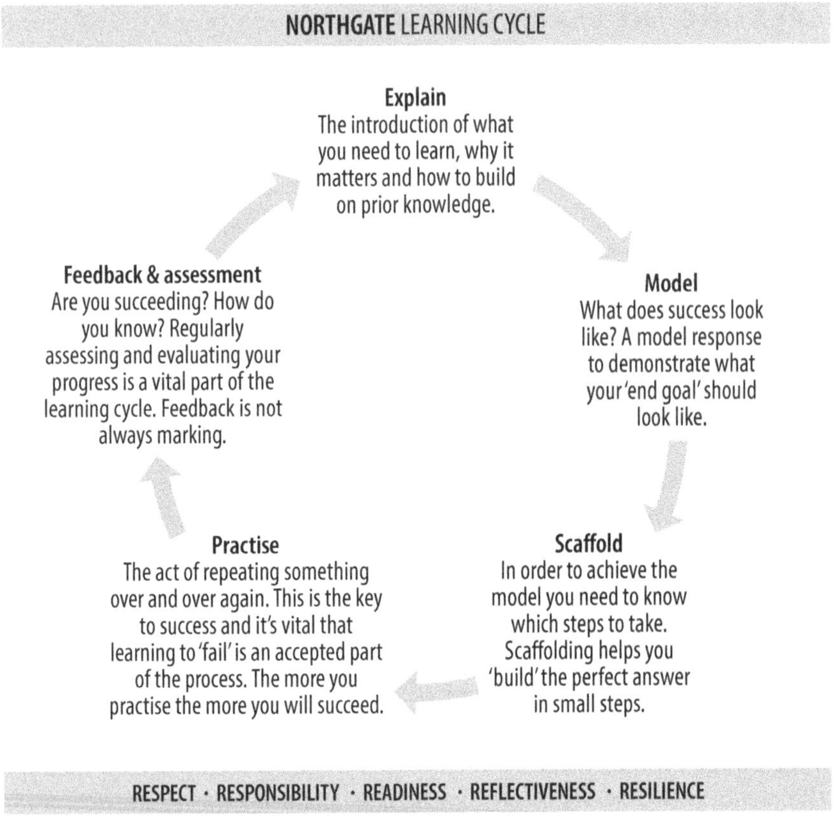

NORTHGATE LEARNING CYCLE

Explain
The introduction of what you need to learn, why it matters and how to build on prior knowledge.

Feedback & assessment
Are you succeeding? How do you know? Regularly assessing and evaluating your progress is a vital part of the learning cycle. Feedback is not always marking.

Model
What does success look like? A model response to demonstrate what your 'end goal' should look like.

Practise
The act of repeating something over and over again. This is the key to success and it's vital that learning to 'fail' is an accepted part of the process. The more you practise the more you will succeed.

Scaffold
In order to achieve the model you need to know which steps to take. Scaffolding helps you 'build' the perfect answer in small steps.

RESPECT · RESPONSIBILITY · READINESS · REFLECTIVENESS · RESILIENCE

Figure 2.7 Northgate School's learning cycle

PART 2:

ALL THE MOVING PARTS

CHAPTER 3:
THE STORY IS ALWAYS ABOUT MORAL PURPOSE (AND STRATEGIC ACTION)

INTRODUCTION: ON THE IMPORTANCE OF NARRATIVE

In the previous chapter, we highlighted the important role that narrative can play in the Unleashing Greatness school improvement framework, noting that the right story stimulates people to act. In a strategic sense we need to tell several stories: there is a story that resonates for an individual school, one for school networks, one for the system, and one for the wider group of stakeholders. The challenge for school leaders is to relate these stories so that they are consistent, relevant to each audience, and galvanise people to act.

Our moral purpose may vary little between schools from one end of the nation to the other. The elements of our school improvement strategy may not vary greatly across systems or between schools. What will vary is how the elements of school improvement are organised into a plan for each school. Local context is telling: where we stand now will directly influence which steps we take next, and what path we follow so that our moral purpose is better enacted.

It is leaderships task to develop and introduce a narrative, or story, which describes the way the school thinks about and enacts teaching and student learning. The story is informed by detailed strategic planning. Over time the story is embedded in the school, guiding our interactions, plans, and practice.

Leaders must determine how to align system and school narratives. The narrative a school adopts is sensitive to three factors as seen in table 3.1.

It is these three factors – an honest diagnosis, a desired outcome and a clear plan – that will provide much of the discussion in this chapter. However, it is narrative that gives authenticity and form to the link between moral purpose and strategic action. This must be underpinned by values and principles that are clearly articulated and by a model that provides coherence, reliability and a guide to action. We also need to be crystal clear that the school's key priorities (their 'non-negotiables') reflect their moral purpose and are in an action-oriented and implementable form through a process of development planning. This planning also needs to realistically reflect the current performance phase that the school is in. The purpose of this chapter is to illustrate how neither moral purpose nor strategic action are sufficient by themselves: we realise our moral purpose through strategic action, and strategic action is the means of delivering on our moral purpose.

Factors driving the narrative	What this means in practice
An honest diagnosis	The school undertakes a thoughtful appraisal of current orientations to student learning.
A desired outcome	The school embraces an ambitious and achievable orientation to student learning.
A clear plan	The school frames and implements actionable strategies for getting to the desired outcome.

Table 3.1 A school's narrative is sensitive to three factors

The focus of this chapter is on three of the first four steps in the Unleashing Greatness framework: clarify moral purpose, decide on the non-negotiables, and articulate the narrative. For reasons of sequencing, the second ('focus on classroom practice and the instructional core') and fifth of the steps ('utilise instructional rounds and theories of action') form the substance of chapters 4 and 5 respectively. As I said at the outset, there is not a linear sequence to the eight steps, they inevitably interact, and the three steps discussed in this chapter set the conditions for high quality teaching and learning. More than that, they are the expression of a school's moral purpose and provide the means for realising it through strategic planning and action.

In this chapter we expand on this line of argument by:

- discussing in more depth the link between moral purpose and school improvement;

- outlining the principles underpinning and the model of school improvement that follows from such a value position;

- proposing an approach to school development planning that highlights the 'non-negotiables' and distinguishes between maintenance and development;

- describing our approach to differential reform and the school improvement pathway; and,

- in the coda, providing some examples of how schools do this in practice and asking the key Unleashing Greatness questions.

MORAL PURPOSE AND SCHOOL IMPROVEMENT

As much of this book is about strategic action, it is worth spending a little time at the outset in reflecting on the nature of moral purpose. As I noted in *Exploding the Myths of School Reform* (Hopkins 2013:4), we see in the following words from Plato and Aristotle that the concern for moral purpose has a long and honourable tradition. This is both in terms of education and more broadly in considering aspirations for society as a whole:

The direction in which education starts a person will determine their future in life ... If a person neglects education s/he walks lame to the end of their life ... No person should bring children into the world that is unwilling to persevere to the end in their nature and education. (Plato)

Moral excellence comes about as a result of habit ... We become just by doing just acts, temperate by doing temperate acts, brave by doing brave acts ... The moral virtues, then, are produced in us neither by nature nor against nature. Nature, indeed, prepares in us the ground for their reception, but their complete formation is the product of habit. (Aristotle)

It was Michael Fullan (2004) who was one of the first to popularise the concept of moral purpose in school reform and he defined it as follows:

1. A commitment to raising the bar and closing the gap of student achievement.
2. Treating people with respect – which is not to say low expectations.
3. An orientation to improving the environment, including other schools in the local authority.

We will reflect on Fullan's third criteria in the final two chapters of the book. What is critical here is bringing the discussion of school improvement down to the level of the individual, to their development as learners within a context of high expectations. Moral purpose in education is not just about achieving academic success. It is also about the underlying skills, dispositions and confidence that result in such success and sustain it. In our work with the *Adventure Learning Schools* charity in the UK (Hopkins 2012a), we have been using the term 'life script' to describe this broader aspiration of moral purpose. We all have life scripts; some of us choose to develop them and others are forced to do so. Life scripts evolve as the individual confronts direct experience and adapts and assimilates it with their self. As Mahatma Gandhi said, 'You must be the change you wish to see in the world'.

According to cognitive psychology, each of us has a life script or schema – whether we are aware of it or not. A life script is another way of describing the meaning we attribute to the events that happen to us. Depending on our particular script, we can interpret an event in a number of different ways.

With its roots in psychology, the concept of the life script is credited to the forefather of transactional analysis theory, Eric Berne (2010) in his seminal work *Games People Play*. Berne's contention in his later book, *What Do You Say After You Say Hello?* (2018), was that in early childhood each person writes the script that will govern the general course of their lives. Forming part of the vocabulary of transactional analysis, our life script is an unconscious pathway created in childhood, reinforced by our parents, and strengthened with evidence sought throughout life ensuring our beliefs are justified.

This is similar to what the humanistic psychologist Carl Rogers (1977) called 'personal power'. Despite the fact that psychologists suggest that one's life script is mostly complete by the age of seven: 'Fortunately, scripts can be changed, since they are not inborn, but learned' (Dusay 1981). As early enthusiasts of script analysis have claimed, 'most people with a loser's script can change to a winner's script' (Abell 1976), although many practitioners suggest that this is much more often 'a matter of learning to exercise new choices' (Stewart and Joines 2000). As the psychotherapist Emmy Brunner (2021) recently wrote:

> *For me, the work always begins with identifying the internal narrative we each have and highlighting the limiting thoughts and belief systems that are holding us back. I call this our "life script". ... You weren't born with this narrative, it's been put together over a number of years and if aspects of it aren't working for you, then you CAN rewrite the script.*

Almost by definition, we would expect professional educators to have positive life scripts, otherwise they would not have developed the skills and personal competencies to become educators in the first place. Sadly, for whatever reason, not all the students who enter our schools, or indeed their parents or carers, have such positive narratives and, on occasion, not all our members of staff do either.

In school improvement, one expression of moral purpose is when teachers and school leaders acknowledge the influence they can exert in formulating, challenging and enhancing the life scripts of the young people in their care. Life scripts evolve as the individual confronts direct experiences, enjoys consequent success, and adapts and assimilates such behaviours into their 'self', creating a positive cycle of development. As we shall see in chapters 4 and 5, there are specific approaches to learning and teaching that have the ability to develop life scripts in the most immediate way. We will also see in the discussion on leadership for learning in chapter 7 that one aspect of the contemporary role is to create situations where others can develop their own life scripts.

It should be clear by now that moral purpose, in the sense that the term is being used here, has great depth to it. Although it is fundamentally about enabling our students to reach their potential, it is also about acquiring those skills and dispositions that enable individuals to become effective global citizens and this, in turn, is sustained and underpinned by nurturing a positive life script. On reflection, perhaps the use of the word 'enabling' is too imprecise. What we do as educators is create reliable conditions and practices in schools whereby the realisation of moral purpose becomes the norm.

This is why moral purpose provides the starting point for the Unleashing Greatness framework and why we give its practical implementation so much prominence in our school improvement strategies. Moral purpose in education is manifest in the development of a positive life script that is realised through helping our students become powerful learners. So, for example, in *The System and Powerful Learning* (Hopkins and Craig 2018a:3) we emphasise the three primary purposes of education and define our goal as helping our students:

- acquire useful and important bodies of knowledge;
- become powerful learners by expanding and making articulate their repertoire of learning strategies; and,
- become fine, caring and principled citizens.

We define *Powerful Learning* as the ability of learners to respond successfully to the tasks they are set and the tasks they set themselves. This ability comprises the capacities to (Hopkins 2013:92):

- integrate prior and new knowledge;
- acquire and apply a range of learning skills;
- solve problems individually and in groups;
- think carefully about their successes and failures, and learn from both;
- evaluate conflicting evidence and to think critically; and,
- accept that learning involves uncertainty and difficulty.

Deploying such a range of learning strategies, as we see in chapter 4, is often referred to as metacognition – the learner's ability to take control over their own learning processes. This is at the heart of enhancing a student's positive life script and, by that same token, realising moral purpose in school improvement.

This is why in our school improvement networks and with Unleashing Greatness, we make the challenge more concrete and our goal more tangible when we invest them with a clear set of values that inform what we do every day, in every school, and every classroom. Table 3.2 is an example of the values that we encourage our schools to adopt and provides the starting point for Unleashing Greatness (Hopkins and Craig 2018a:3).

We believe that:
— student achievement and student wellbeing are the *fundamental* pursuits of schools.
— every student can succeed *regardless* of personal circumstances.
— it is our *responsibility* to act in ways that make individual success a reality.
— the *harder* you work the *smarter* you get.
— given *sufficient challenge and support*, all students can learn and achieve at high levels.
— *learning is a social activity* and all students can learn from each other.
— all schools must consciously choose to be on a *journey to excellence*.
— schools which are *open to all* and which *celebrate diversity* offer rich learning resources that benefit all students.
— our school improvement strategy, and each action flowing from it, must be open to scrutiny — we are *accountable* for implementing the strategy and each associated action.

Table 3.2 Unleashing Greatness: the values base

It is this discussion of the moral purpose of school improvement and the values related to the Unleashing Greatness framework that leads in the following section to a discussion of the principles underpinning our model of school improvement.

UNLEASHING GREATNESS MODEL OF SCHOOL IMPROVEMENT

In chapter 1, we described eight proposals for strategic action that informed our overall strategy for school and system reform that were the antithesis of the 'myths' that I have previously described (Hopkins 2013).

These proposals were also couched as a series of theories of action to help signpost the future direction of the field of school and system improvement in an action-oriented way. As theories of action are used as a means of focusing implementation of the school improvement strategy in the classroom, the school and the system throughout the book, it is important to define them a little more clearly.

ON THEORIES OF ACTION

A theory of action is a guide for identifying, designing, implementing, and evaluating effective responses to the challenges of school improvement. A theory of action connects the actions of teachers and school leaders with consequences – the effects their actions have on quality and performance in their schools and classrooms. Essentially, they are hypotheses that guide our action.

We are always learning. The validity of a theory of action must be tested and retested by gathering evidence about the effects of the action we take. We must evaluate the evidence and then we must make a judgment about whether the theory of action is sound or needs adjustment. Importantly, a theory of action must be stated before it can be shared. It must stand as a common reference point by providing for all members of the school community a common language about the purpose, direction and content of change.

We will revisit theories of action again in chapter 5 when we describe our ten theories of action for teaching and learning – the four whole school theories of action together with the six theories of action for teachers.

PRINCIPLES UNDERPINNING THE MODEL OF SCHOOL IMPROVEMENT

Based on the proposals outlined in chapter 1 a series of principles have been generated that inform the overall Unleashing Greatness model of school improvement. They are described here briefly and related to the relevant chapters of this book.

PRINCIPLE 1: CHAPTER 3

WHEN schools and systems are driven by moral purpose,

THEN all students are more likely to fulfil their potential.

We ensure that the achievement and learning of students is at the centre of all that teachers do. This is our moral purpose. Enacting it requires a focus on those strategies that have a track record of accelerating student achievement, such as:

- building student learning capability;
- personalising learning and the curriculum;
- assessment for learning; and,
- giving students a voice in their own learning.

PRINCIPLE 2: CHAPTER 4

WHEN teachers and schools, in their search for improvement, reflect deeply on their own and their student's performance and act on evidence about learning,

THEN the student becomes a more powerful learner and outcomes improve.

Student and school performance is enhanced when teachers and school leaders:

- clearly understand the links between the key elements of the instructional core;
- frame the curriculum as a process of enquiry;
- consistently develop students learning and social skills; and,
- establish a culture of personalised learning in the school.

PRINCIPLE 3: CHAPTER 5

WHEN the focus of policy and practice is on the quality of teaching,

THEN student achievement will increase.

The central theme of any improvement strategy is to enhance the quality of teaching, rather than to be distracted by structural change. The quality of teaching is necessarily related to system goals and targeted support which will emphasise:

- the use of instructional rounds for non-judgmental observation;
- developing theories of action for teaching across the school;

- utilising models of teaching to give greater depth to the instructional core; and,
- developing the student's learning skills and nurturing their curiosity.

PRINCIPLE 4: CHAPTER 6

WHEN teachers constantly acquire a richer repertoire of pedagogic practice,

THEN students' learning constantly deepens.

Appropriate, ongoing and sustained professional learning opportunities are put in place.

Such opportunities help develop a common 'practice' of teaching and learning. They are characterised by:

- a conscious blending of theory, evidence and action;
- skill-oriented workshops;
- peer observation on a regular basis; and,
- networking with other schools on developing on pedagogic practice.

PRINCIPLE 5: CHAPTER 7

WHEN leadership is instructionally focused and widely distributed,

THEN both teachers and students can capitalise fully on their capacity to learn and achieve.

This kind of leadership capability and practice relies on constantly developing professional practice, frequent and thoughtful reflection on data, and delivering early intervention using differential strategies. These characteristics are present in schools where the leadership:

- reinforces very high expectations for both teachers and students;
- adopts an unrelenting focus on quality learning and teaching;
- creates structures that ensure an orderly learning environment and generate professional responsibility and accountability; and,
- when appropriate, supports leadership development across neighbouring schools.

PRINCIPLE 6: CHAPTER 8

WHEN the system as a whole takes student learning seriously,

THEN moral purpose is achieved.

System level structures are established that reflect the processes described in the previous principles. The structures link the various levels of the system, including the school and classroom. Effective structures support capacity development by:

- takes seriously its responsibility to ensure both equity and excellence;
- balancing professional autonomy and mutual accountability;
- promoting disciplined innovation as a consequence of networking; and,
- using differential strategies at classroom, school and system level.

We now turn to a discussion of how these principles and theories of action combine dynamically in our school improvement model.

THE UNLEASHING GREATNESS SCHOOL IMPROVEMENT MODEL

The *Unleashing Greatness* school improvement model brings together in a coherent way all the elements of a comprehensive school improvement strategy (adapted from Hopkins 2013:14). The model expresses the context and process of school improvement through the image of a series of concentric rings. It is important to note however, that the model should not be followed slavishly. It is presented as an action framework to help education practitioners and school leaders to think strategically about school improvement, rather than telling them what to do!

The school improvement model comprises of:

- the core – curiosity and powerful learning;
- an inner ring of four elements;
- a middle ring of six elements; and,
- an outer ring of four elements.

At the centre of the model, curiosity and powerful learning is recognised as being at the heart of the school's moral purpose. This represents the goal that every student will reach their potential and that they acquire a range of knowledge, skills and dispositions that will equip them, not only to meet the challenges of the 21st century but also to help them shape it. The participation of students and the inclusion of the 'learner voice' is encouraged from the outset of the Unleashing Greatness journey.

The next ring is comprised of those essential ingredients of effective classroom practice that focus on the instructional core so necessary for personalised learning. This is the teacher's repertoire of teaching and learning strategies, the organisation of curriculum in terms of frameworks and standards and the ways in which students are involved in their learning.

Such classroom practice is found in schools that have *organisational capacity* supportive of high levels of teaching and learning – these key elements are found in the next ring.

In today's educational systems, it is recognised that 'no school is an island'. Schools exist within a broader systemic context, represented in the outer ring of the diagram.

This model of school improvement is more than the sum of its parts. There are four implications for viewing the process of school improvement in this way:

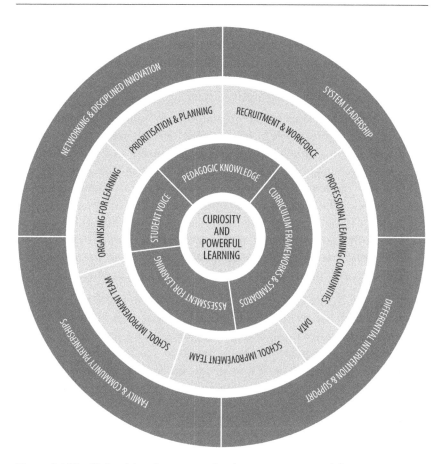

Figure 3.1 The Unleashing Greatness school improvement model

1. The first is that when all the circles are pulling in the same direction, then the aspirations of school improvement have much more chance of success. All need to exist in a reciprocal relationship if student attainment is to be enhanced.

2. The second is that this way of working places great demands on school leadership. It requires the courage to collaborate; the abandonment of activities that do not best serve student achievement; the creation of a culture of mutual interdependence and trust; and, being open to evidence of what works in school reform. The role of the school improvement team is crucial here.

3. The third is that schools need to develop a deep appreciation of their current performance along with their particular strengths and weaknesses (with external assistance as required) to determine where in the model to focus their energies and hence, where their improvement journey needs to start.

4. The fourth relates to the crucial issue of where the initiative for improvement comes from. As noted earlier, most school reform assumes that change comes from the 'outside in'. In those schools that have made the jump from 'good to great' the linear logic of policy implementation has been inverted – they start from the centre of the circle and move outwards. They survey the range of policy initiatives confronting the school to see which they can most usefully mould to their own improvement plans. Paradoxically, schools that work from the 'inside out' appear to be the most effective at interpreting the centralised reform agenda.

As is implied by the outer circle, successful reform is neither singularly system-led nor led by individual schools – it is best achieved by one supporting the other in an actively interdependent, mutually beneficial relationship. Consequently, schools involved in Unleashing Greatness will network together to share knowledge, skills and transferable practice. These school leaders clearly understand what Aristotle meant when he said, 'We are what we repeatedly do. Excellence, therefore, is not an act but a habit.'

It is important also to stress that the Unleashing Greatness strategy is not just another school improvement project – something to be done in addition to what teachers and schools are already doing. It is often described as 'not so much a program, but more a way of life'. Unleashing Greatness is successful to the extent that it helps teachers and schools achieve their existing educational goals but more efficiently and with increased depth and precision. There is one pre-condition, however, that the school and its community is driven by a moral purpose that has the enhancement of student potential as its ultimate goal.

In summary, Unleashing Greatness is designed as an inside out approach to school improvement. This does not mean schools that adopt the approach ignore the policy context within which they work. Far from it, as Unleashing Greatness aligns sympathetically with the school development agenda of all states in Australia, the UK and elsewhere. What it does mean however is that the school focuses unrelentingly on the learning needs of all students and builds the learning environment and curriculum outwards from that starting point. In so doing, the school adapts external change for internal purpose. To make sense of the complexity of change, schools are encouraged at any one point in time to select a small number of high value educational goals that lead to the fulfilment of their moral purpose. Unleashing Greatness schools do these activities as well as they possibly can and, as we have said previously, everything else as well as they would have done anyway!

This, however, requires an approach to school development planning that puts the moral purpose of the Unleashing Greatness model into action, highlights the non-negotiables, and distinguishes clearly between maintenance and development (Hargreaves and Hopkins 1991). This is the focus of the following section.

SCHOOL DEVELOPMENT PLANNING THAT HIGHLIGHTS THE 'NON-NEGOTIABLES' AND DISTINGUISHES BETWEEN MAINTENANCE AND DEVELOPMENT

As we saw clearly in the previous section, when schools work 'inside-out' their starting point is virtually always student learning. It is as if they ask, 'What changes in student learning and performance do we wish to see this year?' They then decide on priorities for change, the non-negotiables, and select the teaching strategies that will most effectively bring them about. They also pinpoint the modifications required to the school's organisation to support these developments.

NON-NEGOTIABLES

In exploring the Unleashing Greatness framework in chapter 2, we discussed the importance of:

- determining what is non-negotiable, and
- securing resources for the non-negotiables.

The discussion of moral purpose and strategic action in the previous section of the chapter delineates clearly the boundaries around the identification of the non-negotiables or key priorities for development. So, agreement on the key priorities should not be too contentious for schools utilising the Unleashing Greatness framework.

Some years ago, David Hargreaves and myself were commissioned by the UK government to develop protocols and advice on school development planning. Four booklets were widely disseminated, and we then expanded and published the work in *The Empowered School* (Hargreaves and Hopkins 1991). This book still contains sound advice on the school development planning process. The practical discussion that follows builds on this and figure 3.2 illustrates the flow of action in constructing the development plan.

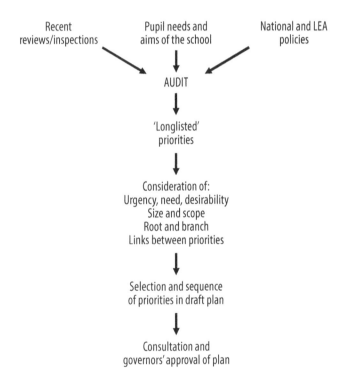

Figure 3.2 The construction of the development plan

DISTINGUISHING BETWEEN MAINTENANCE AND DEVELOPMENT

In order for the Unleashing Greatness strategy to work, it is imperative that schools and their leaders in their planning process distinguish, clearly both strategically and practically, between maintenance and development. As was discussed in chapter 2 (and seen in figure 2.3), schools obviously need to not only maintain their existing organisational functions to a high level, but also have the capacity to develop and change at the same time. The maintenance structure is concerned with relatively permanent systems and processes that are necessary for the school to get its work done as efficiently as possible. The development structure is there to adopt new ways of working (the non-negotiables) that add value to the school over time, as new practices become common practice.

Separating maintenance activities from development work is essential for continual school improvement. Maintenance and development need separate infrastructures – separate organisational and management arrangements – because they need to work in different ways, as seen in table 3.3.

The school maintenance structure	The school development structure
Comprises relatively permanent systems and processes necessary for the school to do its work efficiently.	Purposefully develops new ways of working that, over time, add value to the school.

Table 3.3 Distinguishing between maintenance and development

For example, the development structure is inclusive and fluid. Teams and partnerships are assembled to design, implement and embed specified school improvement priorities. The composition of the teams will change depending on what tasks need doing and what skills are required to do them well. It is not a structure of permanent committees and fixed roles. Yet permanent committees and fixed roles are essential for efficient school maintenance.

CENTRAL TO A SCHOOL'S DEVELOPMENT STRUCTURE IS A SCHOOL IMPROVEMENT TEAM

An effective school improvement team creates the capacity for development, while retaining the existing structures required both for organisational stability and efficiency. The school improvement team provides the organisational framework for resolving the tensions caused by the conflicting demands of maintenance and development. An effective school improvement team creates development capacity, whereas the existing maintenance structures provide organisational stability and efficiency.

As was discussed in chapter 2, the school improvement team is cross-hierarchical. It could have three to six members in small schools, and between six and ten members in large schools. The head or principal is likely to be a member. It is important that other team members are genuinely representative of the range of perspectives and ideas available in the school. Team members should not come together in any already existing group within the school.

THE SCHOOL DEVELOPMENT PLANNING PROCESS

There is a danger of being overly prescriptive in giving advice on development planning. As was intimated earlier, the purpose is to help colleagues to think strategically rather than tell them what to do. That was our approach in *The Empowered School* (Hargreaves and Hopkins 1991) and is the intent here also.

The key priorities (the non-negotiable) must be rooted in evidence about student progress and achievement. With that evidence to hand, a school can begin generating a plan that encompasses:

- specific targeted improvements in student outcomes;
- changes in teaching practices that arise from the theories of action (see chapter 5); and,
- modifications to whole school organisation and management arrangements that will underpin improvements in the classroom.

It's the last of these points that we need to dwell on here. If we are to make changes in each classroom to improve student outcomes, we must also modify the operations of the whole school and the system to ensure those changes are successful and sustainable.

We have already underscored the importance of maintaining clear distinctions between the school's organisational and management arrangements for both maintenance and development work. The right modifications ensure maintenance and development functions are fit for purpose. There is practical, symbolic and strategic value in implementing arrangements that align with the priorities for development set out in the school's development plan.

At first glance, making such modifications can appear complex. It is true that school improvement is a jigsaw, but it is not an impossible puzzle. When it comes to modifying whole school organisation and management arrangements, we should recognise that the number of pieces is not infinite. We have a good idea of what they are.

Figure 3.3 presents the interface between classroom practice and the school's management arrangements. There are ten items in the outer ring of the diagram. School leaders must modify some, or all, of these constructs in ways that:

- maximise the impact of action taken on the school's priorities for development; and,
- reduce the attraction or availability of old ways of doing things.

Securing sustainable changes in student outcomes and teacher practices is only possible when whole school organisation and management arrangements back them up. Traditional arrangements are deeply embedded in how schools operate, if only because they have been with us for a long time. Clear thinking needs to be given to:

- diagnosing the impediments that existing arrangements put in the way of making rapid process on the school's priorities for development;
- designing new whole school organisation and management arrangements that facilitate progress; and,
- transitioning from old whole school arrangements.

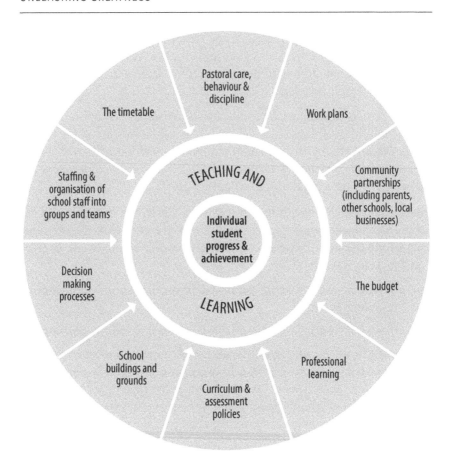

Figure 3.3 The interface between classroom practice and the school's management arrangements (Hopkins and MacGilchrist 1998)

As one progresses on the school improvement journey, the planning framework (table 3.4), together with the crucial eight questions, may help you shape the strategic scope of the work ahead. The questions are foundational to strategy development. They can be used to begin sketching out the school improvement narrative, what the school's priorities for development might be, and what modifications to whole school organisation and management might need to be considered. The school improvement team can also use the questions as prompts in conversations with colleagues about school improvement.

These questions can be returned to as the school improvement journey unfolds. Additionally, they provide a strategic reference point for the annual renewal of the school improvement plan.

Consideration	What is involved?	What organisation & management modifications are necessary?	How much will it cost? (Consider staff time, professional learning, and other resources)	What support & resources in the school network & school system can help us here?
1. What specific, near term, unambiguous targets will we set for student learning, progress and achievement?				
2. What evidence will we collect so that we can assess our progress in achieving our targets?				
3. How should we sequence the targets? How much time will it take to meet each target?				
4. What teaching & learning strategies related to the theories of action will ensure we deliver on our targets?				

5. What kinds of professional learning will develop teacher behaviours that enact the theories of action?				
6. What immediate tasks must we complete to move towards our targets? Who is responsible for the tasks?				
7. How will we evaluate over time the impact of our school improvement plan on student learning?				
8. Who is responsible for monitoring progress on our school improvement plan & priorities for development?				

Table 3.4 A school development planning framework

DIFFERENTIAL REFORM AND THE SCHOOL IMPROVEMENT PATHWAY

The discussion to this point has mainly assumed that all schools are uniformly effective and have the capacity to manage and implement a school improvement strategy such as described here. Unfortunately, this is not always the case. Indeed, it is now well established that schools, and indeed all organisations, are at various stages or phases of development.

The clear implication from our school improvement research is that there is a developmental sequence that needs certain building blocks to be in place before further progress can be made (Hopkins 2001; 2007; 2013; 2022a). This contention finds support in other research that identifies a clear iterative process in most successful school improvement efforts (see Gray et al 1999; Day et al 2011; Barber and Mourshed 2007). We have previously described the three phases of the school improvement journey, as 'awful to adequate', 'adequate to good' and 'good to great' (Hopkins et al 1997; Hopkins 2013). The implication is that different strategies and combinations of strategies are necessary at different phases of the process. So, a clear and accurate diagnosis of where the school is at on the performance cycle is necessary in defining appropriate strategies for change. The school improvement pathway also described in this section is a diagnostic tool.

PHASE ONE: AWFUL TO ADEQUATE

By definition, schools in this phase cannot improve themselves. They are 'stuck' and such 'failing' schools require a high level of external support. Within these schools, several early interventions and changes need to be made that have a direct focus upon basic organisational issues. These would include (Hopkins 2013):

- **Change at leadership level.** It is too sweeping to say that all heads or principals of failing schools do not have the capacity to be effective school leaders. Often though, new leadership opportunities will need to be created for new and different staff, using new models, to achieve new goals.

- **Provision of early, intensive outside support.** Schools in a failing situation are likely to be isolated and in a state of cultural stasis. They are unlikely to have the potential for constructive self-analysis or evaluation and will need support from outside to provide knowledge about school improvement strategies and models of ways of working.

- **Surveying staff and student opinion**; gathering and disaggregating data on student achievement. The collection of data will help find out why the school is unsuccessful, and where to direct efforts for greatest improvement. In addition to inspection reports, data needs to be gathered at whole-school and classroom level, as well as from students. This potentially gives the school community ownership of the improvement agenda.

- **A short-term focus on (relatively) easy to change targets.** Changes to the school environment, attendance and uniform will be short-term changes, but can result in tangible gains. Following a period of low morale, such visible changes will demonstrate that things are to be different in the school. These changes should reflect the core values that the new leadership is articulating.

- **A focus on managing learning behaviour, not on behaviour management.** This means creating the conditions where learners can learn most effectively. Strategies for managing learning behaviour would inevitably include a focus upon praise and positive reinforcement, as well as consistent and well scaffolded teaching rather than punishment and discipline, throughout the school.

- **Intensive work on re-skilling staff in a specific repertoire of teaching and learning styles.** In the first instance, the focus for staff development could be quite simple, for example: seating arrangements, classroom organisation, the phasing of lessons or active use of resources. Staff could explore these skills in teams to lay the basis for subsequent peer coaching.

PHASE TWO: ADEQUATE TO GOOD

Schools in this phase need to refine their developmental priorities, focus upon specific teaching and learning issues and build capacity within the school to support this work. Developmental strategies for this type of school include:

- **Changing leadership strategies.** This change incorporates both leadership styles and range. Restructuring will be necessary in order to diversify leadership opportunities and unlock static structures and systems. This enables the process of management to become more dynamic and to be geared towards increasing the capacity for change.

- **Lengthening the lesson unit.** Some curriculum restructuring occurs to support the re-skilling of teachers. Time is given to focus on a wider repertoire of teaching and learning styles and on the learning behaviours. The longer the time unit, the more time staff will have to plan together and practise different teaching approaches.

- **Targeting particular students at certain thresholds across the ability range.** If achievement is to matter, then underachievement at all levels should be targeted. Data about performance will provide opportunities to generate dialogue with staff and with students – in groups and individually, by gender and by ability.

- **Talking to pupils about their aspirations; giving their achievement meaning.** Schools are good at internally assessing pupil effort and achievement, but less skilled at assessing potential, and it is in this gap that the potential for improvement lies. So formal mechanisms for rewarding all types of pupil achievement are important and should be built into any school restructuring programme.

- **Harnessing the energy and optimism of new staff.** Morale will inevitably be low, but new members of staff who have accepted jobs at the school within the last year or two will have done so with optimism and hope for what they might achieve. These staff can be used to re-energise others and can become a catalyst for change.

- **Generating an ongoing dialogue about values.** The values and beliefs, both of the profession and the school, need to be articulated and re-affirmed. All staff members need to be clear about the values dimension in their everyday work. All professional decisions will have their roots in the values and beliefs of the school community – and they need to be shared and debated.

PHASE THREE: GOOD TO GREAT

It is imperative that those schools that are effective remain so. Consequently, in this third phase there is a need for specific strategies that ensure the school remains a 'moving' school that continues to enhance pupil performance. These strategies include:

- **Articulating values, developing narrative and disseminating eloquence.** 'In effective schools, school leaders disseminate eloquence' to use Weick's (1985) felicitous phrase. It is a school leader's role to articulate the school's values and to reinforce them at every opportunity. These values need to be embedded and shared by staff, parents and pupils. The generation of narrative is discussed further in the coda of this chapter.

- **Raising expectations and defining achievement; creating an achievement orientation.** Schools need to be explicit, eloquent and prolific in their definition of achievement. Such a process will ignite the enthusiasm of staff and generate motivation among students. It is important to give pupils and the wider community ownership of the school's achievements, involving them in regular celebrations of the school's success.

- **Involving and empowering students in the focus on learning; developing a student charter.** It is important that students feel involved and empowered in the process of learning. By providing their constructive feedback and views about how their learning can be improved in the individual classroom, within the department and within the school, students are contributing to the improvement process.

- **Using networking and system leadership to develop leadership skills, team-building, and teaching and learning.** A learning school will seek out best practice elsewhere, share their own practices and initiate networks. The development of system leadership can offer alternative curricular practices and new ways of teaching and learning. Staff become skilled in these new processes by working alongside others in and beyond the school.

- **Generating a common language around learning and achievement.** Developing common understandings about learning and achievement is important. Members of staff that have a shared language concerning learning and achievement, say, through the use of the theories of action (chapter 5), are more likely to work together and to be committed to understanding and improving the processes of teaching and learning.

- **Giving teachers space to experiment, share and celebrate successes.** Effective schools encourage experimentation and risk-taking with the knowledge that real learning lies in understanding the failures rather than the successes. All schools, at whatever stage in their development, should also take joy in every demonstration of success and aim to orchestrate optimism and celebration of achievement at all levels.

There are four interrelated points to be considered here:

- First is that all the elements within each phase need to be worked on at the same time.

- Second, together they combine to create a distinctive school–work culture and address both a substantive focus on teaching and learning as well as capacity building.

- Third, as progress is being made, the move from one phase to another reflects a deepening of work on each dimension.

- Fourth, three phases of improvement have been described here, but there is an argument for extending this to a fourth phase in order to give greater opportunity for differentiation. This is the case with the school improvement pathway that we now describe.

SCHOOL IMPROVEMENT PATHWAY

In order to assist with this process of adaptation and contextualisation, we have developed the school improvement pathway[2] as seen in figure 3.4. The school improvement pathway is a framework that assists school leaders and teachers to diagnose current orientations to student learning, and from that diagnosis map a pathway to excellence. Each school begins its improvement journey at a different point on the school improvement pathway.

As is seen in the previous section, it is now clear that when standards are too low or variable, more central direction is needed initially to improve a school. Over time, as school practice and student performance improve,

---

2   The school improvement pathway is found in: Hopkins, D. and Craig, W. (2018c) *Leadership for Powerful Learning*. Sydney: ACEL, McREL / Kindle edition, Cambridge; Pearson (available from Amazon) pages 24-28 and can be downloaded from my website www.profdavidhopkins.com.

then less prescription is needed as the school enhances its professional capability. Through this work, we have also gained specific knowledge about the combination of strategies needed to move a school along the continuum. When systems and schools use this knowledge strategically, they make significant and rapid progress.

The performance continuum describes schools as moving along a pathway from:

- Awful to adequate
- Adequate to good
- Good to great
- Great to excellent

The pathway also specifies five improvement dimensions:

- Curriculum
- Teaching
- Learning
- Assessment/data and accountability
- Leadership

The school improvement pathway is illustrated in figure 3.4. Each phase along the improvement continuum has a commentary on the five improvement dimensions noted above. For each dimension there are a set of key issues that provide criteria to identify which phase it is on for each of the improvement dimensions. It then poses a series of diagnostic questions to help progress development from one phase to another. So, to provide an example and contrast, tables 3.5 and 3.6 illustrate the key issues and diagnostic questions related to curriculum and teaching at the 'awful to adequate' and the 'great to excellent' phases.

AWFUL TO ADEQUATE

Schools that are moving from 'awful to adequate' lack the internal capacity to improve. To get the basics in place, and to establish the pre-conditions for success, they need a high level of external support and direction.

Improvement dimension	Key issues	Diagnostic questions
Curriculum	- Usually there is no comprehensive view of the curriculum that is progressive, individualised, or inquiry oriented. - Commonly, the curriculum is an amalgam of the 'favourite things' of individual teachers, or materials they have used for some time and with which they are comfortable. - The curriculum lacks coherence and encourages little engagement from students.	- Has a curriculum determined how well the curriculum meets mandated requirements? - Is introduction of such materials preceded by professional conversations about curriculum that establish the rationale for change and how the change links to the school's emerging narrative? (Establishing clear curricular guidelines and scaffolding is of urgent important. This cannot be matter for debate.) - Is there a clear process for importing structured and proven curriculum materials where they are lacking? - Is the importance of literacy and numeracy in every classroom emphasised? - Are planning cycles implemented? - Have students' views been shared with teachers as additional motivation for change?
Teaching	- Teaching is often highly individualised, inconsistent, lacking in pace and informed by the teacher's own prior experience. - Debate about teaching is not a common professional practice in the school, and teachers are allowed or encouraged to 'do their own thing'. - There is a great variation in teaching practice and consequently student progress and performance is highly variable.	- Has an audit of teaching practice been conducted and presented (without attribution to individual teachers) as a picture of the school's common professional practice? - Has the audit resulted in development of a 'good lesson' template that is the initial basis of common teaching practice? - Does the 'good lesson' reflect what research about good practice, such as the theories of action for teachers? - Are there clear descriptions of what performance looks like at commencing, intermediate, accomplished, and expert levels? - Are these descriptions use as a key reference for conducting classroom observations and discussing observation data?

Table 3.5 Curriculum and teaching in the 'awful to adequate' phase

GREAT TO EXCELLENT

The signal characteristic of 'great' schools and schools that sustain excellence is the way in which they search for excellence internally, and offer support to other schools undertaking an improvement journey.

Improvement dimension	Key issues	Diagnostic questions
Curriculum	- All schools, including excellent schools, can tend to towards didacticism (the impulse to teach something) rather than inquiry (a preference for finding things out). - The key challenge is to build into the curriculum: problem solving and the application of knowledge.	- Is an inquiry focus present across the curriculum? - Does the curriculum entitlement for all students include: leadership opportunities; adventurous activities; and, cultural activities? - Do teachers have time and resources to reconstruct their curriculum and schemes of work using inquiry and fertile questions as the dominant curriculum forms? - Are research 'lesson study' and peer observation the main mode of professional development and learning? - Does the design of curricular tasks for students incorporate: problem solving, inquiry, sustained collaboration, appropriate scaffolding, and worthwhile and intrinsically motivating products?
Teaching	- The challenges for teaching are the same as those noted for learning. - The journey to excellence necessarily involves teachers becoming increasingly autonomous in professional judgment within an educational system dominated by external criteria and accountability.	- Is there shared understanding across the school about learning and achievement? - Do teachers have a shared language for learning and achievement through applying theories of action? - Is experimentation and risk tasking encouraged in the knowledge that real learning lies in understanding the failures rather than the successes? - Is joy taken in every demonstration of success? - Is optimism and celebration of achievement apparent across the whole school?

Table 3.6 Curriculum and teaching in the 'great to excellent' phase

The key issues and diagnostic questions assist school leaders and school improvement teams to:

- complete an honest diagnosis of their school's current performance – this is essential preparation for precise strategic decision making and planning; and,
- prepare a plan for progress towards excellence.

What excellence means for each school continues to evolve. It is important to adapt the school's narrative and improvement plans so that they remain relevant to changing context. Ongoing adaptation is facilitated by regularly reassessing where the school is situated on the school improvement pathway.

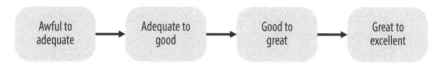

Figure 3.4 The school improvement pathway

Schools may elect to use the school improvement pathway as a framework for discussion, decision making, and planning with system leaders, their own school leadership team, school improvement team, all teachers and even students and the community. Knowing when and how to engage others in working with the pathway may be among one of the school's early strategic decisions. Crucially, it can also inform the development of the school's narrative, as we discussed in the introduction to this chapter.

In the following two chapters, we get to the heart of the matter by first discussing the instructional core and then pedagogy.

CODA: MORAL PURPOSE AND BUILDING THE NARRATIVE

In this chapter, we have considered three of the initial steps in the *Unleashing Greatness* process that are loosely related to the 'planning' phase of the strategy. In helping school leaders and school improvement teams plan for action at this stage of their school improvement journey, the following questions may be found helpful.

MORAL PURPOSE

- Does your school's version of moral purpose link aspiration to action?
- Does your school's version of moral purpose reflect the values of students, parents and the community?
- Is your school's version of moral purpose widely accepted by the whole school staff?

NON-NEGOTIABLES

- Is the whole staff clear about what the non-negotiables are in your school and are actively working on them?
- Is there a distinction between the maintenance and development functions in your school, particularly the purposes, funding and responsibilities involved?
- Is there a school improvement team in your school and how do they operate?

NARRATIVE

- Does your school's narrative link moral purpose to action?
- Does the core story describe the direction the school is moving in and what success will look like – the desired state?
- Is your narrative understood and owned by all sections of the school community – students, staff, parents and governors?

Here are three cameos from schools in our Curiosity and Powerful Learning programme in New South Wales that have adopted the *Unleashing Greatness* framework. These three primary schools, Smithtown Public School, Eungai Public School and South West Rocks Public School, describe how they responded to these steps in the journey.

FOCUSING ON MORAL PURPOSE AND BUILDING THE NARRATIVE

SMITHTOWN PUBLIC SCHOOL, EUNGAI PUBLIC SCHOOL AND SOUTH WEST ROCKS PUBLIC SCHOOL, NEW SOUTH WALES

Smithtown Public School, Eungai Public School and South West Rocks Public School are three highly unique schools with completely different contexts that have been able to collaborate, observe practice, provide feedback and have narrow and deep focus on whole school improvement. Principals have collaborated to build unified, streamlined, student-centred model guided by the Curiosity and Powerful Learning Framework underpinned by Unleashing Greatness framework and the theories of action and models of practice. As a collective, we are building the foundations of high performance through the use of the triads and instructional rounds, drawing upon cross school expertise and using social learning as a tool to redevelop, redesign and re-engage effective whole school improvement that is in parallel to each individual school. The key foundation of our model is the principal as instructional leader, developing a principal triad model that has resulted in cross-school collaboration and a united approach to school excellence.

In developing our narrative, each school collectively discussed and clarified their moral purpose and their 'why.' This was then followed by a discussion regarding our narrative, our current practices and identifying our successes and challenges. An understanding of progress toward the shared goals (aspirations) for our schools and students was developed.

The ten theories of action were then prioritised for engagement over time. These were ordered to build on current school strengths and strategically introduced others over time. We see C&PL and *Unleashing Greatness* as 'big picture' thinking, and a 'framework' to prioritise, provide focus and achieve short and long-term improvement in pedagogy, culture and student achievement.

SMITHTOWN PS
UNPACKING THE
NARRATIVE

To begin our C&PL journey at SPS, at an initial staff meeting we discussed our moral purpose and our narrative for our school improvement journey.

As SPS sits on the banks of the Macleay River and has been impacted by recent flooding events, this was chosen the narrative for our whole school improvement journey with our successes and challenges being described as our flows and ebbs. These are interchangeable depending upon what is occurring at the school.

We then ranked the ten Theories of Action according to priority beginning with prioritising high expectations and authentic relationships as we are a relatively new staff. Priorities may change over time.

EUNGAI PS
UNPACKING THE NAR[...]
-EPS sailing for school improvement success, we are using these guiding 10 theories of action to Navigate the journey.
-The ship is a metaphor for our whole school improvement journey, sailing together using our USS protocols- unified, streamlined and student centred.
-Each element of the ship represents a symbol e.g. Connecting feedback to data is the win in the sails.
Compass- commitment to assessment for learning, ensuring all students reach their destination.

South West Rocks PS
UNPACKING THE NARRATIVE

We first affirmed our collective 'whole-staff' moral purpose. This was followed by a shared understanding of progress toward the shared goals (aspirations) for our school and students.

Current NSW DoE educational research recommendations were reviewed and direct links between C&PL and these to the SEF, WWB document and APST made.

The ten C&PL Theories of Action were then prioritised for engagement over time. These were ordered to build on current school strengths and strategically introduced others over time at SWRPS.

We see C&PL as 'big-picture' thinking, and a 'framework' to prioritise, provide focus and achieve short and long-term improvement in pedagogy, culture and student achievement.

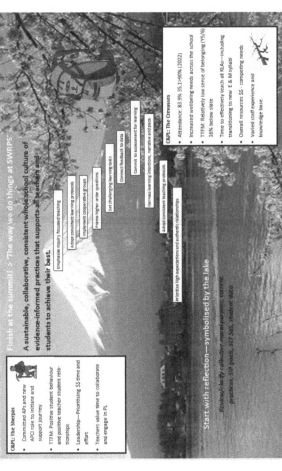

At SWRPS, we were inspired by Professor Hopkins' own mountaineering metaphors in visualising our school narrative.

CHAPTER 4:

THE INSTRUCTIONAL CORE AND PERSONALISED LEARNING

INTRODUCTION: THE NATURE OF PROFESSIONAL PRACTICE

The elephant in the room of school improvement, and it has been resident for some time, is the lack of a professional practice that provides a language and a set of behaviours or processes to connect teaching to learning. There are two key problems here: the first the individualised and atomised nature of teaching as a profession; the second that teaching is a profession without a practice. These two tendencies intertwine in intricate and resilient ways. It is difficult to realise moral purpose through strategic action or unleash greatness whilst this is still the case.

I was helped to understand the nature of this complexity through conversations with Richard Elmore, and through reading the book he co-authored entitled *Instructional Rounds in Education* (City et al 2009). In that book they contrast the individualism that too often characterises teaching, where the person and the practice are intertwined, with professionals who are those that share a common practice and open it up to public scrutiny.

Professionals believe that the only way to improve one's practice is to allow yourself to think that your practice is *not* who you are. It is, instead, a way of expressing your current understanding of your work, your knowledge about your work, and your beliefs about what is important about the work. All these things can change (*should* change if you are a professional) as your knowledge, skill, expertise and understanding of your work increases.

The real insight here is that you can maintain all the values and commitments that make you a person and still give yourself permission to change your practice. Your practice is an instrument for expressing who you are as a professional; it is not who you are.

How we define practice is therefore critical, and Elmore and his colleagues (City et al 2009:3) mean something quite specific:

> *We mean a set of protocols and processes for observing, analyzing, discussing and understanding instruction that can be used to improve student learning at scale. The practice works because it creates a common discipline and focus among practitioners with a common purpose and set of problems.*

It is the lack of such a practice that has inhibited recent reform efforts from realising the potential of our students. This is at the heart of the failure of policy implementation to authentically raise standards that we noted in chapter 1. We need to reach down into the classroom and deepen reform efforts by moving beyond superficial curriculum change and policy prescriptions to a more profound understanding of how teacher behaviour connects to learning. It requires a direct and unrelenting focus on the 'instructional core'. It is important to note that here and in the remainder of this chapter, the words instruction, pedagogy and teaching are used synonymously, reflecting as they do American, European, and British definitions of the same concept.

So, in this chapter we discuss the nature of the instructional core and the dimensions of classroom practice phase of the Unleashing Greatness journey. In the following chapter, we explore the nature of pedagogy. Without a clear understanding of these constructs, both conceptually and practically, the aspiration of unleashing greatness remains a chimera.

Here the focus is on:

- defining the instructional core and using this as a basis for constructing a framework for classroom practice and its implications for our whole-school theories of action;
- exploring contrasting approaches to the curriculum and propose the use of fertile questions as a means of curriculum development;
- briefly reviewing the research on learning and learning skills with an emphasis on metacognition;
- advocating for personalised learning as a whole school approach for the implementation of the instructional core consistent with Unleashing Greatness; and,
- in the coda, providing some examples of how schools do this in practice and asking the key Unleashing Greatness questions.

INSTRUCTIONAL CORE AND WHOLE-SCHOOL THEORIES OF ACTION

As previously introduced in chapter 2 and seen in figure 2.2, in its simplest terms, 'the instructional core is composed of the teacher and the student in the presence of content' (City et al 2009). Although there are several principles associated with the definition of the instructional core, two features require emphasising again.

The first feature is that one element of the instructional core cannot be changed without impacting directly on the other two. Yet most change efforts focus on only one – curriculum innovation, or assessment. The three need to be regarded as a whole, if authentic change in student achievement is to occur. It is the relationship between the teacher, the student and the content – not the qualities of any one of them by themselves – that determines the nature of instructional practice. Each corner of the instructional triangle has its own particular role and resources to bring to the instructional process.

The second feature is more subtle but as we saw earlier, even more important. It is an understanding that the 'instructional task' is at the centre of the instructional core. The instructional task is the actual work that students are asked to do. It is not what teachers think they have asked students to do, nor what the prescribed curriculum says they should be doing, but what students are actually doing and the sense they make of it which is fundamental.

It is the interaction of the core elements of the instructional core that is crucial. That is why in *Models of Learning: Tools for Teaching* (Joyce, Calhoun and Hopkins 2009:7) we said:

> *Learning experiences are composed of content, process and social climate. As teachers we create for and with our children opportunities to explore and build important areas of knowledge, develop powerful tools for learning, and live in humanizing social conditions.*

Unless we make the instructional task the focus of our enquiry, then we can have no confidence that learning will be enhanced and consequently, the outcomes of educational reform will remain capricious. We must also continuously remind ourselves that it is the tasks that students undertake that predict their performance (Doyle 1983).

The model of the instructional core provides the basic framework for thinking about classroom practice and how to enhance the instructional process so as to improve the quality and level of student learning. Elmore and his colleagues propose the following seven principles to guide the work (City et al 2009). They are:

1. Increases in student learning only occur as a consequence of improvements in the level of content, teachers' knowledge and skill, and student engagement.

2. If you change any single element of the instructional core, you have to change the other two.

3. If you can't see it in the core, it's not there.

4. Task predicts performance.

5. The real accountability system is in the tasks that students are asked to do.

6. We learn to do the work by doing the work, not by telling other people to do the work, not by having done the work at some time in the past, and not by hiring experts who can act as proxies for our knowledge about how to do the work.

7. Description before analysis, analysis before prediction, prediction before evaluation.

As a corollary to this, Elmore also says there are only three ways to improve student learning at scale – in other words, more than just one or two classrooms:

1. increase the teacher's instructional knowledge and skill (capacity).
2. increase the level of complexity of the content students must learn.
3. change the role of the student in the instructional process.

Taken together the potential contained in the implementation of these principles is to create a new instructional culture within the school. This requires adopting strategies that have the ability to build a common language of instructional practice as well as of building within and across schools – the connective tissue by which the culture is propagated – and of focusing greater attention on the knowledge and skill requirements of doing the work. The approach works iteratively from the existing knowledge base of individual teachers to develop theories of action that discipline and deepen the culture of teaching and learning of all teachers in the school.

In our own Unleashing Greatness work, we have linked closely together the understanding of the instructional core with the practice of instructional rounds and, from that, the generation of theories of action for teaching and learning. This provides the focus for much of chapter 5. Without wishing to presage that discussion too much, it is important here to describe how the Unleashing Greatness strategy has built in practical ways, on Elmore and his colleagues' original articulation of the instructional core. There are two that are crucial to our way of working.

First, and as already noted, critical to the success of the Unleashing Greatness approach has been the development of 'theories of action'. A theory of action is a link between cause and effect: *if* we take a particular action, *then* we expect that action to have specific effects. A theory of action connects the actions of teachers with the consequences of their actions – the learning and achievement of their students. We describe in detail the theories of action for teaching and learning in chapter 5, but we have also generated a series of 'whole school' theories of action emerging from the instructional rounds process (Hopkins and Craig 2018b). They are as follows:

1. When schools and teachers set **high expectations** and develop authentic relationships, then students' confidence and commitment to education increases and the school's ethos and culture deepens.

2. When teacher directed instruction becomes more **enquiry focused**, then the level of student achievement and curiosity increases.

3. By consistently adopting **protocols for teaching**, student behaviour, engagement and learning is enhanced.

4. By consistently adopting **protocols for learning**, student capacity to learn, skill levels and confidence are enhanced.

These whole school theories of action give more texture to the discussion of the nature and implementation of the instructional core and are discussed further in chapter 8.

Second, we have extended and elaborated somewhat Elmore and colleagues original conception of the instructional core as seen in figure 4.1.

The four components of high-quality classroom practice are profoundly interrelated. Figure 4.1 emphasises several features of these interconnections:

- we cannot change one component without impacting directly on the other three;

- we must regard the four components as a whole if significant change leading to powerful learning is to occur – success is unlikely if we focus on three or fewer components; and,

- powerful classroom practice results from the quality of the relationship between the teacher, the student, the content, and the feedback from assessment – such practice cannot emerge from any one component alone, no matter how strong its individual qualities.

This leads to our overarching theory of action related to powerful classroom practice:

- **When** we increase teacher knowledge about high quality instruction and generate a shared view of effective practice,

- **Then** we will improve teacher capacity to translate that knowledge into effective practice for every student in every classroom.

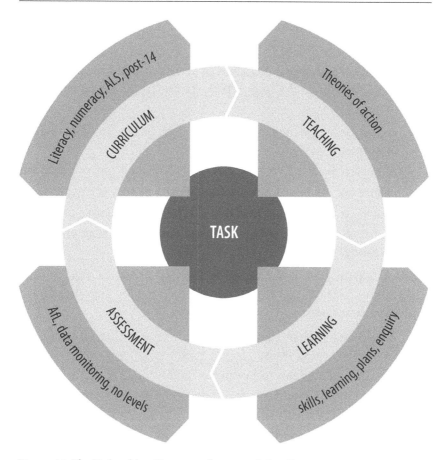

Figure 4.1 The Unleashing Greatness framework for Classroom Practice

THE FOUR POWERFUL CLASSROOM PRACTICE COMPONENTS

Pedagogic knowledge. The Unleashing Greatness approach to teaching is based on the six teacher theories of action described in chapter 5:

- Harness learning intentions, narrative and pace.
- Set challenging learning tasks.
- Frame higher order questions.
- Connect feedback to data.

- Commit to assessment for learning.
- Implement cooperative groups.

Assessment for learning is described in detail in Curiosity and Powerful Learning (Hopkins and Craig 2018b). Its underpinning principles are that we:

- collect clear evidence that informs us about how to lift individual attainment;
- offer clear feedback to, and seek clear feedback from, our students;
- ensure our students know what grades/levels they are working at;
- provide transparent criteria that enables peer coaching; and,
- make evidence-based links between student learning and lesson planning.

Student learning is about students playing an active role in their education and schooling. The impacts of encouraging and attending to student voice include:

- developing student capacity to reflect on learning and acquire a range of learning skills;
- making our students feel respected and listened to;
- developing student capacity to take up more demanding roles and responsibilities;
- giving students a sense of belonging; and,
- students seeing teachers positively.

Curriculum frameworks. In the following section, we provide an overarching perspective on the curriculum then introduce our approach to curriculum development that draws on the use of fertile questions. A fertile question frames the curriculum as a proposition, a problem to be solved, and a question to answer. Fertile questions develop student metacognition capability by constantly providing opportunities for reflection and discussion about the 'how' as well as the 'what'.

CURRICULUM DEVELOPMENT AND FERTILE QUESTIONS

Obviously, the curriculum is a central component of the instructional core and is often the key focus for both policy change and innovation in many educational contexts and systems. The curriculum is often regarded as the means for every school to become a great school and for every student to realise their potential. Yet, in many educational systems, the curriculum is often a barrier to achieving the forms of personalised learning so necessary for such a transformation. It is partially for this reason that the curriculum per se does not feature centrally in the Unleashing Greatness strategy.

The other reason is, as we have already argued, it is high quality pedagogy that has a direct and proven effect on student learning and outcomes and within a much shorter time frame. The interval between a decision to mandate a specific curriculum, however potentially powerful, and its implementation often takes years, and students need more immediate support on their learning journeys. That is why chapter 5 is devoted to the discussion of high-quality pedagogy.

This is not to say, of course, that curricular issues are unimportant or irrelevant, but such a complex discussion is beyond the scope of this book. It is necessary though to acknowledge the importance of the curriculum here and I will do so by firstly, discussing curriculum entitlement, secondly, identifying the two key approaches to curriculum development, and thirdly, describing an approach to curriculum development – fertile questions – that puts enquiry at the heart of the curriculum experience and can be implemented expeditiously within most policy contexts.

WHAT DOES IT MEAN TO BE EDUCATED?

One way of both pinpointing the curriculum issue and of drawing the argument together is to pose the question 'What does it mean to be educated?' at any particular phase of education. Being educated at any phase of learning has four central elements (Hopkins 2013):

- a breadth of knowledge gained from a curricula entitlement;
- a range of skills on a developmental continuum that reflects increasing depth at ages 7, 11, 14, 16 and in many cases, 18;

- a range of learning experiences; and,
- a set of key products, projects or artefacts.

It also means that students are sufficiently articulate to:

- sustain employability through basic skills;
- apply their knowledge and skills in different contexts;
- choose from and learn in a range of post-14 study (assuming an entitlement curriculum up until then); and,
- draw on wider experiences to inform further learning and choice.

Most national curricula do not meet these desiderata. Although the following proposals were originally based on my original work on the Key Stage 3 (11–14) curriculum in England, they represent a broader attempt to imagine a structure that enables schools and teachers to personalise the curriculum across all stages of education.

The first is to **focus on core study**. Functional literacy, numeracy and communication could be clarified as expected attainment at the end of the Key Stage 3 curriculum. ICT would also need to be explicitly added to a suggested core of language, maths and science. Functional skills would similarly need to be embedded across the curriculum.

The second would be a **condensed statutory curriculum in non-core subjects combined with an optional entitlement**. In many countries this is referred to as the 'essential curriculum'. This means that the statutory curriculum content and processes in non-core subjects would be reduced. As a rule of thumb, in most national systems this would mean that the content removed would be approximately 20–25% of current specifications. The reduction could be re-designated as an optional entitlement. The entitlement would make up several components in the breadth of study currently set out for each subject. Schools would be required to teach a minimum number of components.

Third, the flexibility of an **optional entitlement** would allow schools to guarantee time to:

- secure essential knowledge and teach common learning skills through the curriculum

- organise the curriculum to meet the needs of a range of abilities, tailoring support for underachieving and underperforming students, and to stretch gifted and talented students.

Fourth, there needs to be **clarity on common learning skills**. This requires that a common framework of skills be identified across the whole curriculum. As is seen later in the chapter, this would include: enquiry, problem-solving, creative thinking, information processing, reasoning, evaluation and communication. Students would develop each skill to a deeper level as they progressed through each stage of the curriculum. It is also necessary to look systematically across non-core subjects to consider how the spread and transmission of skills could best be improved to develop learning and raise attainment.

Finally, is the need to **champion effective pedagogy**. There needs to be external support to help schools organise the curriculum to meet the needs of a range of abilities. It must also help teachers bring curriculum knowledge and common learning skills together in the classroom.

The clear prize from pursuing these actions would be a curriculum tailored to the needs, talents and aptitudes of all students. This would ensure that every student had the core and common skills required to learn at each stage of education, and that the best students were properly stretched.

ALTERNATIVE APPROACHES TO CURRICULUM DEVELOPMENT

There is a long and distinguished tradition on the theory and practice of curriculum development that is again well beyond the scope of this book. It is worth, however, just spending a little time discussing the two main trends in curriculum development over the past half century or so as it will help the reader get a perspective on current debates and to gain some more insight as to how to fully exploit the potential of the instructional core. The first of the two approaches is associated with Ralph Tyler. The second with Lawrence Stenhouse.

THE TYLER MODEL

The best known of the curriculum models is that associated with Ralph Tyler, derived from his seminal book *Basic Principles of Curriculum and*

Instruction (1949). So ubiquitous is Tyler's model that many claim that it is the only way to develop curricula. Somewhat dismayed by the capricious and whimsical – if not downright sloppy – approach to curriculum development that he witnessed in the US in the 1940s, Tyler, a school inspector, proposed as an antidote a systematic and beguilingly simple approach to curriculum planning based around four questions:

1. What educational purposes should the school seek to attain?
2. What educational experiences can be provided that are likely to attain these purposes?
3. How can these educational experiences be effectively organised?
4. How can we determine whether these purposes are being attained?

The so-called Tyler rationale is often expressed in an even more simplified form:

Objectives
↓
Content
↓
Organisation
↓
Evaluation

The Tyler model has been enormously influential, so much so that most curriculum or lesson plans appear to be based on this approach to some extent. Two points should be made about the model at the outset.

The first is that by beginning with objectives one begs the question: where do they come from? Some of Tyler's students who became important curriculum theorists in their own right provided some answers. Benjamin Bloom (1956) and his colleagues produced a taxonomy of educational objectives that provide a ready-made solution for the problem. Hilda Taba (1962) proposed a needs assessment stage that precedes the derivation of objectives. These solutions have served to satisfy most practitioners, but in many ways the problem remains a real one.

The second point relates to the evaluative aspect of the model. The only way to evaluate this type of curriculum scheme is through observing some change in behaviour on the part of the student that signifies achievement of the objective. In turn, that objective must be expressed in behavioural terms so that the achievement can be observed and evaluated. In its pure form, the model looks something like the diagram shown in figure 4.2.

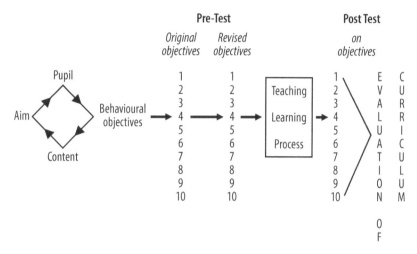

Figure 4.2 A more elaborated version of Tyler's Curriculum Model

In the diagram, behavioural objectives result from some interaction between the general aim of the curriculum, the content to be taught, and the perceived pupil characteristics. The resulting list of objectives is then tested on the class and as a consequence possibly changed. This provides a base line measure of the pupils' achievement. The teaching/learning process then ensues, and the curriculum episode ends with another test that serves to assess the overall pupil achievement on the curriculum. Rarely is the process like this. Testing, particularly the original test, is often omitted. So too is the revision of objectives. Also, the objectives are usually not established with any degree of precision. But the objectives approach is seen in one form or another in most curriculum designs.

Unfortunately, the objectives model is no panacea. Although it is suitable for certain teaching/learning situations its almost universal application is deleterious. There are now a number of well-established critiques of the behavioural objectives model (e.g. Eisner 1979; Hardarson 2017; Stenhouse 1975; Rudduck and Hopkins 1985), but I will briefly rehearse some of the objections here.

- First, the objectives model trivialises the nature of knowledge. By fitting a subject into an objectives format there is the danger that the essence of, say, history will be reduced to a recitation of the kings and queens of England. It is very difficult to represent the deep structure of a subject in an objectives format.

- Second, the objectives models tend to make for predictable pupil outcomes. This is to be welcomed when one is concerned with mathematical or scientific formulae, but to be regretted when one is concerned with poetry or art appreciation.

- Third, the model does not accord with reality. The teaching/ learning process in general does not work like that. We teach in a more idiosyncratic and capricious way; often long periods of effort are followed by a sudden burst of understanding. It is only infrequently that we learn in carefully packaged, uniform and relatively short periods of time.

- Fourth, the approach, although it often increases the clarity of educational programmes, does little, for reasons already outlined, to increase the quality of educational performance. Finally, the model ignores the ethical, moral and political imperatives surrounding schooling. Questions such as, 'Is this the appropriate content to teach?' are of no importance in this approach.

In discussing the objectives model, we have tried to point both to its advantages and its drawbacks. It is the most common form of curriculum design. It has had enormous influence, but is appropriate only in certain, often instrumental, subject areas.

THE PROCESS MODEL

This model stands in contrast. This name was coined by Stenhouse to describe his alternative approach to curriculum development as exemplified in the Humanities Curriculum Project (vide Stenhouse 1975, Rudduck and Hopkins 1985). The process model does not specify the behaviour the student is to acquire after having engaged in a learning activity, rather it describes an educational encounter. It identifies a situation in which children are to work, a problem with which they are to cope, or a task in which they are to engage. Using the process model, teachers can formulate educational encounters that respect both the student and the integrity of the knowledge with which they interact.

There are three basic approaches to developing a curriculum on a process model.

The first is the approach identified with the work of Elliot Eisner in *The Educational Imagination* (1979; Irwin and Reynolds 2010). Like many others, Eisner was dissatisfied with the behavioural objectives approach, for reasons similar to the ones previously discussed. He advocated the use of expressive objectives in the areas where behavioural (or in his terms, instructional) objectives were inappropriate. The expressive objective defines an educational encounter without specifying what the pupil is to learn from that encounter. Eisner (quoted in Stenhouse 1975) says that an expressive objective provides both the teacher and the student with an invitation to explore, defer, or focus on issues that are of peculiar interest or import to the inquirer. An expressive objective is evocative rather than prescriptive.

Second, a more satisfactory avenue for the process model is provided by Jerome Bruner in his book *Toward a Theory of Instruction* – particularly his concept of structure (Bruner 1960; 1966). Following the logic of philosophers like Paul Hirst, Bruner argues that each discipline has a structure that determines the way knowledge evolves or is produced within it. In history, for example, knowledge is produced through locating, analysing and making judgments based upon evidence. This historical method determines the way in which historical knowledge is developed. Similarly, in science, knowledge advances through controlled experimentation commonly known as the scientific method. Bruner argues that this structure provides an effective model for teaching and learning. Curricula can be formulated by following the method of 'real' historians or scientists – using the historical or scientific method to structure the curriculum. Instead of teaching historical or scientific knowledge we teach how to do history or science and accumulate our knowledge in this way. Many of the Schools Council curriculum projects were built on this model. The history 13-16, science S-13 and, of course, Bruner's influential 'Man: A Course of Study' are all examples of these (Stenhouse 1980).

Third, not all curriculum subjects are dignified by the label 'discipline', so how does one proceed here? 'Principles of procedure' was the approach that Stenhouse and his colleagues adopted in the Humanities Curriculum Project (Stenhouse 1970; 1975; Rudduck and Hopkins 1985). Faced with producing a curriculum on controversial issues for pupils of school leaving age in an area with no established tradition, they began by specifying the principles upon which the curriculum should be based. The Humanities Curriculum Project was based upon five major premises:

1. Controversial issues should be handled in the classroom with adolescents.
2. Teachers should not use their authority as teachers as a platform for promoting their own views.
3. The mode of enquiry in controversial areas should have discussion rather than instruction as its core.
4. The discussion should protect divergence of view among participants.
5. The teacher as chairperson of the discussion should have responsibility for quality and standards in learning.

From these considerations a set of highly specific principles were developed that provided a structure for both pupils and teachers despite the open-ended nature of the curriculum and the radical teaching/learning process it adopted.

In contrasting the behavioural objectives and process models, we are not arguing that one is necessarily better than the other. They are complementary approaches – each has the potential of working well but in different contexts and with different goals. I appreciate that this discussion may appear to be an historical diversion, but it is important to an understanding of current curricula debates. The moral purpose and values underpinning the Unleashing Greatness strategy obviously sees much virtue in the process model and a practical way of customising these principles to contemporary lesson plans and curriculum content is found in the discussion of fertile questions that follows.

THE FERTILE QUESTION: WHAT IS IT?[3]

Planning using fertile questions prevents the curriculum from becoming a series of isolated 'bore holes' or bits of information taught but not connected. It ensures students develop a meaningful and useable framework for each subject. Fertile questions allow students to replicate the thoughts and actions of experts within that field. They create opportunities for students to see how knowledge has been created and how it is often contested whilst enabling them to apply knowledge to solving meaningful problems. Fertile questions are naturally engaging – questions demand answers and problems, solutions. They do not focus on 'learning' snippets of information but on turning information into knowledge through applying it to a problem and testing how far it resolves that problem or tension.

An approach based around a fertile question engages pupils and helps them to see the links between concepts and knowledge. It also goes beyond traditional models and instead promotes the idea that the enquiry is a journey that helps pupils to *think* historically, *think* scientifically, *think* geographically, *think* mathematically. The approach addresses the importance of balancing students' knowledge of facts against their understanding of concepts. In history, they are learning about change and cause, not just dates and events. It helps teachers transform straightforward science experiments into a true understanding of scientific principles in the way that a scientist at CERN might apply them. In maths it balances the quest for absolutes with the need for multiple approaches. Fertile questions model the kind of thinking and intellectual habits we want from the students and make it much safer for them to ask questions and take risks. A fertile question is a planning device for knitting together a sequence of lessons, so that all of the learning activities – teacher exposition, narrative, source-work, role-play, plenary – all move toward the resolution of an interesting and meaningful *historical/scientific/mathematical/RE* problem by means of a substantial motivating activity at the end.

---

3 This section is based on Bright Byte – The Fertile Question by Oliver Knight (2014).

THE '6 WEEK' PLANNING FRAMEWORK

The key to designing a good fertile question is to ensure that it is connected to both the students' current thinking and the desired kind of thinking – that of expert practitioners. Just as with a good lesson plan, it starts with what the students can currently do and explores what they need to be able to do next – framed as a problem to be solved. There are four principles for structuring a route through the fertile question:

1. Start with a **big**, essential question that is debated in the world and is used by practitioners of the discipline. In other words, a question that a professional mathematician or historian might ask before venturing into the unknown for answers or a real-world engineering issue that needs resolving.

2. It is essential that the question is framed within the concept it is focused on. For example, a fertile question about evidence will revolve around a '*How do we know*' type question or a fertile question about perspective will revolve around '*developing multiple perspectives on the problem presented.*'

3. Identify a concluding activity that requires a constructed response to the question (a *performance of understanding*) that will create a tangible product that solves the problem posed by the question.

4. Plan backwards from the end product by deciding what activities will develop the conceptual understandings and abilities essential to address the question and create a meaningful response to it. What needs to happen in each phase to allow for resolution of the problem?

THE '6 WEEK' TEACHING AND LEARNING CYCLE

The teaching and learning cycle is a way of ensuring that every fertile question has an impact on progress and attainment. The cycle forms the overarching scaffold for every lesson and enquiry. The cycle works by posing seven key questions that enshrine the construction of each enquiry, as seen in figure 4.3. It is the simplest and most effective way of enshrining the medium-term planning process into a manageable and accountable model for all teachers. These questions provide the rigidity of ensuring that the needs of the curriculum are met whilst being loose enough to allow for creativity and freedom in the planning and delivery from both teacher and learner.

Figure 4.3 The fertile question teaching and learning cycle

The eight stages of the fertile question. One of the reasons why fertile questions provide such leverage is because they emphasise the aspects of learning that make the most difference to student progress. The main focus is on developing student metacognition by constantly providing opportunities for reflection and discussion about 'how' as well as 'what', and on providing opportunities for a constant feedback cycle to be built into the process. The focus of this feedback is always against the criteria outlined at the beginning of the enquiry, and focuses on the three key factors: *where am I going, how am I doing, where to next?*

Once the fertile question has been created, these eight stages need to be followed:

1. Introduce the new fertile question – engage and motivate pupils, discover what they already know, and check out their existing preconceptions. Outline and focus on the concept that frames the question and plan to build on their current thinking. Make this known to the pupils and set clear outcomes and challenging goals = acceleration happens when expectations are high. You can activate undergraduate level thinking in Year 8 students by creating a fertile question that creates a junior version of an expert problem.

2. Allow pupils to decide what research question(s) they might like to formulate that answers the fertile question. This does not always have to be co-constructed and can be set by the teacher. This stage enables metacognition by allowing students to work out where they are and what they need to do next. This stage needs to be carefully planned to allow for a reduction in scaffolding over time. This stage also consists of direct instruction – giving students the fingertip knowledge they need to solve the problem by moving from acquisition to application.

3. Start the process of inquiry with a focus on dialogue not monologue: *what small questions do we need to answer to formulate a response to the BIG question? Can we divide the BIG question up? What happens if we disagree? Where might we go for information? What will we do if we get stuck? How will we know if we are on the right track? How much information do we need? How do we turn the information into knowledge? What language is essential to answering the question? How are we going to display our thinking? What are the success criteria? Who is the intended audience? What is the purpose of this piece of learning?* Use of strategies like reciprocal teaching and home and expert groups to enable meaningful dialogue to occur are important here.

4. Come back as a whole class to discuss findings so far and any problems that have arisen. Use teacher and peer review to critique current thinking and plan where to go next to ensure we solve the problem posed by the question.

5. Create an initial (draft) response to the question in groups or individually – tentative answers and provocative feedback to encourage deeper reflection. (Oral rehearsal) Use this stage to model and deconstruct the language required to replicate 'expertise'.

6. Peer review and re-drafting of first draft in light of feedback and moving from every day to more formal language.

7. Group/individual concluding performance of the solution to the problem. Use or real (peer, teacher) or virtual (ICT) audience to give the response meaning and purpose.

8. Class concluding performance and feedback/review – *can we settle on one final answer, what does this prepare us to do next?*

What does a good performance or understanding look like? Fertile questions need outcomes – concrete endpoints where the students demonstrate what they have learned. These are called 'performances of understanding'. If understanding something is being able to think and act flexibly with it, we need to design approaches to assessment that allow for this to happen – applying their learning to an unseen problem or case. The key word here is performance – it must require the students to do something, and preferably something new. So, the performance of understanding must be more than recital or re-wording. It must require students to be able to demonstrate that they can use and apply, not replicate. It should require them to (amongst other things and not all at the same time):

- synthesise
- predict
- critique
- construct/create something new
- question
- interpret

It is important that the culminating piece of work is something that can be *seen, heard* or *read*. It is equally crucial that not all humanities questions finish with an essay and all maths questions finish with some questions to answer! How can we assess understanding and thinking if it is a representation of the work and thinking of the teacher? Instead, the role of the teacher throughout the different stages of a fertile question is a changing one.

Fertile questions, as an example of a process curriculum, provide a framework for ensuring that students constantly revisit prior learning and use what they have learned previously to help them answer other smaller lesson questions, which are building toward the resolution of the BIG fertile question. The hidden agenda here of course is that students acquire learning skills as well as mastering curriculum content. It is this essential component of the instructional core that we turn to in the following section.

LEARNING SKILLS AND METACOGNITION

The clear conclusion to be drawn from the previous discussion on the curriculum is that:

> At the heart of personalised learning is its impact, not just on test scores and examination results, but also on students' learning capability. If the teacher can teach the student how to learn at the same time as assisting them to acquire curriculum content, then the twin goals of learning and achievement can be met simultaneously (Hopkins 2010:230).

There is now an increasingly sophisticated literature on how children learn (Wood 2007), the different types of multiple intelligences (Gardner 2003) and the descriptions of a range of learning styles (Kolb 1984). As increasing numbers of educators have taken on board learning to learn programs, these reference points have been extended to also embrace understandings about the application of emotional intelligence theory in classrooms and schools (Goleman 2005; Kress and Elias 2006). This trend has also encouraged the development of skills for building learning power such as those captured in Guy Claxton's (2017) – popular 4 R's model resilience, resourcefulness, reflectiveness and reciprocity – which has been widely adopted in the UK (Simms 2006). Although a discussion of these literatures is beyond the scope of this chapter, it is instructive to acknowledge how they have influenced the way in which personalised learning is currently defined.

A fundamental aspect of the instructional core is the ability of learners to respond success-fully to the tasks that they are set, as well as the tasks they set themselves. In the Unleashing Greatness strategy, we define powerful learning as the ability to:

- integrate prior and new knowledge;
- acquire and use a range of learning skills;
- solve problems individually and in groups;
- think carefully about their successes and failures;
- evaluate conflicting evidence and to think critically; and,
- accept that learning involves uncertainty and difficulty.

The deployment of such a range of learning strategies is commonly termed metacognition, which can be regarded as the learner's ability to take control over their own learning processes (Hopkins 2010:230). Although a full discussion of metacognition is also beyond the scope of this chapter, it is important to define our terms carefully, because sloppy thinking leads to poor and confused implementation. It is also important to note the power of metacognition to impact on student performance. In his meta-analysis, Hattie (2009; 2023) calculates an effect size of 0.69 for 'metacognitive activities (thinking about thinking) that include planning how to approach a given learning task, evaluating progress, and monitoring comprehension'.

Daniel Muijs and David Reynolds (2018:80) define metacognition as:

The metacognitive approach starts from the premise that performance can be improved through a better understanding and awareness of one's own thought processes. Teaching pupils this self-awareness is the mainstay of this approach.

In commenting further on metacognition, Muijs and Reynolds (2018:84) maintain that:

Metacognition shouldn't be taught as a standalone skill or in separate lessons but needs to be embedded in subject teaching. It needs to be part of regular subject lessons (e.g. in science, mathematics or history).

Pupils need to know why they are learning metacognitive skills, otherwise they may lack motivation to use them.

In order to improve the likelihood of pupils using metacognitive strategies, one off approaches are not sufficient, Training needs to take place over a lone period of time and ideally be a permanent feature of teaching and learning across pupils' school career.

This certainly accords with the approach that is taken within the *Unleashing Greatness* strategy and one that I have been advocating for some time (Hopkins 2010b:230):

The key point is that within whatever context learning takes place, it involves an active construction of meaning. This carries implications for the management of learning opportunities, in particular that an active construction of meaning requires [the application of] practical, cognitive and other learning strategies. As learning is [interactive] it can occur only as the learner makes sense of particular experiences in particular contexts. This making sense involves connecting with an individual's prior knowledge and experience. Thus, new learning has to relate to, and ultimately fit with, what individuals already understand.

Even such a brief discussion of metacognition as this requires mention of the seminal contribution of the Russian psychologist, Lev Vygotsky's (1962) and his articulation of the 'zone of proximal development'. There are two key ideas here.

The first relates to the necessity to focus instruction at that margin between what the learner already knows and what they potentially can learn. Ensuring that teaching occurs within the learner's zone of proximal development is a 'meta principle' for personalising learning.

The second aspect of Vygotsky's theory is not just identifying the learning zone, but how to operate within the zone. It is here where the concept of scaffolding is so powerful. Scaffolding refers to the interactional support in order to maximise the child's learning. A scaffold is a temporary support that is used to assist a learner. These scaffolds are gradually withdrawn as learners become more competent, although students may continue to rely on scaffolds when they encounter particularly difficult problems. Providing scaffolds is a form of guided practice. Scaffolds include modelling the steps by the teacher, or thinking aloud by the teacher as he or she solves the problem. Scaffolds also may be tools, such as cue cards or checklists, that complete part of the task for the students, or a model of the completed task against which students can compare their own work (Structural Learning 2021)[4].

Throughout this discussion a continuing theme is that the student needs to become increasingly self-conscious about the importance of them expanding their range of leaning skills. Many schools in our Unleashing Greatness networks reinforce and articulate a consistent set of learning skills in displays around the school, within classrooms and in the rubrics that students use. The articulation of learning skills is critical to the implementation of the instructional core as it has been discussed in this chapter.

For example, the International Baccalaureate (IB) is an internationally recognised qualification. The IB movement aims to develop inquiring, knowledgeable, and caring young people who help to create a better and more peaceful world through intercultural understanding and respect. To this end they have developed the IB Learner profile that students can assess themselves against. As seen in table 4.1, IB learners strive to be:

Inquirers	They develop their natural curiosity in learning.
	They actively enjoy learning – this love of learning will be sustained throughout their lives.
Knowledgeable	They explore concepts, ideas and issues that have local and global significance.
	In so doing, they acquire in-depth knowledge and develop understanding across a broad and balanced range of disciplines.
Thinkers	They exercise initiative.
	Through applying thinking skills critically and creatively, they can recognise and approach complex problems.
	They make reasoned, ethical decisions.

4   For a practical and comprehensive review of scaffolding see https://www.structural-learning.com/post/scaffolding-in-education-a-teachers-guide.

Communicators	They understand and express ideas and information confidently and creatively, in more than one language and in a variety of modes of communication.
	They work effectively and willingly in collaboration with others.
Principled	They act with integrity and honesty, with a strong sense of fairness, justice and respect for the dignity of the individual, groups and communities.
	They take responsibility for their own actions and the consequences that accompany them.
Open-minded	They understand and appreciate their own cultures and personal histories.
	They are open to the perspectives, values and traditions of other individuals and communities.
	They are accustomed to seeking and evaluating a range of points of view and are willing to grow from the experience.
Caring	They show empathy, compassion and respect towards the needs and feelings of others.
	They have a personal commitment to service.
	They act to make a positive difference to the lives of others and to the environment.
Risk-takers	They approach unfamiliar situations and uncertainty with courage and forethought.
	They have the independence of spirit to explore new roles, ideas and strategies.
	They are brave and articulate in defending their beliefs.
Balanced	They understand the importance of intellectual, physical and emotional balance to achieve personal well-being for themselves and others.
Reflective	They give thoughtful consideration to their own learning and experience.
	They are able to assess and understand their strengths and limitations in order to support their learning and personal development.

Table 4.1 The IB Learner Profile (from Hopkins and Craig 2015:17)

We have attempted to be more specific and accessible in the Unleashing Greatness strategy. We have developed the 'Being a Learner Framework'. Much like the IB learner profile, it details a series of learning skills and dispositions:

- Being creative
- Being a participator
- Being an enquirer
- Being reflective
- Being a self-manager
- Being a team worker

In addition, however, the framework identifies the range of practical skills that constitute each element and then describes them practically at three levels of performance. An example is given of what it means to 'be creative' in table 4.2. Elaborating the range of learning skills in this way, enables students to be more explicit and specific about their acquisition of metacognitive capabilities at three increasing levels of performance.

Being creative	Bronze	Silver	Gold
Generate ideas, explore possibilities and alternatives	I can identify the key parts of issues within a situation and generate a list of alternatives or possibilities for each one.	I can compare and contrast information or ideas and, from these, generate new alternatives or possibilities.	I can apply a range of creative problem solving skills to develop new ways of thinking through situations or problems.
Make inventive connections	I can make concrete connections between pieces of information, including identifying similarities and differences.	I can make more abstract connections between concepts including linking cause and effect.	I can use a range of thinking approaches to make links between concepts including lateral and emotional thinking.
Questioning assumptions	I can identify different viewpoints in relation to a given assumption.	I can find ways of challenging an assumption by collecting information and evaluating it.	I can apply abstract thinking (emotional and metaphorical) to question assumptions.

Adapting to changing circumstances	I can identify different consequences of change.	I can interpret different consequences of change.	I can evaluate different consequences and implications of change.

Table 4.2 Example of 'being creative' from the 'Being a Learner Framework'

There are a further range of specific teaching techniques that we emphasise in the Unleashing Greatness strategy. The approach to generating fertile questions as seen in the previous section is replete with metacognitive content, which is also the case with the theories of action and models of teaching pedagogic strategies that we discuss in chapter 5. I need to add parenthetically that assessment for learning and task setting, two of the other elements of our approach to the instructional core are described in detail there.

In the final section of the chapter, we discuss how this approach to defining the instructional core can be taken to scale through an overarching 'personalised learning' strategy at the school and system level.

PERSONALISED LEARNING

Personalised learning is an idea that has been capturing the imagination of teachers, parents and young people around the world for some time. It is an idea that has its roots in the best practices of the teaching profession, and it has the potential to make every young person's learning experience stretching, creative, fun and successful. Its essence is found in the way in which the instructional core has been described in this chapter. In this concluding section, we look a little more at how personalised learning can be taken to scale (Hopkins 2019).

In education, personalised learning is the drive to tailor schooling to individual need, interest, and aptitude. This emphasis provides a bridge from prescribed forms of teaching, learning skills, curriculum, and assessment to an approach to classroom practice that is predicated on enabling every student to fulfil their potential. This is the achieved by adopting the version of the instructional core described in this chapter.

In one sense, personalised learning represents a logical alternative to what Pasi Sahlberg characterised as the GERM virus (Sahlberg 2021) as seen in chapter 1. The key GERM policies – standardisation, focus on core subjects, search for low-risk ways to reach learning goals, use of corporate management models and test-based accountability policies are ubiquitous in current neoliberal education policy debates. It may be that these strategies serve a function in the first phase of a long-term large scale reform effort (Hopkins 2013). However, in order to sustain system-wide improvement, societies are increasingly demanding strategies characterised by diversity, flexibility and choice.

It is moral purpose that drives personalisation. We see it most vividly in the concern of the committed, conscientious teacher to match what is taught, and how it is taught to the individual learner as a person. That is not just a question of 'sufficient challenge', of aligning pedagogy to the point of progression that each learner has reached, even though that is vitally important. It is also part of the teachers' concern to touch hearts as well as minds, to nourish a hunger for learning and help equip the learner with a proficiency and confidence to pursue understanding for themselves.

At one point in my career, I was fortunate to serve in the UK government as Chief Adviser to the Secretary of State and Head of the Standards and Effectiveness Unit. For much of that time, I worked very closely with David Miliband, the Minister of State, during the second term of New Labour when we were introducing the concept of personalised learning into the English educational system. David described personalised learning like this (Miliband 2004): 'Giving every single child the chance to be the best they can be, whatever their talent or background, is not the betrayal of excellence; it is the fulfilment of it.'

One can summarise this approach to personalised learning as follows:

- As an educational aspiration, personalised learning reflects a system-wide commitment to moral purpose, high excellence and high equity and to every school being or becoming great.
- As an educational strategy, personalised learning relates to and builds on the learner's experience, knowledge, and cognitive development, develops their confidence and competence, and leads towards autonomy, emancipation and self-actualisation.

- As an approach to teaching and learning, personalised learning focuses on individual potential, develops the individual's learning skills (particularly digital), and enhances creativity and social skills.
- As a curriculum orientation, personalised learning offers an approach to subject teaching that balances societal aspirations and personal relevance, and unifies the curriculum offer across sectors and age groupings.

This leads directly to the following implications that can help guide day-to-day practices:

- **For children and young people**, it means clear learning pathways through the education system and the motivation to become independent, e-literate, fulfilled, lifelong learners.
- **For schools**, it means a professional ethos that accepts and assumes every child comes to the classroom with a different knowledge base and skill set, as well as varying aptitudes and aspirations; and, because of that, there is a determination for every young person's needs to be assessed and their talents developed through diverse teaching strategies.
- **For school governors**, it means promoting high standards of educational achievement and wellbeing for every pupil, ensuring that all aspects of organising and running the school work together to get the best for all pupils.
- **For local authorities and multi-academy trusts**, it means a responsibility to create the conditions in which teachers and schools have the flexibility and capability to personalise the learning experience of all their pupils; combined with a system of intelligent accountability so that central intervention is in inverse proportion to success.
- **For the system as a whole**, it means the shared goals of high quality and high equity.

The rationale of these principles is clear: to raise standards by focusing teaching and learning on the aptitudes and interests of pupils and by removing any barriers to learning. The key question is, how collectively do we build this offer for every pupil and every parent?

Personalised learning occurs within an 'in and out' of school context where schools in a local community and beyond share both staff and curricular resources increasingly within a framework of shared accountability. Figure 4.4 illustrates the central components of personalised learning within and beyond the school.

This leads to an operational definition of personalised learning around six key components:

- Assessment for learning
- Powerful learning and teaching
- Self-directed learning
- Customising the curriculum offer
- The contribution of digital technologies
- Organising the school and system for personalised learning

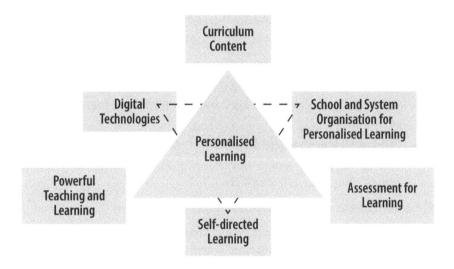

Figure 4.4 Central components of personalised learning within and beyond the school (from Hopkins 2019)

Assessment for learning implies:

- that the school, its teachers and the system develop a high-level capacity for using data to promote student learning.

- the process of seeking and interpreting evidence for learners and teachers to decide where the learners are in their learning, where they need to go, and how best to get there.
- shared objectives and feedback that identifies targets for improvement, 'higher order' questioning, and self and peer assessment.

Powerful learning and teaching implies:

- the curriculum should focus on understandings and competencies that have enduring and intrinsic value.
- high expectations and challenging targets should be set for all, but while standards should remain constant, time and support should be varied according to individual student need.
- teachers should show students how to incorporate new information into their existing knowledge through activities that induce critical thinking and solving conceptual problems.

Self-directed learning implies:

- that self-directed learning contracts provide the basis for project work that is an essential and ongoing feature of the curriculum offer.
- individual learning profiles.
- strong emphasis on cooperative group learning and social interaction, counter intuitively.

Customising the curriculum offer implies:

- modifying the framework of any centralised curriculum to ensure a continuum for personalised learning across the three phases of education: foundation, middle and 14–19.
- using the enquiry into subjects within the context of standards as the building block of curriculum provision.

- involving students in the formulation of their own educational goals. This is the key to them establishing engagement in learning and establishing a long-term commitment to schooling.

The contribution of the 'new' technologies implies:

- opportunity for personal creativity, the ability to match curriculum to individual learning styles and putting the pace of learning under the individual's control.
- concurrent and extended learning opportunities outside of normal school day.
- building diagnostic assessment for learning with different pathways to follow.

Organising schools for personalised learning implies:

- differentiating the workforce for student learning, enhancing the role of the learning mentor and providing each learner with the link to an adult.
- block timetabling and grouping students on basis of learning need, within and between schools to ensure network and community learning.
- establishing a system of transferable learning profiles and credits to underpin assessment and to ensure flexibility.

To meet the full range of individual needs and aspirations inherent in the goal of personalised learning requires extensive, but disciplined, innovation of many different kinds and at different levels in educational provision and professional practices. This entails changes at the level of the classroom, for example through enquiry led curricula, rubrics to scaffold learning and develop skills: for example, at the level of the school, through peer coaching that utilise protocols for the theories of action that ensure consistent teacher practice, as well as at system level, with the creation of networks between schools and other collaborative arrangements.

It should by now be clear that the dissemination of the outcomes of innovation and new methods of personalised learning cannot be achieved by a policy led model alone but requires new mechanisms of lateral transfer through networks. This is an issue that we will address in subsequent chapters of this book.

The purpose of this chapter has been to describe the professional practice that conditions the Unleashing Greatness school improvement strategy. It has focussed principally on an elaboration of the instructional core and its key components as originally proposed by Richard Elmore. It is the instructional core or the framework for 'Powerful Classroom Practice' in our vocabulary that provide the essential architecture for creating those learning experiences for students that ensure both equity and excellence. It is the instructional core that translates moral purpose into strategic action.

CODA: CLASSROOM PRACTICE

In this chapter, we have considered the nature of the instructional core and the dimensions of classroom practice phase of the Unleashing Greatness process. In helping school leaders and school improvement teams plan for action at this stage of their school improvement journey, the following questions may be found helpful:

- Does your school staff understand the importance of the instructional core both strategically and operationally?
- How confident are you that all the tasks that your student's undertake are located within their zones of proximal development?
- Are the teaching practices employed in the school well specified, consistently applied and directly applicable to the learning needs of your students?

The following two cameos are from schools who are members either of the University of Bolton Laboratory School network or the Curiosity and Powerful Learning network in New South Wales. Beaumont Primary School, Bolton and James Meehan High School, Sydney illustrate how they approached this phase of the Unleashing Greatness process.

ENHANCING PUPIL OUTCOMES THROUGH METACOGNITIVE STRATEGIES

BEAUMONT PRIMARY SCHOOL, BOLTON

The primary objective of this cameo is to demonstrate the effectiveness of implementing metacognitive approaches. It aims to underscore how these strategies have contributed to pupils becoming self-regulated learners, fostering metacognitive knowledge, and improving overall academic outcomes.

The implementation of metacognitive approaches was monitored and assessed over an academic year. Qualitative and quantitative data collection methods, including classroom observations, teacher and pupil interviews, and academic performance assessments, were used to evaluate the impact.

Findings and recommendations:

1. **Self-regulation and awareness:** Pupils at Beaumont Primary became more aware of their strengths and weaknesses as learners. They demonstrated increased self-motivation and engagement in their learning processes.

2. **Developing metacognitive knowledge:** Explicit teaching of metacognitive strategies enhanced pupils' understanding of how they learn, various strategies, and the tasks at hand. Pupil outcomes improved as they applied metacognitive knowledge to their studies.

3. **Support for planning, monitoring, and evaluation:** Teachers played a pivotal role in supporting pupils to plan, monitor, and evaluate their learning. Pupils learned to set goals, assess their progress, and adjust strategies effectively.

4. **Explicit teaching and modelling:** The explicit teaching of metacognitive strategies within classroom instruction proved to be beneficial. Teachers modelled their own thinking processes to demonstrate metacognitive strategies to pupils.

5. **Reflection and planning:** Pupils were encouraged to reflect on their strengths and areas of improvement. They learned to plan how to overcome current difficulties, fostering resilience in the learning process.

6. **Providing appropriate challenge:** Teachers at Beaumont Primary set an appropriate level of challenge for pupils. This encouraged pupils to develop effective learning strategies without feeling overwhelmed.

The successful implementation of metacognitive approaches at Beaumont Primary has led to significant improvements in pupil outcomes and metacognitive growth. These strategies have created an environment in which pupils are not only aware of their learning processes but also equipped to navigate and improve them.

In conclusion, Beaumont Primary School's commitment to implementing metacognitive approaches has yielded substantial benefits. Pupils have become self-regulated learners, capable of planning, monitoring, and evaluating their learning effectively. By embracing explicit teaching, modelling, and fostering reflection, Beaumont Primary has created an enriched learning environment that nurtures metacognitive growth.

Based on the success of these strategies, for our next steps, we will:

- continue prioritising metacognitive strategies and explicit teaching within classroom instruction.
- maintain a focus on teachers modelling metacognitive thinking processes.
- encourage ongoing reflection and planning opportunities for pupils.
- ensure that appropriate challenge levels are consistently set for learners to promote effective strategy development.

By sustaining these practices, Beaumont Primary School can continue to enhance pupil outcomes, foster metacognitive growth, and cultivate self-regulated learners prepared for academic success.

FOCUSING ON THE INSTRUCTIONAL CORE
JAMES MEEHAN HIGH SCHOOL, SYDNEY

In 2021, James Meehan High School (JMHS) embarked on a transformative school improvement journey to enhance student learning by fostering high-impact professional development with a specific focus on what Richard Elmore called the instructional core. The timely introduction of Curiosity and Powerful Learning (CPL) played a pivotal role in the school's success. This achievement was facilitated by a dedicated leadership team who embraced a growth mindset, prioritised student-centred leadership with an unrelenting focus on classroom practice, i.e. the instructional core.

Key to our success was the invaluable contribution by Professor David Hopkins, who introduced the school to the CPL and Unleashing Greatness frameworks. He also provided guidance and professional development to our instructional leaders to equip them with the tools to drive model practices within the school. Working collaboratively through ongoing classroom peer observations and sharing of practice, our instructional leaders have over the past 24 months designed comprehensive protocols for classroom practice and feedback mechanisms. These have enhanced the quality of instruction in all classrooms through the implementation of the theories of action.

Regular interactions and check-ins with Professor David along our school improvement journey, together with joint professional development sessions with the Laboratory School network, have served as a wealth of inspiration for our instructional leaders. It has enabled the school to continually refine processes and foster professional dialogue in non-threatening supportive environments. This has encouraged our classrooms practitioners to delve deeper into the instructional core and become intrinsically motivated to improve their classroom practice.

CHAPTER 5:
PEDAGOGY

INTRODUCTION: THE MYTH THAT
TEACHING IS ART OR SCIENCE

One of the myths that I addressed in *Exploding the Myths of School Reform* (Hopkins 2013), was that teaching is either an art or a science. My response was that it is neither one nor the other. It is both. This is the theme that I explore in this chapter that relates specifically to the 'instructional rounds' and 'pedagogy' phases in the Unleashing Greatness framework.

Let me come clean from the outset and also try to put it simply:

- **Teaching is a science** insofar as that there are strategies and practices that a body of research has shown to be effective in enhancing learning. Just like doctors and other professionals, teachers should use research to inform their practice.

- **Teaching is an art** insofar as teachers must bring themselves fully into their teaching – their values, passion and *joie de vivre*. But they must also expand their personal repertoire of practices so that through a process of reflection they discover how to construct the most powerful learning experiences for their students.

- **Teaching is an art and a science when teachers** are first (science) continually observing their students in order to see how they learn best, and then (art) using their professional judgment to adapt their teaching practice(s) to fit the learning needs of their students.

Perhaps the clearest finding from the contemporary research on system reform is, as we have seen, that the quality of an education system cannot exceed the quality of its teachers. The corollary to this is that the only way to improve learner outcomes is to improve teaching. In terms of moral purpose, social equity requires every child to succeed. That is why the highest performing systems and providers focus relentlessly on ensuring high teaching quality while reducing the variability in the learning experiences of every student.

Great teachers are those that share a common practice and as was argued in the previous chapter, open it up to professional scrutiny. They understand that their practice is an instrument for expressing who they are as a professional. One of the confusions that leads to the binary choice between teaching as an art or science lies in the individualism that too often characterises teaching, where the person and the practice are intertwined and confused.

In terms of our own work, the theories of action that have been developed inductively from the work of thousands of teachers, are presented in the form of rubrics or protocols (Hopkins and Craig 2018b). It is the use of protocols for peer coaching, professional development and educational improvement that allows teaching simultaneously to be both an art and a science. In doing this, we remain mindful of Lawrence Stenhouse's (1975:142) caution of many years ago, that such proposals are not to be regarded 'as an unqualified recommendation, but rather as a provisional specification claiming no more than to be worth putting to the test of practice. Such proposals claim to be intelligent rather than correct.'

So let me extend slightly the art and science distinction in terms of the argument of this and the following chapter. There are four essential elements in the infrastructure that enables teaching to be simultaneously an art and a science.

- Initially, there is the instructional round process that generates theories of action inductively from the work of teachers – art informed by professional judgment.
- Second is their translation from hypotheses to frameworks for action in the form of rubrics and protocols – art informed by science.

- Third is the use of high-quality research evidence, such as that associated with the work of John Hattie (2023), that disciplines and informs the specifications contained in the protocols – science.

- Finally, it is the use of the protocols within authentic professional development settings, such as peer coaching triads, that ensures the expansion of teaching skill that leads inexorably to the enhancement of student learning through the creation of increasingly powerful learning experiences – art.

To give more depth to these contentions and explain further our approach to pedagogy, in this chapter, I will:

- propose a simple framework for thinking about teaching and populating it by reference to some key texts on teaching strategies and the *Visible Learning* meta-analyses of John Hattie (2023).

- describe the instructional rounds approach to non-judgmental classroom observation that we have used a means for generating our theories of action on teaching and learning.

- outline the theories of action themselves and illustrate some of the associated protocols of rubrics (Hopkins and Craig 2018b).

- review the models of teaching approach associated with the work of Bruce Joyce (Joyce and Calhoun 2024).

- in the coda, provide some examples of how schools do this in practice and asking the key Unleashing Greatness questions.

A FRAMEWORK FOR TEACHING

The argument I am making in this chapter, reflected in my previous work on teaching and learning, is that the various theories of action and models of teaching and learning are simply tools that teachers can use to create more powerful learning experiences. But such research and strategies should not be regarded as panaceas to be followed slavishly. Research knowledge and the various specifications of teaching can have limitations, especially if they are adopted uncritically. In line with the Unleashing Greatness strategy, such knowledge only becomes useful when it is subjected to the discipline of practice through the exercise of the teacher's professional judgment. So, in beginning this section, I refer to the framework for thinking about teaching (as seen in figure 5.1) that I have been using for some time (Hopkins 2014:191).

The three perspectives on high quality teaching in the outer circles reflect, as we shall see later in the chapter, propositions based on research and practice that relate the impact of different aspects of teacher behaviour to the learning of students. It is the routine of fine teachers to combine these elements through a process of reflection to create an individual style. Consequently, it may be that critical systematic reflection is a necessary condition for quality teaching. This is not reflection for reflection's sake, but to continue to develop a mastery of one's chosen craft. As John Dewey once memorably said, 'One does not learn from experience, but by reflecting on experience.'

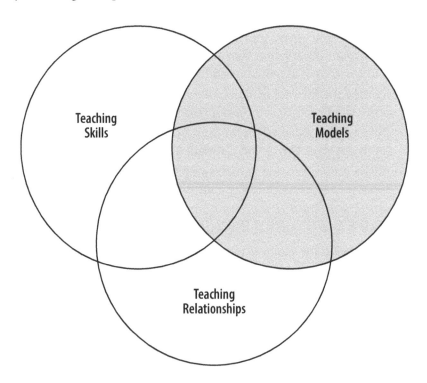

Figure 5.1 Four ways of thinking about teaching (Hopkins 2014)

TEACHING SKILLS

I start with 'teaching skills' because these are the basic building blocks of teacher competence. These are the everyday classroom management skills that most teachers became familiar with during their initial training and that they continue to refine as part of their reflection on professional practice. These are behaviours such as: content coverage, engaged time (i.e., students learn more when they are on task for a high proportion of class time), active teaching, structuring information, wait time and effective questioning. These teaching skills are very similar to our theories of action that are described in detail later in the chapter. The difference being is that our theories of action were generated from our non-judgmental instructional rounds process and then validated by reference to research evidence, rather than the other way round!

There is an extensive research literature on teaching effects that are replete with cues and tactics necessary for effective teaching. As we shall discover in relation to the work of John Hattie, consistently high correlations are achieved between student achievement scores and classroom processes (Hattie 2023). The research evidence on those teaching behaviours most closely associated with student achievement gains is now extensive and very sophisticated. These are all, of course, essential aspects of the skill sets that teachers need to personalise learning. Excellent summaries are found in the research literature. The sources that I have found most valuable, as have the schools that we work with, are:

- *Looking in Classrooms* by Tom Good and Jere Brophy (2008; Good and Lavigne 2017). *Looking in Classrooms* (now in its 11th edition) is a teacher friendly, authoritative, and well organised primer on all the core aspects of effective teaching. The ideas are well presented and that enables easy transfer to classroom practice. This is a good source for strategies for building positive teaching relationships.

- *Effective Teaching* by Daniel Muijs and David Reynolds (2018). Mujis and Reynolds are leading UK researchers and policy influencers with extensive experience in the fields of both teacher and school effectiveness. This book is both comprehensive, authoritative, and scholarly with detailed and well-structured analyses of the evidence and practice of effective teaching.

- *The New Art and Science of Teaching* by Robert Marzano (2017). Marzano is a well-known and published educational researcher in the United States. His work blends reliable research and conceptual analysis into practical strategies that teachers find helpful. He is particularly well known for his work on fostering and sustaining system-wide teaching strategies, providing effective feedback to students, and building a strong student academic vocabulary.

- *Principles of Instruction* by Barak Rosenshine (2012). Rosenshine's principles have been widely disseminated and many of the schools that we work with find them well focused, practical and impactful. The principles referred to come from three sources: (a) research in cognitive science, (b) research on master teachers, and (c) research on cognitive supports.

TEACHING MODELS

Bruce Joyce developed this approach in his pioneering work on *Models of Teaching* that was first published in 1972 and is now in its tenth edition (Joyce and Calhoun 2024). Joyce describes and analyses over thirty different models of teaching, really models of learning, each with their own 'syntax', phases and guidelines. These models are designed to bring about particular kinds of learning and to help students become more effective learners. It is in this way that the use of 'teaching models' form part of an overall strategy for enhancing teacher professionalism and the key tool for personalising learning. They are described in more detail later in the chapter.

Earlier I made the point that it is the teacher's task to not only 'teach' but also create powerful contexts for learning. In our book *Models of Learning: Tools for Teaching* (Joyce et al 2009:7), we phrased the argument in this way:

> *Our toolbox is the models of teaching, actually models for learning that simultaneously define the nature of the content, the learning strategies, and the arrangements for social interaction that create the learning environments of our students.*

> *Through the selection of appropriate models, content can become conceptual rather than particular, the process can become constructive*

inquiry instead of passive reception, and the social climate can become expansive not restrictive. Our choices depend on the range of our active teaching repertoire and our efforts to expand it by developing new models and studying those developed by others.

It is the integration of 'content, process and social climate' that explains how the learning experience can be organised and personalised to make a positive difference to students. The impact is not just on test scores and examination results, but also on the students' capacity to learn. As I have already said, if the teacher can teach the student how to learn at the same time as assisting them to acquire curriculum content, then the twin goals of learning and achievement can be met at the same time.

TEACHING RELATIONSHIPS

The third component of the framework is what I have called 'teaching relationships'. These are less technical and are more related to the teacher's commitment to their students and belief in the power of high expectations. A supportive, rigorous, and optimistic learning environment is fundamental for high levels of student achievement. For me, a key aspect of teaching is the teacher's ability to generate and sustain an authentic relationship with their students. For example, the teacher 'who made a difference' is a common topic of conversation following an admission that 'I am a teacher'. To many educators, a prime indicator of the 'effective' school is one in which a high proportion of pupils have a good or 'vital' relationship with one or more teachers.

The influence of expectations is often a subtle one and is felt within a myriad of classroom interactions. The ways in which the teacher sets tasks, arranges groups, locates the responsibility for learning and provides feedback, are all illustrations of how teachers can give messages of high expectations and support that condition and enhance student behaviour. It implies establishing the classroom as a safe and secure learning environment in which pupils can expect acceptance, respect and even warmth from their teachers, without having to earn these. Both *Looking in Classrooms* (Good et al 2017) and *The New Art and Science of Teaching* (Marzano 2017) are replete with cues and strategies for doing just this. They are intrinsic rights that are extended to all pupils, without prejudice, simply because they are there.

TEACHER REFLECTION

It is the practice of fine teachers to combine these three elements through a 'process of reflection' to create an individual style (Pollard et al 2018). This is the fourth element of the framework. Instead of focusing on discrete teacher behaviour, as does much of the research associated with specific teacher effects, this research explores the relative effectiveness of different teaching styles or collections of teacher behaviours. Consequently, it may be that critical systematic reflection is a necessary condition for quality teaching. This is not reflection for reflection's sake, but in order to continue to develop a mastery of one's chosen craft. It is through reflection that the teacher harmonises, integrates and transcends the necessary classroom management skills and the personal aspects of their teaching into a strategy that has meaning for their students.

Spalding and Wilson (2002) cited five benefits of being a reflective teacher:

- Reflection is at the heart of effective professional development.
- Self-reflection helps teachers create and experiment with new ideas and approaches.
- Reflective practice helps teachers better understand their students, their abilities, and needs.
- Reflective teachers are more likely to develop reflective learners. If teachers practise reflection they can more effectively encourage learners to reflect on, analyse, evaluate and improve their own learning.
- Self-reflection acts as a constant reminder to stay humble and continue working hard to achieve results.

Some years ago, we conducted a comparative study of policies aimed at improving teacher quality for the OECD. Six characteristics of high quality teachers (Hopkins and Stern 1996) were identified:

- commitment
- love of children
- mastery of subject didactics
- a repertoire of multiple models of teaching
- the ability to collaborate with other teachers
- a capacity for reflection

Although it is convenient to group teachers' desired capacities and behaviours into categories, these attributes all interact in practice. For example, one French teacher elegantly defined teacher quality as '*savoirs, savoir-faire, et savoir-être*'. This is translatable perhaps as 'knowledge, knowing how to do, and knowing how to be' (Hopkins and Stern 1996:503). This phrase reflects the essential fusion of the meshing of art and science in teaching.

VISIBLE LEARNING

Those of us who work in the fields of teacher effectiveness and school improvement owe an enormous debt of gratitude to John Hattie and his books *Visible Learning* and more recently *Visible Learning: The Sequel* (Hattie 2009; 2023). These books, contribute enormously to the knowledge base on effective teaching, containing as they do a synthesis of over 2100 meta-analyses, covering over 130,000 studies and involving some 40 million students. Hattie's work, is based on the simple proposition: 'To improve schools, draw on the best evidence available' has become globally influential. He and his team produce 'meta-analyses of meta-analyses' in order to calculate the effect size of a wide range of educational interventions on student achievement.

In the more recent book Hattie, moves beyond claiming what works to what works best, by asking questions such as: Why is the current grammar of schooling so embedded in so many classrooms, and can we improve it? And, how can we incorporate research evidence as part of the discussions within schools? These questions reflect a theme that he presaged in his paper, *What doesn't work in education: the politics of distraction*, Hattie (2015). Here he takes on some of the most popular approaches to reform such as small classes, high standards, more money. These popular and oft-prescribed remedies from both the right and the left wings of politics, he argues, have not been shown to work as well as alternatives.

He continues this line of argument in his ACEL Monograph, *Implementing, scaling up, and valuing expertise to develop worthwhile outcomes in schools* (Hattie 2019). In this paper Hattie (2019:3) writes (I have inserted the bullet points for sake of emphasis):

- *The influences from the Visible Learning research clearly show that the greatest investment needs to be directed towards the expertise of the educators to maximise their collective impact on students, and particularly on teaching students the various strategies of learning within the context of the various subjects.*

- *The investments at government levels, however, have traditionally been into the "things" or structures of schools. Yes, these structural influences have positive impacts, but they are small relative to investment in developing the expertise of the educators: governments tend to be more interested in buildings than expertise, "things" rather than people.*

- *For example, Table 1 provides some of the lower influences, mainly structural on the left-hand side, with the higher influences on the right-hand side. These are mainly expertise by teachers, particularly teaching the strategies of learning within the content domains.*

Hattie's 'Table 1' (Hattie 2019:3) is seen as table 5.1. In the left-hand column, he contrasts examples of low-impact investments in building academic achievement with the right-hand column examples of high-impact influences on student achievement. What is so striking about these two contrasting sets of examples is how often the low-impact influences are currently used and become part of the established educational rhetoric than those in the right-hand column. Yet moral purpose and Unleashing Greatness resides unrelentingly in the right-hand column. This explains the heavy emphasis in this book on the instructional core, theories of action and models of teaching.

This point assumes even more relevance when one realises that in Hattie's rankings, socioeconomic status has an effect size of 0.57 (Hattie 2009). This means that a student growing up in poverty may be expected to perform roughly a year and a half behind an otherwise similar student who grows up more in wealthy circumstances. This is bad news for a socially just society, for schools with a moral purpose, and of course for the students themselves. But there is an upside. Look again at the teaching behaviours in the right-hand column of table 5.1 and acknowledge the range of resources and strategies that the school and the teacher have at their control to compensate for what students brings with them into the classroom. This is where Unleashing Greatness surely lies.

Influence	d	Influence	d
Retaining back a year	-0.32	Collective teacher efficacy	1.57
Suspension	-0.20	Student assessment capability	1.22
Charter schools	0.04	Cognitive task analysis	1.29
Teacher performance pay	0.05	Response to intervention	1.09
Single-sex schools	0.08	Conceptual change programs	0.99
Modifying calendar/ timetables	0.09	Strategies to integrate prior knowledge	0.93
Initial teach education programs	0.10	Self-efficacy	0.92
Tracking/streaming	0.12	Success criteria	0.88
School choice	0.12	Transfer strategies	0.86
Reducing class size	0.16	Classroom discussion	0.82
Growth vs fixed mindset	0.16	Deliberate practice	0.79
One-to-one laptops	0.16	Teacher clarity	0.75
Home school programs	0.16	Feedback	0.74
Web-based learning	0.18	Reciprocal teaching	0.74
Within-class grouping	0.18	Rehearsal & memorisation	0.73
Systems accountability	0.20	Building student confidence	0.71
Adding finances	0.21	Goals/success criteria	0.68

Table 5.1. Hattie's examples of low- and high-impact investments in building academic achievement

A NOTE ON EFFECT SIZE

Effect size refers to the impact that a specific teacher practice has on the curve of normal distribution, moving it, as seen in figure 5.2, more to the right. The curve can of course move to the left when the teacher behaviour or context is ineffective or negative. Effect size provides a means of gauging the impact of a particular school, change in teaching method or classroom organisation on learning and achievement. By the same token, it can also be used to predict what can hope to be accomplished by using that practice. The computation of effect size involves the meta-analysis of those empirical studies that measure the impact of a specific teacher behaviour on student learning. First developed as a statistical technique by Gene Glass and colleagues, it was subsequently adopted by Bruce Joyce to measure the impact of models of teaching on learning and by ourselves, in relation to the theories of action (Glass, McGaw and Smith 1981; Joyce et al 2009; Hopkins and Craig 2018b). The concept has of course received global recognition through the work of John Hattie (2009; 2023).

Figure 5.2 illustrates the effect size of using higher order questions. In this case it is 0.73 of a standard deviation that is the metric utilised by effect size analysts. This means that the average student in the 'experimental group' – where the teacher used higher order questions – would be performing at the about the 65th percentile level, compared with the 50th percentile level in the 'control group' where the teacher was using closed questions.

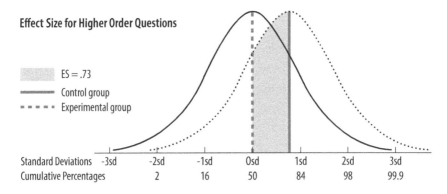

Figure 5.2 Effect size for higher order questions (reproduced from Eisner 2002)

In *Visible Learning*, Hattie introduced his own 'barometer of influence' that provides a heuristic way of expressing the concept. Although both developmental and teacher effects are important, we should always aim to be adopting practices that are in the zone of desired effects. As he (Hattie 2009:19) comments:

The development of this barometer began not by asking whether this or that innovation was working, but whether this teaching worked better than possible alternatives; not by asking whether this innovation was having positive effects compared to not having the innovation, but whether the effects from this innovation were better for students than what they would achieve if they had received alternative innovations.

For each of the many attributes investigated in Visible Learning, the average of each influence is indexed by an arrow through one of the zones on the barometer. All influences above the 0.40 point are labelled in the 'zone of desired effects' as these are the influences that have the greatest impact on student achievement outcomes.

In terms of our own work discussed later in this chapter, both our theories of action and models of teaching have high empirical support. John Hattie generously allowed us to use his 'barometer of influence' with the theories of action. As seen in figure 5.3, five of the teacher theories of action described later are in the zone of desired effects, according to Hattie's barometer of influence.

The effect size for direct instruction is 0.59 – in the zone of desired effects

The effect size for questioning is 0.46 – in the zone of desired effects

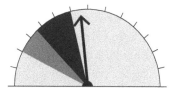

The effect size for feedback is 0.73 – in the zone of desired effects

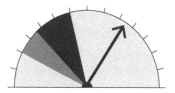

The effect size for providing formative evaluation is 0.90 – in the zone of desired effects

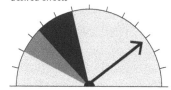

The effect size for cooperative learning is 0.41 – in the zone of desired effects

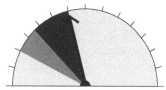

Figure 5.3 Hattie's Barometer of Influence and the theories of action

Bruce Joyce was an early adopter of effect size and a means of measuring the impact of *Models of Teaching* on student learning (Joyce et al 2009). This is a summary of the effect sizes of the four families of the models of teaching:

- **information processing** – a mean effect size over 1.0 for higher order outcomes.
- **cooperative learning** – a mean effect between 0.3 to 0.7.
- **personal models** – a mean effect of 0.3 or more for cognitive, affective and behavioural outcomes.
- **behavioural models** – a mean effect between 0.5 to 1.0 – best representatives are for short-term treatments looking at behavioural or knowledge of content outcomes.

The increasingly widespread use of effect size provides an understandable, accessible and reliable methodology for linking together the art and science of teaching in the pursuit of ever higher levels of student learning. The challenge for all school improvers is to develop increasingly powerful specifications and strategies for teaching that will push the normal curve of distribution way to the right.

We turn now in the rest of the chapter to a discussion of our particular contribution to the theory, research, and practice of pedagogy – theories of action and models of teaching (practice). Before we do however, it is important to note that our approach has stemmed from practice, rather than research and statistical analysis. The theories of action in particular have emerged from the extensive non-judgmental observations of teaching that we have conducted through the instructional rounds process in many countries. These theories of action have been generated inductively through professional observation and tested against the meta-analyses computed by Hattie and others. In this way we are keeping faith with the 'inside-out' character of Unleashing Greatness but disciplining it by ongoing engagement with the evidence base. It is necessary therefore to review the instructional rounds strategy before going into more detail on the theories of action and models of teaching (practice).

INSTRUCTIONAL ROUNDS

Central to implementing the Unleashing Greatness strategy is the establishing of a professional practice in the school that can create a new culture of teaching and learning. The question is, how do we create this new culture of teaching and learning that embraces the instructional core?

Our response was to refine the generic instructional rounds strategy associated with the work of Richard Elmore and his colleagues (City et al 2009). Our approach works iteratively but systematically, from the existing knowledge base of individual teachers to develop theories of action that discipline and deepen the culture of teaching and learning of all teachers in the school and their network. Critical to the success of the instructional rounds approach has been the development of 'theories of action'. A theory of action, as we have seen, is a link between cause and effect: *if* we take a particular action, *then* we expect that action to have specific effects. A theory of action connects the actions of teachers with the consequences of their actions – the learning and achievement of their students. It is these collectively that provide the basis of the protocols that ensure precision, consistency and engagement in the classrooms of our schools.

The process works like this:

- The network convenes in the host school for an instructional round visit. The purpose of the instructional round is to generate a series of theories of action that present a positive picture of the pedagogic practice of the school. The emphasis is solely on description, not evaluation or judgment.

- There are usually a maximum of 24 participants, although post-covid, we have become more imaginative at how to organise rounds virtually. In the morning, the network divides into groups of four that visit a rotation of six classrooms for approximately twenty minutes. In each classroom network participants collect descriptive evidence of the practices – teacher, students and classroom environment – they observe.

- After completing the round of classroom observations, in the afternoon, the entire group assembles in a common location to work through the process of description, analysis and prediction.

The group analyses the evidence for patterns and look at how what they have seen explains or not the observable student performance in the school.

- There are three phases to this process:

  ▫ First, participants individually analyse their own data searching for common themes across the classrooms they visited and producing a composite list.

  ▫ Second, participants share their list of themes (or hypotheses) in groups of four, but not the same group with which they did the observations.

  ▫ Third, the whole group comes together, and each group proposes an observation in sequence. The aim is to develop a series of 'theory of action' principles from the analysis of the observations under the leadership of a skilful facilitator. Skilful because it is quite challenging to synthesise the discussion and simultaneously translate it into a theory of action. We find it helpful to have someone type the theory of action onto a screen as the facilitator articulates it. Once it is on the screen the whole group can debate and edit the proposed theory of action before moving on.

- Finally, the network provides feedback to the school and teachers involved in the rounds visit. No comments are made about the behaviours of individual teachers, except to say – look what we have learned from you! The focus is unrelentingly on describing the practice, how it can be enhanced and lead to the next level of professional work in the school.

This approach enables the knowledge base and practice of teachers to be used to develop theories of action that discipline the culture of teaching and learning in the school and across the network. As our experience with instructional rounds has deepened through experience in schools in the UK, Australia, Sweden and elsewhere, five important lessons have been learned (Hopkins and Craig 2018b:6):

- The first was that despite the phase or context of schooling, the theories of action generated by each school were in most cases very similar.

- Second, this is not a 'pick and mix' approach – all the theories of action must be integrated into the teacher's professional repertoire if they are to impact in a sustained way on student learning.
- Third, and most importantly, all the theories of action are characterised by an approach to teaching that has enquiry and personalised learning at its centre.
- Fourth, some of the theories of action relate to the school and some to the practice of individual teachers.
- Fifth, all the theories of action, as we saw in the previous section, have a high level of empirical support in the educational research literature.

SUGGESTIONS FOR CLASSROOM OBSERVATION

The visit is not focused on what individual teachers are doing per se, but more on observing the common strategies and practices in place at the school and the observable evidence of the enhancement learning within the classroom. The purpose of the round is to look for evidence on setting of expectations, classroom culture, structure and delivery of lesson, questioning of students, student understanding of the lesson and the tasks they are engaged in, as well as individual student learning behaviour.

Recall that the last two of Elmore's principles cited in chapter 4 (City et al 2009) are:

- 'We learn to do the work by doing the work, not by telling other people to do the work, not by having done the work at some time in the past, and not by hiring experts who can act as proxies for our knowledge about how to do the work.'
- 'Description before analysis, analysis before prediction, prediction before evaluation.'

This is why we emphasise non-judgmental observation in our rounds process, as well as the fact that judgments always hinder growth and development. It also explains why I am loathe to use observation schedules as they often, in my experience, lead both to a narrowing of focus and some form of assessment. Despite this, many participants ask for observation guidelines and so we usually provide suggestions as seen in table 5.2.

Essentially, this is professional development in the workplace rather than the workshop – it is 'learning the work by doing the work'. We should also remember that this is similar to the rounds approach associated with medical training but applying it to work in the classroom. As such, it engages participants in practising the two essential skills of the professional: diagnosis and treatment. In educational terms these might be phrased as 'What are the necessary educational goals for this student?' and 'How can we bring to bear the most powerful curriculum and instructional strategies to achieve them?'. It is this diagnostic approach that leads to the generation of the theories of action that we describe in the following section.

- Each classroom visit will be of 20 minutes duration.
- To gain a snapshot of common practices at the school, each individual in the team will observe:
  - **What teachers are doing and saying**

    Examples:
    - Using a range of strategies for learning, e.g. open ended tasks, open-ended questions, clear learning intentions and success criteria.
    - Gaining assessment evidence through e.g. questioning, asking students to explain their thinking, providing opportunities for discussion between students.
    - Establishing high expectations for all students through differentiated activities.
    - Organising the classroom space to promote, e.g. cooperative learning, individual learning, whole class teaching.
    - Exercising appropriate authority and has good relationship with learners.
    - Displays demonstrate and support learners' progress and achievement.
    - Question and supportively challenge students to explain their ideas.
    - Use praise and feedback on learning to help students understand their 'next steps' and successes.
  - **What students are doing and saying**

    Examples:
    - Able to explain the task, what they are doing and the success criteria for the lesson.
    - Explain the tools and strategies they use to help themselves when they get stuck.
    - Aware of the assessment criteria and understand how teacher feedback supports them.
    - Can explain how they know what they are doing is of high quality.

- ◻ Opportunities to explain their thinking and application to the task.
- ◻ Able to ask questions and seek clarification.
- ◻ Able to apply themselves to the task purposefully and autonomously.
- ◻ Feel praised and encouraged through formative assessment and feedback – self, peer and teacher assessment.
- ◻ Know how they have progressed in learning and what to do to improve and the next steps they need to undertake.
- ◻ Use the classroom environment e.g. displays to support their learning.
- ◻ Are confident, motivated and want to do their best. Proud to show their learning.

- **What is the nature of the task students are engaged in**
  Examples:
  - ◻ Can respond to whether the task is too easy or hard and can say which they prefer.
  - ◻ Able to say what they will know after doing the task.
  - ◻ The tasks provide explicit criteria for the quality of the work the students are. expected to produce and are reference points for assessment and feedback.

- **The team may talk to and ask questions of students but should not disrupt the class.**
  Examples of questions:
  - ◻ What are you doing?
  - ◻ What do you do if you get stuck?
  - ◻ How do you know if what you are doing is of a high quality?
  - ◻ What will you know after doing the task that you may not have known before?
  - ◻ How difficult are you finding the task? Do you prefer easy or hard tasks?

- The team should not speak to each other during the classroom observation and should not discuss anything observed or the process until the afternoon debriefing with the larger group.

Table 5.2 Instructional rounds suggestions for observations

THE SIX THEORIES OF ACTION FOR TEACHERS

So, as we have seen, the instructional rounds process supports school heads and leadership teams in developing a shared understanding and common language around effective teaching practices. It enables them to recognise what good teaching and student learning looks like; and to identify the next level of work for the school and network, in terms of professional development and school improvement. The currency of the instructional rounds process is the theories of action that emerge inductively form the analysis of the non-judgmental observations. In any typical rounds morning, 144 pieces of observational data will be generated – 24 observers x 6 classrooms. In line with the overall argument therefore, our overarching theory of action is:

When teachers explicitly and consistently incorporate the theories of actions in their own teaching,

then the learning skills, the spirit of enquiry, and the achievement of our students will be greatly enhanced.

When I first began incorporating instructional rounds into my school improvement programmes in the mid to late 2000s, the principals and teachers involved were uniformly excited by the opportunity to discuss teaching and learning in a safe space and in an authentic way. That encouraged me to do more, and I began to involve primary and special schools as well as secondary and then began to conduct them in colleges as well. I also expanded the range of contexts in which I did them, so besides Australia and the UK, I conducted rounds in Beijing, Chile, South Africa, as well as my own country of Wales. The response from participants continued to be exceptionally positive.

Then a curious thing happened. As I reflected on the range of rounds conducted in different phases of schooling and in contrasting global contexts, I began to realise that the more rounds that I did, the less I learned. What I mean by this is that the outcomes of the rounds – the theories of action generated – were remarkably similar and consistent, phase to phase and country to country. I began to realise that high quality teaching travels well throughout the phases of schooling as well as globally.

That reflection encouraged me to synthesise the outcomes of the first 50 or so rounds that I had conducted. In doing this I then realised that some of the theories of action related to the whole school and represented in many ways the decisions of leadership whereas the others were related to the behaviours of individual teachers. The ten theories of action are seen in table 5.3.

The four whole school theories of action were described alongside the instructional core in the previous chapter and the six theories of action for teachers are the focus of the discussion below. Taken as a whole, the ten theories of action are highly consistent with the summaries of research on effective teaching practice seen earlier and as previously noted. Our colleague John Hattie generously encouraged us to use his work to illustrate the likely effect size associated with each of the theories of action (Hattie 2009; 2023). This is the science. The art lies in selecting and combining the theories of action to suit the learning needs of students. The theories of action and models of teaching in the following section are simply tools that teachers can use to create increasingly powerful learning contexts. The theories of action however have emerged authentically from the work of teaches.

Four whole school theories of action	Six theories of action for teachers
Four whole school theories of action support teaching for curiosity and achievement. They are fundamental in every school and for all teaching practice. They create a reliable, consistent, supportive environment for implementing the six theories of action for teachers.	These theories of action are about teaching. They form the core teaching protocols for the whole school.
Prioritise high expectations and authentic relationships **When** schools and teachers prioritise high expectations and authentic relationships, **then** curiosity will flourish.	**Harness learning intentions, narrative and pace** **When** we harness learning intentions, narrative and pace so students are more secure about their learning and more willing to take risks, **then** achievement and understanding will increase and curiosity will be enhanced.

Emphasise inquiry focused teaching	Set challenging learning tasks
When inquiry is a defining characteristic of a school's culture, **then** the level of student achievement and curiosity will increase.	**When** learning tasks are purposeful, clearly defined, differentiated and challenging **then** all students will experience powerful, progressive and precise learning.
Adopt consistent teaching protocols	Frame higher order questions
When we adopt consistent teaching protocols, **then** student behaviour, engagement, learning and curiosity will be enhanced.	**When** we systematically employ higher order questioning, **then** levels of student understanding will deepen and levels of achievement will increase.
Adopt consistent learning protocols	Connect feedback to data
When we adopt consistent learning protocols in all classes, **then** all students will experience an enhanced capacity to learn and to develop skills, confidence and curiosity.	**When** we connect feedback to data about student actions and performances, **then** behaviour will be more positive, progress will accelerate, and curiosity will be enhanced.
	Commit to assessment for learning
	When we commit to peer assessment and assessment for learning, **then** student engagement, learning and achievement will accelerate.
	Implement cooperative groups
	When we implement cooperative group structures and techniques to mediate between whole class instructions and students carrying out tasks, **then** the academic performance of the whole class will increase.

Table 5.3 The ten theories of action (Hopkins and Craig 2018b)

I then decided to disseminate them more widely and published the *Curiosity and Powerful Learning* manual (Hopkins and Craig 2018b). The manual has a two-page spread devoted to each theory of action: the left-hand page contains a description of the individual theory of action, and the right-hand page contains a protocol or rubric. Each rubric provides a precise description of the habits, behaviours and ways of doing that characterise teacher practice at four phases of a professional development continuum – commencing, intermediate, accomplished and expert. An example is seen in table 5.4.

Teacher often asks questions that require students to repeat information.	COMMENCING PRACTICE	INTERMEDIATE PRACTICE	Teacher often asks questions that allow students to demonstrate their thinking.
Most teacher questions are low order, relating to task compliance, knowledge acquisition and comprehension. Some questions are directed at developing thinking skills and knowledge application. Response to student answers is often 'yes', 'no', or praise for correct answers rather than praise for effort and thinking strategy. Student responses occasionally inform pace and direction of a less, and occasionally develop a lesson's narrative. Teacher asks around one question a minute, and frequency produces low engagement. Teacher may ask questions to manage off-task behaviour.			The ratio of low order and high order questions is about 50/50. Most teacher questions are referenced to the fertile question, the learning intention and task objectives. Some questions are not referenced and students and teachers may lose sight of the lesson's narrative. Responses are not always well acknowledged or validated. The teacher uses questioning to tease out evidence of student thinking. Teacher sometimes asks volunteers to answer a question, enabling some students to take a back seat or disengage. Teacher uses questioning that encourages discussion, such as wait time.
Teacher uses questions skilfully to check understanding and uses student responses to intervene in ways that have a noticeable impact on learning.	EXPERT PRACTICE	ACCOMPLISHED PRACTICE	Teacher usually asks questions that assist teacher and students to revise tasks and review explanations in ways that improve learning.
Teacher drives learning through questioning technique. Teacher poses big, fundamental questions that require students to apply their knowledge and to think in complex ways. Questions are used to focus attention on the learning intention and the lesson narrative. Student responses and student questions directly influence the lesson's pace and direction. Teacher asks only a few, powerful questions and student responses demonstrate their grasp of how these powerful questions connect to the fertile question. Students are supported to close knowledge gaps by creating multiple draft responses to questions, seeking feedback and clarifying learning intention and task objective.			Teacher uses strategies to ensure students demonstrate thinking skills in their answers. The teacher uses student responses and student questions to control the direction of the lesson. Teacher uses high order questions to identify and address misconceptions and gaps in understanding. Teacher uses questions to determine how ready students are to move more deeply into an idea, and to judge the pace of escalation and level of complexity. Students are encouraged to respond to questions with analysis and explanation. Teacher uses questioning strategies that focus students on their responsibility to think carefully about their responses.

Table 5.4 Example of theory of action protocol related to questioning

The teacher protocols or rubrics have four primary purposes:

- to set out clearly the habits, behaviours and performance expectations that characterise teaching of the highest quality, as reflected in the expert phase.
- to support personal reflection by teachers about where their practice falls on the continuum.
- to provide a common reference point and language for teachers and school leaders to use when they discuss teaching practice and teacher performance.
- to inform planning for professional learning and development for individual teachers, groups of teachers, and for the whole school.

Each rubric incorporates three objectives that apply to every student:

- **Ensuring mastery** – teachers plan with an unrelenting focus on high standards to ensure all students achieve mastery.
- **Continual development** – every action and every communication is focused on the individual student's ability to constantly grow and improve.
- **Longevity** – all students set and achieve their goals, and all students are ready for post-school education and employment.

Using a common language and structure, the rubrics support professional conversations and collective inquiry. They contribute to professional learning by grounding peer observation and collective reflection in what teachers and students actually do in a lesson. They indicate stepping-stones from current practice to improved practice. The rubrics provide tools for situating and evaluating current practice and mapping a pathway for productive improvement.

The rest of this section includes a brief description of the six theories of action for teachers, with the exception of 'learning tasks' and 'assessment for learning'. These are part of our interpretation of the instructional core and, as noted in chapter 4, are described in a little more detail, together with their associated protocol, here. The *Curiosity and Powerful Learning* manual (Hopkins and Craig 2018b) provides further detail on all theories of action.

HARNESSING LEARNING INTENTIONS, NARRATIVE AND PACE

When teachers set learning intentions and use appropriate pace and have a clear and strong narrative about their teaching and curriculum, then students are more secure about their learning, and achievement and understanding is increased.

It has become very clear from the instructional rounds that when teachers are clear about their learning intentions, then the students become more engaged and feel more secure in their learning. But it is about more than just setting a learning intention or goal. Importantly, it is also about linking the intention to the learning outcome and success criteria for the lesson, as well as ensuring curricula progression. This becomes the basis for the narrative of the lesson. Teachers with a strong sense of narrative can engage with deviation, knowing how to bring the discussion back on track. Pace is also necessary to keep the lesson lively and through increasing tempo, deal with potential low-level disruption.

A learning intention for a lesson or series of lessons is a statement that describes clearly what the teacher wants the student to know, understand and be able to do as a result of the learning and teaching activity. In formulating the learning intention, it is essential to consider three components:

- An action word that identifies the performance to be demonstrated.
- A learning statement that specifies what learning will be demonstrated.
- A broad statement of the criterion or minimum standard for acceptable performance, e.g. 'By the end of the lesson you will be able to describe foundation concepts and questions in ...'.

SETTING CHALLENGING LEARNING TASKS

When learning tasks are purposeful, clearly defined, differentiated and challenging then the more powerful, progressive and precise the learning for all students. In many of the instructional rounds conducted, we found that by and large, most students did not find the tasks they were set very challenging. Yet it is the tasks that students do that predict their performance. This requires setting tasks that are within the student's 'zone of proximal development' if their learning is to progress. Usually, this involves having three or four 'graded tasks' available for each group with scaffolding around the task to ensure success.

Each task we set our students must contain challenges that extend metacognitive skills and their domain knowledge. An attribute of challenging learning tasks is that they attract our students to questions rather than push them towards answers. All tasks should seek to inspire and sustain curiosity and inquiry through interest and engagement. Task scaffolding ensures that each student can work towards a successful performance of understanding.

In *Looking in Classrooms*, Good and Brophy (2008) identified the six components listed below as central to scaffolding support for pupils carrying out tasks:

1. Develop student interest in accomplishing the intended goal of the task.
2. Demonstrate an idealised version of the actions to be performed.
3. Simplify the task by reducing the steps.
4. Control frustration and risk.
5. Provide feedback that identifies the critical features of discrepancies between what has been produced and what is required.
6. Motivate and direct the student's activity to maintain continuous pursuit of the goal.

Closely associated with scaffolding is the gradual transfer of responsibility for managing learning. As students develop expertise, they begin to assume responsibility for regulating their own learning, by asking questions and by working on increasingly complex tasks with a concomitant increase in learner autonomy.

The protocol for *Challenging Tasks* is seen in table 5.5.

	COMMENCING PRACTICE	INTERMEDIATE PRACTICE	
Teacher is aware of strategies that create challenge in the classroom Tasks allow many students to avoid challenge while still meeting success criteria. Teacher uses subject-specific language to explain concepts. Some students use subject-specific language to explain concepts. Some students are often passive and display off-task behaviour. A minority of students engage in higher level cognitive tasks. Teacher sets low level cognitive tasks that ask students to repeat, reproduce, match or sequence. Students are occasionally asked to develop or apply their thinking.			**Teacher uses teaching strategies that are usually matched to most students' needs.** Most tasks set by the teacher challenge students and require them to use subject-specific language to explain concepts. Some students are challenged to demonstrate subject expertise. Occasionally the teacher mismatches challenges and students' levels of understanding. This is apparent from flagging pace, engagement, motivation. Students demonstrate some autonomy. They often require teacher input before deciding what they need to do to improve their performance.

	EXPERT PRACTICE	ACCOMPLISHED PRACTICE	
Teacher uses well-judged and often inspirational teaching strategies. Students learn optimistically and independently. All tasks are precisely targeted. Each student makes greater than expect progress. All students understand the desired learning outcome and regulate their performance against it. Students are engaged by, and able to complete, tasks that require them to find contradictions or tensions in knowledge, and to expose assumptions in knowledge. Students know subject-specific language and use it to talk about their thinking. Students confidently formulate counter-knowledge and generate new knowledge. Students have the autonomy and expertise to monitor their learning. They ask questions and work independently on increasingly complex tasks.			**Teacher matches teaching strategies to most students' needs.** Most tass are differentiated and set within the ZPD for all students. All students demonstrate progress. Students are encouraged and supported to use subject-specific language to explain their thinking. Students are asked to perform high level cognitive tasks, such as arguing, justifying, analysing and evaluating. Students demonstrate autonomy through task choice. Students can talk about the gap between their current performance and the desired performance.

Table 5.5 Rubric for set challenging tasks (Hopkins and Craig 2018b:21)

189

FRAMING HIGHER ORDER QUESTIONS

When teachers systematically use higher order questioning, the level of student understanding is deepened and their achievement is increased.

John Hattie reports in *Visible Learning* (2009:182) that questioning is the second most prevalent teaching method after teacher talk. Most teachers spend between 35% and 50% of their time in questioning. Questioning has a positive impact on student learning, but this effect is associated more with higher order questioning, which promotes more conceptual thinking and curiosity. The evidence suggests that most teachers ask low-level questions, related more to knowledge acquisition and comprehension. Research studies suggest that 60% of teachers' questions recall facts and 20% are procedural in nature. Bloom's taxonomy of learning objectives is widely used as a basis for structuring questions, particularly higher order questions (Anderson and Krathwohl 2001). The taxonomy provides a way of organising thinking skills into six levels from the most basis to the higher order levels of thinking. These levels can then be used to frame appropriate questions:

- **Knowledge**: recall previous material learned.
- **Comprehension**: demonstrate understanding of facts and ideas.
- **Application**: solve problems by applying knowledge, facts and skills learned in different ways and situations.
- **Analysis**: examine information and break into parts, make connections and support ideas and arguments.
- **Evaluation**: present judgments, recommendations and opinions.
- **Synthesis**: compile information in different, more creative ways; choose other solutions.

The following sequence works well, as this approach makes everyone responsible for generating an answer, particularly when combined with some of the simple cooperative techniques:

- Frame a question to the whole class.
- Allow students time to think, 'wait time'.
- Only then, call on someone to respond.

CONNECTING FEEDBACK AND DATA

When teachers consistently use feedback and data on student actions and performance, then behaviour becomes more positive and progress accelerates.

Feedback is one of the most powerful influences on student achievement. That is clear from both psychological theory and research. In *Visible learning*, John Hattie (2009:173) provides a powerful insight, as he describes his attempts to understand feedback:

> *It was only when I discovered that feedback was most powerful when it is from the student to the teacher that I started to understand it better. When teachers seek, or are at least open to, feedback from students as to what students know, what they understand, where they make errors, when they have misconceptions, when they are not engaged – then teaching and learning can be synchronized and powerful. Feedback to teachers helps make learning visible.*

In considering data and feedback that moves beyond the purely academic, Hattie suggests that a behavioural focus on student performance helps students to recognise the linkage between effort and outcome. In addressing this behavioural dimension of student performance and achievement, it is recommended that the teacher should:

- model beliefs.
- focus on mastery.
- portray skill development as incremental and domain specific.
- provide socialisation with feedback.
- portray effort as investment rather than risk.

COMMITTING TO ASSESSMENT FOR LEARNING

When peer assessment and assessment for learning (AfL) are consistently utilised, student engagement, learning and achievement accelerates.

The generally accepted definition of Assessment for Learning (AfL) is (Assessment Reform Group 2002:3): 'The process of seeking and interpreting evidence for use by learners and their teachers to decide where the learners are in their learning, where they need to go and how best to get there'.

This may be organised differently in different schools, but the rationale is always the same:

1. Clear evidence about how to drive up individual attainment.
2. Clear feedback for and from pupils, so there is clarity on what they need to improve and how best they can do so.
3. Clarity for students on what levels they are working at, with transparent criteria to enable peer coaching.
4. A clear link between student learning and lesson planning.

Assessment for learning is a powerful strategy for improving student performance (Black et al 2003; Wiliam 2009). Practices that characterise formative assessment are:

- sustaining classroom cultures that encourage interaction and use of assessment tools;
- establishing learning goals and tracking individual student progress;
- consciously varying instruction methods to meet diverse student needs employing multiple approaches to assess student understanding;
- providing feedback on student performance and adapting instruction to meet identified needs; and,
- active student involvement in the learning process.

Teachers deepen their understanding of how students learn so they can help them to:

- reflect on how to learn.
- develop learning strategies and apply them in different circumstances.
- engage in high quality classroom dialogue with the teacher, other adults and their peers. High quality dialogue supports them to develop as learners who are effective, resilient, confident and independent.

Teachers need to continue to develop their understanding of how students learn so they can help them to reflect on how they learn, develop learning strategies and apply them in different circumstances, and engage in high quality dialogue with teachers, peers and others.

COMMENCING PRACTICE	INTERMEDIATE PRACTICE
Teachers gather evidence through feedback and uses it after a lesson to assess the progress students are making in their thinking.	**Teacher checks understanding several times a lesson, and if necessary, recaps ideas before moving on.**
Teacher occasionally uses AfL strategies to elicit evidence of student thinking. Teacher occasionally uses evidence gathered through feedback to assist lesson planning and delivery. Teacher often sticks closely to a lesson plan even if students are not keeping up or are venturing down a different pathway. Teacher sometimes defines success vaguely so that students are unable to grasp where they are on their learning journey and where they are trying to get to. Teacher sometimes is unclear about the link between tasks, learning intentions, and the Fertile Question – consequently, students experience difficulty in peer rview and group learning activities.	Teacher clearly describes what success looks like for each learning task and activity. Teacher often uses AfL strategies to elicit clear evidence of student thinking. Teacher often uses evidence gathered through feedback to assist lesson planning and delivery. Teacher uses feedback from students to ensure most students achieve success, and to keep the class on track. Students know where they are in their learning journey, and what the learning intention is for the lesson. Teacher is sometimes unclear about strategies students can use to make progress in their thinking or on a learning task. Teacher provides supported opportunities for peer review.

EXPERT PRACTICE	ACCOMPLISHED PRACTICE
Teacher constantly uses a range of assessment strategies to connect current learning to the big picture.	**The teacher carefully plans for and uses various AfL strategies many times in a lesson and across a series of lessons.**
Students actively maintain a classroom ethos in which students are a resource for one another. Students can explain where they are going, describe their current performance, and identify what they need to do next to keep making progress. Students know how to review one another's work and how to construct appropriate, helpful feedback. Students share an understanding of the model of mastery they are working towards and constantly review their progress against it. Peer feedback is connected to the model of expertise students are working towards. Teacher ensures all students have multiple opportunities for drafting and re-drafting their constructed responses.	Teacher actively cultivates a classroom ethos in which students are a resource for one another. Students are familiar with their role as peer reviewers. Before moving on, teacher elicits feedback to ensure that understanding is consolidated. All students know where they are going and what they need to do next to keep making progress. Teacher uses AfL systematically to develop increased learner autonomy and metacognition. Teacher uses feedback from students to inform lesson planning. Teacher uses feedback from students to alter lesson plans in real time. Students set short-term task completion goals to achieve the overall learning goal for the Fertile Question.

Table 5.6 Rubric for assessment for learning (Hopkins and Craig 2018b:27)

IMPLEMENTING COOPERATIVE GROUP STRUCTURES

If teachers use cooperative group structures/techniques to mediate between whole class instruction and students carrying out tasks, then the academic performance of the whole class will increase as well as the spirit of collaboration and mutual responsibility.

Cooperative group work has a powerful effect in raising pupil achievement because it combines the dynamics of democratic processes with the discipline of academic enquiry. It encourages active participation in learning and collaborative behaviour by developing social as well as academic skills. The approach is highly flexible and draws on a wide range of methods (individual research, collaborative enquiry and plenary activities) and allows the integration of them all into a powerful teaching tool. We advocate its use as part of the direct instruction 'model of teaching', both as part of teacher instruction and the structuring of group activities, although at times the teacher will use the approach to structure a whole lesson or series of lessons (Hopkins 2016a; Kagan and Kagan 2015).

There are a wide range of strategies that comprise cooperative group work. They are all underpinned by the following five principles (Johnson and Johnson 2016):

1. **Positive interdependence:** when all members of a group feel connected to each other in the accomplishment of a common goal – all individuals must succeed for the group to succeed.

2. **Individual accountability:** where every member of the group is held responsible for demonstrating the accomplishment of their learning.

3. **Face-to-face interaction:** when group members are close in proximity to each other and enter into a dialogue with each other in ways that promote continued progress.

4. **Social skills:** human interaction skills that enable groups to function effectively (e.g. taking turns, encouraging, listening, clarifying, checking, understanding, probing). Such skills enhance communication, trust, leadership, decision-making and conflict management.

5. **Processing:** when group members assess their collaborative efforts and target improvements.

Cooperative group work requires pupils to practise and refine their negotiating, organising and communication skills, define issues and problems and develop ways of solving them. This includes, collecting and interpreting evidence, hypothesising, testing and re-evaluating.

TEACHING TACTICS AND MODELS

As we segue from the discussion on theories of action to models of teaching, it is important to clarify the distinction between teaching tactics and teaching models. In many ways the theories of action for teachers are tactics – teacher behaviours that have a direct and precise impact on student learning. They are specific actions that respond to specific classroom circumstances. For example, framing a learning intention sets the context for learning, questioning encourages reflection and problem solving, group work establishes the social conditions for inquiry. Tactics are the core repertoire of teaching skills.

By way of contrast, a model of teaching or model of practice (the distinction will become clear shortly) is a teaching strategy that is far more comprehensive and describes the approach for an entire lesson or curriculum unit. It also has an impact of how students learn, because the way we teach has a large impact on students' abilities to educate themselves. Whole class teaching is the best-known model of practice. The good news is that in different combinations the six theories of action for teachers comprise the essential building blocks for the whole class teaching model and other models of teaching/practice that we discuss in the following section.

MODELS OF TEACHING

We introduced the concept of a model of teaching earlier in the chapter. We noted that a model of teaching is more comprehensive than a theory of action in so far as it defines a whole lesson or series of lesson and can impact more directly on a student's capacity to learn. We have also noted that it was Bruce Joyce who developed this approach in his pioneering work *Models of Teaching*.

In this chapter, we have used the terms models of teaching and models of practice interchangeably. 'Models of teaching' refers to Joyce's original work while 'models of practice' refers to the manuals I wrote with his encouragement that outline six of the models for use in our school improvement and *Unleashing Greatness* programmes (Hopkins 2016a; b; c). To complicate matters further, Bruce Joyce, Emily Calhoun (2009) and I also wrote *Models of Learning: Tools for Teaching* that was intended more for a British audience. In essence all these volumes address the same seminal idea, but with slightly different emphases and detail.

In relation to *Unleashing Greatness* to the models of teaching/practice approach is the impact on student learning. Thus, imagine a classroom where the learning environment contains a variety of models of teaching that are not only intended to accomplish a range of curriculum goals, but are also designed to help students increase their competence as learners. Consider this quote from *Models of Learning: Tools for Teaching* (Joyce, Calhoun and Hopkins 2009):

In such classrooms the students learn models for memorising information, how to attain concepts and how to invent them. They practice building hypotheses and theories and use the tools of science to test them. They learn how to extract information and ideas from lectures and presentations, how to study social issues and how to analyse their own social values. These students also know how to profit from training and how to train themselves in athletics, performing arts, mathematics and social skills. They know how to make their writing and problem solving more lucid and creative. Perhaps most importantly, they know how to take initiative in planning personal study, and they know how to work with others to initiate and carry out co-operative tasks. As students' master information and skills, the result of each learning experience is not only the content they learn but also the greater ability they acquire to approach future learning tasks with confidence and to create increasingly effective learning environments for themselves.

Models of teaching simultaneously define the nature of the content, the learning strategies, and the arrangements for social interaction that create the learning environments of students. Models of teaching are also models of learning. Each model has its own core purpose that relates not only to how to organise teaching, but also to ways of learning. So, for example, if in whole class teaching the teacher uses the advance organiser model to structure a presentation, the student can use the same method as a means of extracting information and ideas from lectures and presentations. Some examples of the relationship between teaching and learning strategy are given in table 5.7.

Model of teaching/practice	Learning skill
Advanced organiser (or whole class teaching model)	Extracting information and ideas from lectures and presentations
Group work	Working effectively with others to initiate and carry out cooperative tasks
Inductive teaching	Building hypotheses and theories through classification
Mnemonics	Memorising information
Concept attainment	Attaining concepts and how to invent them
Synectics	Using metaphors to think creatively

Table 5.7 Examples of the relationship between model of teaching and learning skills

All the models in the box are described in detail in the *Models of Practice* manuals (Hopkins 2016a; b; c). Of these six, three (whole class, inductive and cooperative group teaching) will be touched upon through brief descriptions, but the manuals themselves contain more detailed explanation and examples.[5]

---

5   Please check my website www.profdavidhopkins.com for more information on the Models of Practice manuals and how to obtain them.

WHOLE CLASS TEACHING

In active whole class teaching, the teacher controls pupils' learning and seeks to improve performance through direct instruction, whole class questioning, discussion and learning activities. Whole class teaching relies on good lesson and topic planning. It's essential to have a clear set of overarching learning objectives and a coherent teaching and learning programme that pays close attention to the learning objectives.

Whole class teaching progresses like this:

PLANNING
Before implementing whole class teaching, the teacher must: specify learning objectives and relate the learning and teaching programme to the objectives.

TALK & DEMONSTRATION
Through lecture or demonstration, the teacher formally presents students with: a problem, an issue, an area of knowledge, a set of skills.

INQUIRY & QUESTIONING
Students develop understanding through systematic questioning and disciplined inquiry.

APPLY UNDERSTANDING
Students apply their understanding through a series of set tasks.

Figure 5.4 Whole class teaching steps

For each of the models of teaching and practice, we have specified it's 'syntax'. The syntax of a teaching model refers to the patterns, phases and guidelines that characterise the model. The syntax of the whole class teaching model follows six steps as seen in figure 5.5.

In addition to this overview, the model of practice manual goes into much more practical detail on the components of the four phases in the whole class teaching model. Each stage comprises distinct teaching strategies or activities that are described and populated with practical examples:

STEP 1: REVIEW
Review concepts and skills from the previous lesson (and homework if set).

STEP 2: PRESENT INFO IN A TALK
Outline your talk. Introduce key terms and concepts. Proceed in small steps: start with what is familiar and use lively explanations and illustrations.

STEP 3: DEMONSTRATION (PPRR)
Preliminaries: a guide about what to observe and expect. Preview: outline the purpose. Rehearsal: teacher goes through each step. Reprise: repeat procedures.

STEP 4: STUDENT DISCUSSION
Maintain fast-paced discussion that establishes meaning and promotes student understanding. Assess student comprehension using high quality questioning techniques.

STEP 5: LEARNING ACTIVITIES
Design activities to focus on content. Implement learning activities.

STEP 6: SUMMARY & REVIEW
Students ask follow-up questions. Students share findings and conclusions. Teacher reinforces key points, emphasises central ideas and sums up achievements.

Figure 5.5 The syntax of the whole class teaching model

INDUCTIVE TEACHING

Inductive teaching is a model of teaching that encourages pupils to build, test and use categories. It nurtures logical thinking and allows pupils of all abilities to process information effectively.

The inductive teaching model is a powerful way of helping pupils to learn how to construct knowledge. The model focuses directly upon intellectual capability and is intended to assist pupils in the process of mastering large amounts of information. Within teaching there are numerous occasions when pupils are required to sort and classify data. In many cases, however, the sorting process is viewed as an end in itself. Pupils are usually required to understand the 'one correct way of classifying'. Teachers know that there are usually many ways of classifying, but they choose one for simplicity. The inductive method allows pupils to understand a variety of classifications in a structured way that includes a variety of teaching techniques within one method. Without the opportunity for re-classification or hypothesising, learning potential is limited and the development of higher order thinking is restricted.

Inductive teaching brings purposeful structure to the numerous occasions when learning activities require students to sort and classify data. Inductive inquiry takes time. It is a process that asks students to think deeply about collecting and sifting information, constructing categories or labels, and then allocating data to those categories. It requires students to:

- generate hypotheses based upon their allocation decisions.
- test out their hypotheses by using them to guide later work.

Well planned inductive teaching should mean that the students:

- work collaboratively to solve problems;
- discuss with each other, often using higher order thinking skills;
- teach each other, thus memorising facts and concepts more easily;
- demonstrate their skills by seeking and freely expressing reasons for their views;
- discuss alternatives before deciding, challenging each other, being prepared to compromise and showing a willingness to change their mind; and,

- learn from what other pupils are thinking and respect their ideas and opinions.

The inductive model of teaching consists of a number of discrete phases that cannot be rushed or omitted. Inductive inquiries are rarely brief because the very nature of the inquiry requires pupils to think deeply. The inductive model in synthesis is the collecting and sifting of information in order to construct categories or labels. This process requires pupils to engage with the data and seek to produce categories in which to allocate the data. It requires them to generate hypotheses based upon this allocation and to test out these hypotheses by using them to guide subsequent work. The syntax of the inductive teaching model is characterised by the following six phases as is seen in table 5.7.

Phases in the inductive teaching model	
Phase one: identify the domain	Establish the focus and boundaries of the initial inquiry. Clarify the long-term objectives.
Phase two: collect, present and enumerate data	Assemble and present the initial data set. Enumerate and label items of data.
Phase three: examine the data	Thoroughly study items in the data set and identify their attributes.
Phase four: form concepts by classifying	Classify items in the data set and share the results. Add data to the set. Reclassify the data (possibly many times).
Phase five: generate and test hypotheses	Examine the implications of differences between categories. Classify categories, as appropriate. Reclassify in two-way matrices and by correlations, as appropriate.
Phase six: consolidate and transfer	Search for additional items of data in resource material. Synthesise by writing about the domain, using the categories. Convert categories into skills. Test and consolidate skills through practice and application.

Table 5.8 The syntax of the inductive teaching model

The inductive teaching model has a series of advantages. For students, it supports a variety of learning styles because each phase is taught in different ways. For teachers, the data has longevity and flexibility. Once the data has been assembled:

- it is easily kept from one year to another.
- its availability means you can readily incorporate its use into other classes.
- it is easy to share as a resource for colleagues.

In addition to this overview, the *Model of Practice* manual goes into much more practical detail, particularly on providing a range of worked examples and examples of data sets.

COOPERATIVE GROUP WORK

The cooperative group work is a model of teaching where pupils, working together in small groups on range of academic problems can develop both their social and intellectual skills.

As a model of teaching, cooperative group work has a powerful effect in raising pupil achievement because it harnesses the synergy of collective action. It combines the dynamics of democratic processes with the processes of academic enquiry. It encourages active participation in learning and collaborative behaviour by developing social as well as academic skills. Thus, the model requires pupils to practice and refine their negotiating, organising and communication skills; define issues and problems and develop ways of solving them, including collecting and interpreting evidence, hypothesising, testing and re-evaluating.

Well planned cooperative group work should mean that students:

- depend on each other to get a task completed;
- have individual responsibility to the rest of the group;
- discuss with each other, often using higher order thinking skills;
- teach each other, thus memorising facts and concepts more easily;
- develop better social skills, which encourages positive feelings among group members.

These are reflected in the principles for cooperative group work.

The principles for cooperative group work	
Principle 1: Positive interdependence	All members of a group feel connected to each other in accomplishing a common goal. This means all individual must succeed for the group to succeed.
Principle 2: Individual accountability	Every member of the group is held responsible for demonstrating accomplishment of the learning.
Principle 3: Face-to-face interaction	Group members are close in proximity to each other. They enter into dialogue in ways that promote continued progress.
Principle 4: Exercising social skills	Group members exercise interaction skills. These skills enable groups to function effectively. They include taking turns, encouraging, listening, clarifying, checking, understanding, probing. Interaction skills enhance communication, trust, leadership, decision-making and conflict management.
Principle 5: Collaborative processing	Group members assess their collaborative efforts and collectively target improvements.

Table 5.9 Principles for cooperative group work

The model is highly flexible and draws on a wide range of methods (individual research, collaborative enquiry and plenary activities) and allows the integration of them all into a powerful teaching tool. The teacher is able to conduct a more subtle and complex learning strategy that achieves a number of learning goals simultaneously. Thus, styles can vary from didactic to 'light touch' teaching where teacher is more an adviser and guide than a director.

In summary, cooperative forms of teaching quicken and deepen learning and enhance a wide range of cognitive abilities. In particular:

- The model enhances certain higher cognitive abilities, including the capacity to form and reform concepts and transfer knowledge across domains.
- The model helps pupils develop the basic skills of memorisation – with 'deep' learning the capacity to memorise, hold and recall information is much enhanced.
- The model creates a cohesive context for learning that supports both able and less able pupils alike.
- The model encourages positive feelings among members, reduces loneliness and alienation, builds relationships and provides affirmative views of other people.

BALANCING WHOLE CLASS, SMALL GROUP AND INDIVIDUAL LEARNING

There is ongoing debate about the appropriate balance between whole class, small group and individual activities. Working out that balance depends on what works best for our students. It is the models of learning and teaching we choose that have the greatest direct effect on student achievement. Efficient models of teaching make two assumptions:

- We will organise the whole class to pursue common learning objectives.
- Individual differences in achievement are comfortably met within our organisation of the whole class.

Creators of efficient and effective teaching models have an overall educational scheme in mind – the whole class, small group work and individual work are part of that scheme. As Bruce Joyce elegantly phrased it, 'the operational repertoire of the teacher is the critical element in the calculus of effects'.

CODA: GENERATING A LANGUAGE FOR TEACHING AND LEARNING

In this chapter, we have considered the pedagogical aspects of the Unleashing Greatness framework and the role of instructional rounds in generating a language for teaching and learning that is owned by all staff. In helping school leaders and school improvement teams plan for action at this stage of their school improvement journey, the following questions may be found helpful.

- Does your school staff regularly engage in instructional rounds and appreciate that the focus of the observations is on description not evaluation or judgment?
- How far do the six theories of action reflect common consistent and widespread practice in your school?
- Does your school's school improvement team contextualise and provide examples of the theories of action and models of teaching related to the specific context of teaching and learning in the school?

The following two cameos are from schools who are members of the University of Bolton Laboratory School network. Here Pikes Lane Primary School, Bolton and Bolton School share the pedagogical approaches they have developed as part of engaging in the Unleashing Greatness process.

PIKES LANE PRIMARY SCHOOL, BOLTON

We conducted our instructional rounds as part of the collaborative Laboratory School network in January 2022. This process involved senior leaders from the ten schools in our network and we visited six lessons across a range of subjects and year groups to distil a narrative around practice. This process helped us to build on the pedagogical protocols that we had already started to put into place in our teaching and learning policy.

The appreciative enquiry model for generating the theories of action was a very positive experience for the staff involved. When we disseminated the theories of action, we looked at which needed the greatest development. These then formed the professional development approach, supported by our triad joint practice development. In focusing on specific TOA, we could really drill down into what the best practice looked like, we further developed this through considering WAGOLL (what a good one looks like). These are the rubrics or protocols the staff developed to support peer coaching in different phases/subjects. This is an ongoing piece of work. Following this approach, other senior leaders were able to engage with the instructional rounds process in other schools from the network. They found this to be really helpful when leading their peer coaching/triad approach.

INSTRUCTIONAL ROUNDS/THEORIES OF ACTION

IR in Jan 2022, 11 school leaders visited, saw 15 minute sections of 6 lessons in small groups. TOA generated and shared with staff to create artefact for our curriculum policy.

TOA formed basis of professional development strategy for appraisal targets, reflective coaching and joint practice development (JPD).

WAGOLL/rubric to support staff to reflect on improvements to practice. Development of additional teaching tools when applied to specific subjects.

Small steps

Research

TOA
When teachers carefully sequence new learning in small steps, making it clear what learning is happening and giving pupils opportunity to practice sufficiently at each stage of experiencing new material, then pupils can reduce cognitive load and assimilate new information from working memory into long term memory more effectively.

WAGOLL
Misconceptions are identified and addressed quickly, and pupils are able to move on quickly in the lesson when they are ready to. Lessons are sequences effectively within a unit of learning.

Integrated technology

Research

TOA
When teachers self-consciously and thoughtfully integrate tech into their planning, e.g. helping scaffold learning, being able to share their and students' work visually, utilising apps, then student engagement is higher, learning is more transparent, and they find ways to work more independently and efficiently.

WAGOLL
Technology is used to support learning so all pupils have access to scaffolds to help succeed within the lesson. Appropriate apps can promote pupil engagement.

Collaboration

Research

TOA
When teachers use a variety of collaborative structures for discussion, enquiry and carrying out tasks, then students exhibit a high level of engagement, deepen their learning, and enjoy mutual success building their teamwork skills.

WAGOLL
Fluid grouping are used so all pupils can progress and access the learning at an appropriate level and it removes any barriers to learning. Mixed ability groups provides coaching opportunities which allows children to adopt different roles (leadership/coaching).

Modelling/scaffolding

Research

TOA
When teachers model learning and scaffold activities that move from simple to complex, concrete to abstract (e.g. Ready, Steady, Go), and move through 'I Do, We Do, You Do', then all students feel confident to be able to build their learning forward and achieve more than they expected.

WAGOLL
Lessons are adapted to ensure accessibility so all pupils can access the learning and make progress within the lesson. Targets of pupils with SEND are known so those pupils have the appropriate support and scaffolds to access the required learning.

Learning environment

Research

TOA
When teachers create an environment that celebrates learning and provides visible aspiration and learning clues, strategies, reinforcement and information, then students are motivated and prouder of their work, own their environment and can see the next steps, recognizing the contribution their work makes.

WAGOLL
Working walls include scaffolds and adaptions (including vocabular and examples of decoding) to support pupils with learning.

207

BOLTON SCHOOL, BOLTON

Bolton School, an Independent School Foundation comprising three primary schools and two senior schools, embarked on a school improvement journey through instructional rounds, a process conducted under the umbrella of appreciative inquiry.

To facilitate this, members of the teaching and learning groups (TLG) from each school volunteered to participate in the instructional rounds, either as observers or facilitators, often collaborating with the Bolton University network.

In this process, we ensured that the rounds were perceived as non-threatening, a key factor in gaining staff endorsement for this initiative. An unexpected but welcome side effect was that teachers on both sides of the process became highly motivated participants in research directly relevant to their teaching practices.

In this structured process, each school first identified a list of 10 to 12 pedagogical practices. Subsequently, guided by the school's development priorities, three practices were selected for in-depth exploration. An intriguing aspect of this process was the discovery of shared pedagogical focuses between the schools, including feedback, relationships, modelling, inquiry, language usage and technology integration.

Furthermore, the prioritisation of assessment and collaboration reflected the broader interest in the creation and application of knowledge.

Three of the girls' division pedagogies

Collaboration

When teachers plan opportunities for focused and structured cooperative work, then all students demonstrate enjoyment and self-confidence in collaboration with their peers and will make faster progress through deeper understanding and wider sharing of ideas and solutions.

Student agency

When teachers encourage students to make choices over their learning, both in terms of outcome and presentation, and explicitly plan opportunities to develop a range of personal skills, then students become more independent and take agency over their learning.

Student agency

When teachers explicitly create success criteria and are prepared to deconstruct these with the students to ensure they are clear about expectations, then students are clear about how they can improve their tasks and have a common vocabulary to discuss and share ideas, meaning that all students can make progress.

Three of the boys' division pedagogies

Collaboration

When teachers plan opportunities for focused cooperative work (such as paired work, structured group work and peer assessment) then students demonstrate enjoyment and develop a deeper understanding through wider sharing of ideas and solutions enabling all to make faster progress

Feedback

When teachers allow the opportunity for different forms of feedback, and this feedback is linked to lesson objectives, prior learning, or the bigger picture in a focused and personalised way then students are more engaged, can take ownership of their learning and are aware of their next steps so they know how to progress.

Use of vocabulary

When teachers consistently help students build up subject-specific vocabulary in planned activities and in ad hoc communications by making it explicit, describing it clearly and embedding meaning through questioning and application, then students can retrieve this knowledge readily, feel increasingly secure and confident about using these key concepts in their work, and are able to articulate higher order thinking eloquently.

Instructional rounds

Bolton School (an independent school foundation comprising of three primary schools and two senior schools) embarked on a journey through instructional rounds, a process conducted under the umbrella of 'appreciate inquiry'

CHAPTER 6:
STAFF DEVELOPMENT
AND NETWORKING

Over the years working with schools in several countries on our school improvement programmes, three key learnings have become crystal clear. Those schools that have been most successful at achieving both equity and excellence have had the following characteristics. The first is that the school is driven by a strong narrative that has moral purpose at its core. The second is that teachers have upskilled themselves in the pedagogic strategies that reliably create powerful learning experiences for their students. Lastly, the third is that the school has created an infrastructure for professional learning that all staff opt into. Professional learning is both an expectation and entitlement for being a member of staff in the school.

Without these three elements being articulate and linked together in practical and grounded ways, Unleashing Greatness will not be possible. This thought can be expressed diagrammatically as in figure 6.1.

Figure 6.1 A framework for professional learning

The framework shown in figure 6.1 links together the three critical elements for professional learning required in any school improvement strategy. These are also three of the most crucial steps in the *Unleashing Greatness* framework. The creation of a new culture of teaching and learning in school requires the integration of these three distinct but complementary aspects of the organisation of the school.

- **Moral purpose**: These are the explicit values and commitments that underpin the school's approach to the learning it wants for its students and the expectations that it has for their success. In terms of this book, it is also a reflection of the clear narrative that has been established that defines moral purpose and provides the guide to strategic action.

- **Pedagogy**: These are the precise specifications of practice, both theories of action and models of teaching, that when incorporated into the teacher's repertoire will accelerate student achievement and allow them to become more successful learners.

- **Coaching**: This refers to the culture of professional learning created in the school, the scheduled time it makes available for the learning of staff and the forms of activity involved. Without regular timetabled opportunities for professional collaboration such as peer coaching, it is unlikely that the teaching and learning culture of the school will change.

How the amalgamation of moral purpose, specifications of pedagogic practice and structured professional learning play out will also reflect the stage of development of the school. They are the fundamental building blocks of Unleashing Greatness and are necessary for progression along the developmental continuum. In previous chapters, we have discussed moral purpose and establishing narrative (chapter 3) and the instructional core and specifications of pedagogic practice (chapters 4 and 5). The focus in this chapter is on establishing a culture and infrastructure for professional learning within the school. In particular, we will:

- consider the contribution that intrinsic motivation makes to establishing a culture that prizes professional learning and the importance of understanding the dynamics of implementation in achieving it.

- assess the utility of various models of professional learning and emphasise again the importance of the role of the school improvement team.

- describe what we consider to be the most effective form of professional learning for Unleashing Greatness – coaching and peer coaching, and in so doing reflect on the importance of the workshop/workplace distinction.

- discuss the contribution that networking can make to the professional development of teachers and in Unleashing Greatness.

- in the coda, provide some examples of how schools do this in practice and asking the key Unleashing Greatness questions.

INTRINSIC MOTIVATION AND IMPLEMENTATION

In establishing a professional work culture in a school conducive to Unleashing Greatness, we have found it helpful for leaders and school to incorporate two related frameworks into their strategic thinking. The first is the research evidence around the concept of intrinsic motivation, particularly the work of Dan Pink (2011) in his book, *Drive*, as noted in chapter 2. The second is the research on educational change especially on the process of implementation, that has been well summarised by Michael Fullan (2015) in *The New Meaning of Educational Change*. Although these two frameworks mesh in practice, we will describe them separately.

The underlying theme of this book is that in many ways Unleashing Greatness will not be achieved without a paradigm shift in organisational, social and political culture. The argument was made in chapter 1 that most educational systems are locked into what Habermas would term the 'instrumental' or top-down paradigm which is concerned with instrumental bureaucratic strategies and ways of working. This is the GERM virus as Pasi Sahlberg (2012) terms it that was also described in chapter 1. We will return to Habermas' analysis of paradigms and its implications for the future of schooling in the last chapter. The point being made here is the importance of establishing a professional learning culture compatible with Unleashing Greatness.

In thinking this through in practical terms, I have been helped by the Autonomy, Mastery and Purpose framework of Dan Pink (2011), as outlined in his book *Drive*. Although writing from a business organisation perspective, his ideas and analysis have a direct relevance for schools. His focus is on employee motivation in the workplace and the research-based premise that people perform better when they are motivated. This contention is at first glance self-evident, but Pink argues that it is somewhat more complex than that. In *Drive*, Pink sets out a new vision for workplace motivation that he calls 'Motivation 3.0'. He contrasts this with 'Motivation 1.0' where motivation is a consequence of primitive survival and 'Motivation 2.0' which is the culture of reward and punishment that we find in most businesses (and schools). This is extrinsic motivation driven by external accountability, which is highly consistent with the norms of the instrumental paradigm.

Pink argues that traditional 'carrot and stick' approaches to motivation are outdated and do not adequately meet the needs of a creative or innovative organisation, especially schools committed to Unleashing Greatness. The distinction between extrinsic and intrinsic motivation has been well-researched by organisational psychologists – see for example Ryan and Deci's (2000) authoritative review, *Intrinsic and Extrinsic Motivations: Classic Definitions and New Directions.*

Motivation 3.0 in Pink's analysis relates to intrinsic motivation and the evidence that people become self-motivated when they are given the freedom to do the work that they enjoy and are not constrained by external factors (Mind Tools 2023). Pink's framework for intrinsic motivation comprises three key components as seen in figure 6.2 – autonomy, mastery and purpose.

- **Autonomy** relates to the need to direct one's own life and work. In the workplace, and particularly the school, this does not mean that one can do whatever one likes, that would lead to anarchy. What it does mean is that one is treated as a professional with all the freedoms and obligations that brings. Autonomy implies a principled way of behaving; the consistent meeting of professional practices and expectations, and not feeling that one is always under surveillance and control.

- **Mastery** is the desire to improve and the satisfaction one gets from doing so. When one is motivated by mastery, there are few limits on potential and there is a continual innate desire to improve driven by a curiosity about learning. With competitive athletes for example, the award of medals becomes less important than the knowledge they are improving. With the teacher, it is about ending the day feeling tired yes, but with a deep satisfaction that one has made a positive difference to their students through the powerful learning experiences they have created for them. Mastery is about the satisfaction one gets from doing a task well combined with a continual drive for improvement.

- **Purpose** is the feeling that one is working towards something that is bigger than oneself. It is about aligning one's own values and aspirations with those of the organisation and one's peers. It is about the value of collective endeavour towards a common purpose. That is why in Unleashing Greatness we place so much emphasis on moral purpose and the development of narrative linked to strategic action.

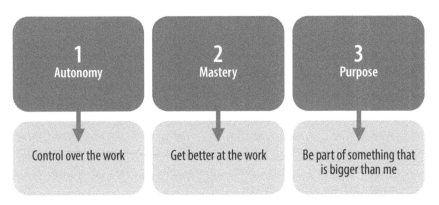

Figure 6.2 Pink's (2011) Intrinsic Motivation Framework

It should be clearly apparent by now that Dan Pink's conception of intrinsic motivation is highly consistent with the Unleashing Greatness strategy. It is one of those overarching frameworks and ideas that we encourage our leaders to keep in mind as they think in both the short and medium term. The medium aspiration is to create and sustain a work culture that embraces these components, and the short-term actions are the everyday decisions and practices that lead towards the establishment of that culture. Figure 6.3 lists various aspects of the Unleashing Greatness strategy that contribute to establishing a work culture predicated on intrinsic motivation.

Autonomy Control over the work	1. Structural change: development & maintenance
Mastery Get better at the work	2. Professional learning: a coaching model
	3. Protocols
Purpose Be part of something is bigger than me	4. Teacher teams
	5. Observation

Figure 6.3 Generating intrinsic motivation through components of the Unleashing Greatness Framework

If Pink's concept of intrinsic motivation is one of those 'meta-frameworks' that leaders and school improvement teams committed to Unleashing Greatness need to keep in mind, then the research-based knowledge on the process of implementation is another.

We have learned a great deal about the managing the process of educational change in recent years. We have also been very fortunate to have had a contemporary scholar like Michael Fullan (2015) who has chronicled this learning and made it accessible for us, most notably in *The New Meaning of Educational Change*, now in its fifth edition. Space precludes even a brief review of the history of educational change, but a succinct summary compatible with the themes of this book is found in *School Improvement: Precedents and Prospects* (Hopkins 2022). Despite the pressure on space, it is important to reflect a little on what has been learned about the process of change; an understanding of this is crucial to one's ability to unleash greatness in educational organisations.

We saw in chapter 1 that educational change strategies are always a combination of top-down and bottom-up approaches. The general rule is that the worse the situation, the more directive and top-down one must be. This accounts for the prevalence of instrumental change strategies in the history of education reform. Sadly, many believe that this is the only way of achieving change – a view that, of course, reinforces the ubiquity of the instrumental paradigm noted already. The critical point is that as the school and system begins to improve and as confidence and competence increases, the balance needs to be adjusted to give more authority and control to those leading the change. Strategies need to become more bottom-up, more empowering to build professional capacity and confidence. One needs to unleash greatness!

One of the reasons why reform efforts have been variously non-linear, arbitrary, political and fragmented is because policy-makers and reformers have not understood the importance of rebalancing top-down/bottom-up change over time in context-specific ways. Top-down, bureaucratic and authoritarian strategies actually reduce performance and create toxic cultures in schools and systems over time. This explains, once again, the need to unleash greatness, and this requires at least a rudimentary understanding of the educational change process.

Unfortunately, the focus of much policy implementation tends to be on structural change or some aspect of curriculum and the production of guidelines or materials. Yet educational changes that directly impact on the learning of students usually involve teachers in not only adopting new or additional teaching materials, but also in (Fullan 2015):

- acquiring new knowledge.
- adopting new pedagogic behaviours.
- sometimes modifying their beliefs or values.

If classroom practice is to be affected, as argued for in previous chapters, then teachers' behaviours and practices, as well as their beliefs and understandings, need to be addressed. There are a few implications for the *Unleashing Greatness* strategy that stem from this (Fullan 2015):

- Change takes place over time.
- Change initially involves anxiety and uncertainty.
- Technical and psychological support is crucial.
- The learning of new skills is incremental and developmental.
- Organisational conditions within and in relation to the school make it more or less likely that the school improvement will occur.
- Successful change involves pressure and support within a collaborative setting.

It is exactly because change is a process whereby individuals need to 'alter their ways of thinking and doing' that many changes fail to progress beyond early implementation. It is this phenomenon that Fullan (2015) has graphically referred to as 'the implementation dip' (see figure 6.4). The 'implementation dip' incorporates that constellation of factors that creates the sense of anxiety and those feelings of incompetence so often associated with re-learning and meaningful change. This is the phase of dissonance – of 'internal turbulence' – that is as predictable as it is at the same time uncomfortable. It also explains why many school improvement initiatives do not progress beyond early implementation.

The implications for unleashing greatness are that conditions need to be created within the school that ensure that individuals are supported through this inevitable but difficult and challenging phase of the process. The school's internal conditions should be organised around the realisation that change is a process whereby individuals alter their ways of thinking and doing. Besides understanding the change process, educators also need to become more skilled in its use. There is now a general acceptance that, as Fullan (2015) has demonstrated, the change process consists of a series of three overlapping phases: initiation, implementation and institutionalisation (also seen in figure 6.4). It is particularly important to understand what happens during each phase and what behaviours within each phase make for success.

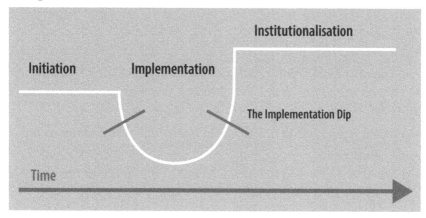

Figure 6.4 The implementation dip and the three phases of change

Initiation is the phase concerned with deciding to embark on innovation and of developing commitment towards the process. The key activities in the initiation phase are the decision to start and a review of the school's current state as regards the particular change. Miles (in Fullan 2015) identified the following factors that make for successful initiation:

- The innovation should be tied to a local agenda and high-profile local need.
- A clear, well-structured approach to change.
- An active advocate or champion who understands the change and supports it.
- Active initiation to start the innovation (top-down is okay in certain conditions).
- Good quality innovation.

Implementation is the phase of the process that has received the most attention. It is the phase of attempted use of a change and is where the 'implementation dip' often kicks in. There are two types of dip as seen in figure 6.4. The first, which occurs fairly early in the process, is when the conditions are not in place to support individual teachers in extending their professional repertoires and they react negatively. In these cases, school improvement efforts fail to progress beyond early implementation. The second is when the change remains a 'pilot' activity with only a relatively small group of staff and the change never becomes fully embedded.

To overcome the 'dip', the key activities that should occur during implementation are the carrying out of action plans, the developing and sustaining of commitment, the checking of progress and overcoming problems. The key factors making for success at this stage are:

- Clear responsibility for coordination (head, coordinator, external consultant).
- Shared control over implementation (top-down not okay); good cross-hierarchical work and relations; empowerment of both individuals and the school.
- Mix of pressure, insistence on 'doing it right' and support.
- Adequate and sustained staff development and in-service training.
- Rewards for teachers early in the process (e.g. empowerment, collegiality, meeting needs, classroom help, load reduction, supply cover, expenses, resources).

Institutionalisation is the phase when innovation and change stop being regarded as something new and become part of the school's usual way of doing things. The move from implementation to institutionalisation often involves the transformation of a pilot project, to a school-wide initiative and often without the advantage of the previously available funding. Key activities at this stage are:

- An emphasis on 'embedding' the change within the school's structures, its organisation and resources.
- The elimination of competing or contradictory practices.
- Strong and purposeful links to other change efforts, the curriculum and classroom teaching.

- Widespread use in the school and local area.
- An adequate bank of local facilitators, (e.g. advisory teachers) for skills training.

Besides the specific activities required during each of the phases of initiation, implementation and institutionalisation, there are also generic skills and abilities identified from research and practice (Schmuck and Runkel 1985; Brown et al 2021) that characterise the behaviours of effective change agents in this context. These are:

- To generate trust.
- To understand and diagnose the state of the school's organisation.
- To plan into the medium term and to see the bigger picture.
- To work productively in groups.
- To access the required technical resources and advice – be it research, good practice or specifications of teaching and learning.
- To give people the confidence to continue.

So far in this section we have largely dealt with organisational frameworks necessary to support professional learning. In order to unleash greatness, we also need to consider the challenge of individual change. As we have seen at length in previous chapters, all the empirical evidence suggests that it is teaching behaviours that most directly enhance student progress. This presents a serious challenge to many teachers because it requires them to expand on what is referred to as their 'circles of competence' and their repertoire of teaching strategies. It is exactly because change is a process whereby individuals need to alter their ways of thinking and doing explains why most change fails to progress beyond early implementation.

We turn in the following two sections to a consideration of those strategies for professional development that enable individual teachers to expand their repertoires of professional practice most effectively.

THE PROFESSIONAL LEARNING IMPERATIVE

It is patently obvious by now that any school committed to unleashing greatness will need to invest heavily in staff development and professional learning. However, many traditional approaches to professional development have a chequered history, so designing the most effective strategies that appropriately support staff as they progress on their learning journeys is crucial. In this section of the chapter, we review the various models of professional learning and emphasise again the importance of the role of the school improvement team. In the following section, we discuss the role of peer coaching that we consider to be the most powerful – although not exclusive – form of professional development for unleashing greatness.

MODELS OF PROFESSIONAL DEVELOPMENT

One of the best kept secrets in school and system reform are the range of staff development strategies available to facilitate more precise and deeper forms of professional learning. What is not sufficiently recognised is the potential of linking the aims of staff development to increasingly more specific strategies that can deliver changes to teacher behaviour that will profoundly impact on student learning. Bruce Joyce and Emily Calhoun (2010) have helpfully surveyed the field in their book *Models of Professional Development*, in which they describe five contrasting families or models of professional learning. In summary, their five models are (Joyce and Calhoun 2010:12–13):

1. **Supporting the individual**: Although all of staff development intends to support individuals, some types focus on the individual as a person and provide avenues for people to grow according to their own lights. They focus on several different but complementary ways in which the school can support individual professional development. The first two are quite specific in terms financial support for external training and the provision of short-term leave. A third would be specific support for implementing a specific curriculum or teaching approach. Fourth would be specific analysis of individual teaching approaches.

2. **Personal/professional service**: Here, some teachers and administrators are designated to provide help to others. In some ways, this type of staff development has evolved from supervision as a part of teacher training programmes. This approach would include mentors for new teachers, generic coaches for school staff, literacy coaches and so on.

3. **Social construction of knowledge and action**: The school as an organisation is on stage with the development of learning communities. This model can be very open-ended as in the form of 'study groups or 'professional learning communities' or take various forms of disciplined action research.

4. **Curriculum/instructional initiatives**: Courses are prominent; developed ways of teaching or the dissemination of curriculums are the content of formal workshops. Such approaches were very popular historically with the curriculum projects associated with the Schools Council and more recently with the literacy and numeracy strategies in primary schools. Specific programmes like 'Success for All' in the US and 'Reading Recovery' originally from New Zealand can be very successful in specific contexts.

5. **The infamous menus of brief workshops**: No treatise on staff development would be complete without contemplation of the currently most criticised and common way of organising people for study – the menus of brief workshops on designated staff development days. Despite the critiques, when properly executed, this mode can be effective. Staff development organisers should not dismiss it out of hand.

This is a helpful taxonomy, particularly for those charged with organising staff development events. It is also supportive of the range of staff development activities involved in our early school improvement programmes that included:

- whole staff development days on teaching and learning and school improvement planning, as well as 'curriculum tours' to share the work done in departments or working groups;
- interdepartmental meetings to discuss teaching strategies;
- workshops run inside the school on teaching strategies by school improvement team members and external support;
- partnership teaching; and,
- the design and execution of collaborative enquiry activities, which are, by their nature, knowledge-generating.

What Joyce and Calhoun's taxonomy does not capture, however, in such an abbreviated description, is the mode of enquiry adopted or the necessity of non-judgmental collaboration emphasised in our approach to instructional rounds. What is also critical to unleashing greatness is the establishing of a school improvement team (SIT). We have already introduced the concept, but now is the place to describe their role in a little more detail.

A FURTHER NOTE ON THE SCHOOL IMPROVEMENT TEAM (SIT)

As we noted in chapter 2, the SIT is a cross-hierarchical team that could be as small as three or four to six in comparatively small schools, to between six and ten in large schools. Though one of these is likely to be the headteacher, it is important to establish groups that are genuinely representative of the range of perspectives and ideas available in the school. It should, ideally, be cross-hierarchical, cross-institutional, and have a mix of ages, experience, gender, length of time at the school, and so on. School improvement team group members should also not come together in any already existing group within the school, such as the senior management team or a heads of department group, so that the problem of pooled rationalisations is minimised.

In organisational terms, the reason a school improvement group is required is because of the tensions in schools caused by the conflicting demands of maintenance and development. One of the underpinning principles of the *Unleashing Greatness* strategy is the separation of maintenance activities from development work. The SIT is essentially a temporary membership system focused specifically upon enquiry and development. One teacher described it as the educational equivalent of a research and development group. The establishing of a SIT creates the research and development (R&D) capacity, whilst retaining the existing structures required also for organisational stability and efficiency. It also unlocks staff potential often stifled within formal structures and opens up new collaborations.

In the same way that SIT members are mutually supportive of one another, the school community (the wider staff and the institutional support of senior management and governing body) make several tacit commitments too:

- To support the work of the SIT in whatever way possible – time, resources, visits to centres of good practice, the adoption of recommendations, etc.
- To agree to remain informed about the progress of work involved in unleashing greatness to maintain collective ownership of the directions being travelled.
- To support the implementation of new practices, new structures, or new ways of working.
- To be open to the research process by contributing ideas, opening up our classrooms for observation, offering our professional support in whatever way required.
- To engage in workshop activity within full staff meetings or staff days in order to contribute to the on-going knowledge creation and learning process.

This description of SIT functioning is perhaps a counsel of perfection. Despite best efforts, in many schools, SIT members seem unsure about how they were selected for the role, and, initially at least, unclear about what will be expected of them. Consequently, there is hesitancy in the beginning. However, they appear to grow in confidence quite quickly, particularly as the school's efforts and resources become focused around priorities they are addressing. The three phases of this cycle of development are as follows (taken from West 2000; Hopkins 2013):

PHASE 1: UNCERTAINTY ABOUT FOCUS

- SIT feeling its way (What is a SIT?)
- What is school improvement?
- What is the role of a SIT?
- How can the SIT work best together as a group?
- Initial reliance on established ways of working.
- Initial reliance on existing structures.
- Initial reliance on key personnel/leaders within the SIT.

- Start to collect data and share it.
- Uncertainty about the theory.
- Where is it all going? It's hard to make things happen.

PHASE 2: CLEARER ABOUT FOCUS

- Using existing structures in new ways, e.g. department meetings with single item research agendas.
- New ways of working.
- Greater openness within the SIT, e.g. voice of main scale teacher.
- Better at making meaning from data.
- Beginning to shift from staff development mode to school improvement mode.
- The theory makes sense.
- Seeing the connections. Learning how to implement.

PHASE 3: CHANGE/RENEWAL OF THE SIT

- R&D establishing its own rhythm – SDP becomes more organic.
- New structures emerge – R&D group.
- New roles emerge, e.g. HOD as facilitator of research, establishing a R&D research post.
- Establishment of research culture within the school:
  - Evidence-based
  - Risk taking
- Involvement of students as researchers:
  - From data-source to partners in dialogue
- Collection of data, making meaning, and supporting research outcomes.
- The school generates its own theory.
- The implementation becomes growth.

This 'summary' of how the SIT develops gives a clear indication of how a structure for dispersed leadership that relates both to instructional leadership and unleashing greatness is established. It also illustrates how it evolves over time, gradually expanding its leadership capacity and increasing its understanding about learning – organisational learning, the learning of SIT members and other teachers and the learning of students.

Where the *Unleashing Greatness* strategy has taken hold and the SIT has had a positive effect, then we have noted a significant and positive shift in the culture of professional learning in the school. In most of these schools the shifts in culture and practice include:

- The opening up of classrooms and classroom practice and the legitimisation of in-class coaching.
- The creation of a language to talk about teaching and school improvement.
- The integration of enquiry and professional development approaches.
- The value and authenticity of the student voice and the significance given to their perceptions as learners.
- The willingness of all staff to embrace the value of the development work emanating from the school improvement group.
- The ownership by the whole staff of the school improvement approach.
- The power of a sustained school improvement journey to win over those initially sceptical or even cynical.
- The expansion of leadership capacity.

In reflecting on the implementation of our various school improvement programmes over the years, we have identified two broad categories of strategies that have a proven track record in building professional learning cultures within schools (Hopkins 2013). The two contrasting approaches are:

1. **Deductive**: where the staff work collectively, through conventional workshops and groupings, to expand their repertoires of professional

practice by using specifications of what is known about effective instruction.

2. **Inductive**: where staff and other invited colleagues work collectively and iteratively from the existing practice in the school to develop theories of action that discipline and deepen the instructional culture of all the teachers in the school. Our use of instructional rounds is a prime example of this.

Both approaches should end up at the same place and the choice often depends on where the school is starting from. For example, it may be more appropriate in a school that has a very weak instructional culture to use a deductive approach initially to master basic knowledge and skill, before moving into the more iterative approach. Similarly, a school with a healthier instructional culture may start by using the inductive approach, and then fairly rapidly assimilate the range of specifications of theories of action and models of teaching into their development work.

In the following section, we look in more detail at these 'inductive' approaches to professional learning in particular the peer coaching methodology.

COACHING AND PEER COACHING

During our over four-decade long conversation on the rudiments of school improvement, Bruce Joyce and I have repeatedly talked about the design of staff development and the transfer of training. During one of those more recent conversations that we consequently published, Bruce talked about the similarities of the training regime he had experienced with Vic Braden, the renowned US tennis coach and contrasted this with the designs for coaching that we were developing for unleashing greatness (Joyce, Calhoun and Hopkins 2014). Consider these quotations from our article on Braden's tennis coaching design:

- 'The course on the backhand began with the rationale for the new stroke … the introduction to a stroke was very conceptual, and the concepts were continually emphasized throughout the instruction.'
- 'Then, there were demonstrations – dozens of them, some live, some on video – all connected to the rationales.'

- 'And then, practice – each of us got a ball machine that delivered about 300 balls an hour. As we practiced, coaches danced around us and continued to demonstrate elements of the stroke, and repeated the rationale, politely but directly. And then back to the classroom, and then again to the courts – practice, think, practice.'

- 'Fascinatingly, Braden's approach conformed to what we were learning about how to design workshops to help teachers learn new curricular and instructional models and how to create their own training for their colleagues.'

- 'In both the tennis and professional development (PD) experiences, **rationale** mixed with **demonstrations** mixed with **practice** makes the difference in building knowledge and skill.'

There are two key points here. First, Braden was not teaching Bruce how to play tennis – he was teaching the backhand stroke, which is a skill. In *Unleashing Greatness*, we develop outstanding teachers by expanding their repertoire of teaching skills. Second, the process of skill development looks very similar whether it is for tennis or teaching – **rationale** mixed with **demonstrations** mixed with **practice**.

In their research on staff development, Joyce and Showers (2002) identify five key training components that, when used in combination, have much greater power than when they are used alone. The major components of training are:

- Presentation of **theory** or description of skill or strategy – when the rationale for the new approach is explained or justified.

- Modelling or **demonstration** of skills or models of teaching – when the skill is demonstrated live, in practice.

- **Practice** in non-threatening simulated and classroom settings.

- Structured and open-ended **feedback** (provision of information about performance) from experts and colleagues.

- **Coaching** for application (hands-on, in-classroom assistance with the transfer of skills and strategies to the classroom) – peer coaching supports teachers to improve their practice.

The five components of effective staff development are seen in figure 6.5.

Theory	Explain and justify the new approach
Demonstrate	Show/model how it can be done in practice
Practice	Teachers practice in non-threatening situations
Feedback	Teachers receive feedback from their triad (professional learning team)
Peer coaching	Triads support professional learning using protocols

Figure 6.5 Joyce and Showers' (2002) Coaching/Peer Coaching Model

Joyce and Calhoun (2010) have also distinguished between the locations in which these various forms of staff development are best located – either in the 'workshop' or the 'workplace'. The **workshop**, which is equivalent to the best practice on the traditional INSET course, is where teachers gain *understanding*, see *demonstrations* of the teaching strategy they may wish to acquire, and have the opportunity to *practice* them in a non-threatening environment.

If the aim is to transfer those skills back into the **workplace** – the classroom and school – then merely attending the workshop is insufficient. The research evidence is very clear that skill acquisition and the ability to transfer vertically to a range of situations requires 'on-the-job-support' (Joyce and Showers 2002). This implies changes to the workplace and the way in which staff development is organised. In particular, this means the opportunity for 'immediate and sustained practice, collaboration and peer coaching, and studying development and implementation'.

The paradox is that changes to the workplace cannot be achieved without, in most cases, drastic alterations in the ways in which schools are organised. Yet the transfer of teaching skills from INSET sessions to classrooms settings will not occur without them. Consequently, staff development is perhaps the most crucial of the enabling conditions for unleashing greatness. This as seen in the following chapter is the key 'adaptive challenge' for school leaders, and the critical positive response is the provision of 'in classroom support' or 'peer coaching'.

The crucial point is that this is not a 'pick and mix' approach, all of the components need to be present in a training design to ensure transfer of practice back into the classroom. This point is underscored by the effect size research conducted by Joyce and Showers (1995:112) as seen in table 6.1.

Professional learning: Effect sizes for training outcomes by training component			
Training components and combination	Knowledge	Skills	Transfer of training
Information	0.63	0.35	0.00
Theory	0.15	0.50	0.00
Demonstration	1.65	0.26	0.00
Theory + Demonstration	0.66	0.86	0.00
Theory + Practice	1.15		
Theory + Demonstration + Practice		0.72	0.00
Theory + Demonstration + Practice + Feedback	1.31	1.18	0.39
Theory + Demonstration + Practice + Feedback + Coaching	2.71	1.25	1.68

Table 6.1 Effect Sizes for training outcomes by training components (adapted from Joyce and Showers 1995)

So, if one's concern is simply knowledge then providing information and demonstration will suffice. If skill development is the goal, then theory, demonstration, practice and feedback are required. However, if the outcome is transfer of training into classroom settings, as is the case with Unleashing Greatness, then peer coaching needs to be added to the mix.

It is the facilitation of peer coaching that enables teachers to extend their repertoire of teaching skills and to transfer them from different classroom settings to others. During the implementation of our various school improvement projects refinements have been made in the use of peer coaching to support student learning. When the following refinements are incorporated into a school improvement design, peer coaching can virtually assure 'transfer of training' for everyone:

- Peer coaching teams of two or three are much more effective than larger groups.
- These groups are more effective when the entire staff is engaged in school improvement.
- Peer coaching works better when heads and senior leaders participate in training and practice.

- The effects are greater when formative study of student learning is embedded in the process.

In summary, the design of staff development that leads to enhanced levels of student achievement needs to be based on the following six principles (Hopkins 2017):

1. Make space and time for enhancing teacher enquiry and creating a 'professional practice'.
2. Utilise evidence from research and practice in developing a range of theories of action and teaching models that impact on student learning.
3. Study the models' impact on student learning and use data formatively and habitually.
4. Invest in school-based processes, both deductive and inductive, for extending teachers' repertoires.
5. Link the classroom focus with whole-school development and embed pedagogic innovation within curriculum plans.
6. Use this emerging 'professional practice' as a basis for networking and system-wide capacity building.

In the following section, we examine in more detail how networking practice can contribute not only to the development of individual schools and their school improvement teams, but to the system as a whole.

NETWORKING FOR SCHOOL IMPROVEMENT

In reflecting on the role of networks in *Unleashing Greatness*, it is important to remember that the construct has a distinguished provenance in education. Although networks bring together those with like-minded interests, they are more than opportunities to just share 'good practice'. My early analysis of effective networks for the OECD (see Hopkins 2022b) yielded this definition:

> *Networks are purposeful social entities characterised by a commitment to quality, rigour, and a focus on outcomes. They are also an effective means of supporting innovation in times of change. In education, networks promote the dissemination of good practice, enhance the*

professional development of teachers, support capacity building in schools, mediate between centralised and decentralised structures, and assist in the process of re-structuring and re-culturing educational organisations and systems.

Those were more optimistic times and more recently there has emerged a tension between networks and autonomy.

Andreas Schleicher (2018:114) in his authoritative text on *World Class* school systems, comments on the findings of recent OECD research:

But all (these systems) flourished because governance and oversight arrangements gave them the freedom to create spaces for experimentation. [...] A (recent OECD) study also underscored the risk of autonomy leading to the 'atomisation' of schools. Working with others can spur innovation and sustain the drive to innovate. However, school autonomy will be self-defeating if it is interpreted as functioning in isolation. Instead, autonomy should take the form of freedom and flexibility to work with many partners.

It is evidence like this that led me to develop a framework for 'Networked Autonomy' (Hopkins 2022b). Autonomous networked schools:

- Put in place substantive collaborative arrangements.
- Understand that they are as strong as the weakest link. Schools that are failing and/or underperforming can expect to receive unconditional support from all network schools, as well as from commissioned external agencies.
- Support and accept significantly enhanced funding for students most at risk.
- Operate within a rationalised system of national and local agency functions and roles that allow a higher degree of coordination for this increasingly devolved system.

Such a set of principles allow schools to use 'networked autonomy' to:

- More fully express their moral purpose of enabling every student to reach their potential.
- Ensure that every teacher has the maximum time to teach and to develop their professional competence.

- Maximise resource allocation to ensure that this happens.
- Explore the full potential of the 'inside-out' school development strategy.
- Enable leadership to work more effectively with the system both within and outside the school and generate sustainable networks that deepen the impact on student learning.
- Move from external to professional forms of accountability.

This 'networked autonomy' proposal is essentially similar to David Hargreaves' (2010; 2011; 2012) vision of the 'Self-Improving School System' (SISS). The SISS concept was originally and elegantly outlined by Hargreaves in three highly influential monographs. In commenting on the new model of national teaching schools in England, as part of his SISS vision Hargreaves (2011:5) wrote:

> *The new teaching schools, based on the concept of the teaching hospital, are to be a critical element in a more self-improving school system. They will:*
>
> - *Train new entrants to the profession with other partners, including universities.*
>
> - *Lead peer-to-peer learning and professional development, including the designation and deployment of the new specialist leaders of education (SLEs).*
>
> - *Identify and nurture leadership potential.*
>
> - *Lead an alliance of other schools and partners to improve the quality of teaching and learning.*
>
> - *Form a national network to support the schools in innovation and knowledge transfer.*
>
> - *Be at the heart of a different strategy of school improvement that puts responsibility on the profession and schools.*

To Hargreaves, the SISS was designed to be genuinely transformative. Here are two practical proposals from Hargreaves and then myself, for establishing networked autonomy within the current English (academy) context and these, of course, can apply to a range of other jurisdictions.

First Hargreaves. His SISS agenda for school reform is based on innovation and networking proposals first made in his monograph *Education Epidemic* (Hargreaves 2003). The essential task, Hargreaves argues, is to create a climate in which it is possible for teachers to actively engage in innovation and change and to transfer validated proposals rapidly within their school and into other schools. This does not mean a return to 'letting a thousand flowers bloom', but a disciplined approach to innovation. This involves moving innovation in education to scale through 'front-line innovation conducted by leading-edge institutions and government-supported "pathfinders", which develop new ideas into original practices' (2003:39). This is then followed by 'transferred innovation', which closes the gap between the least and most effective schools (or subject departments).

Hargreaves (2003:46) suggests that the achievement of such a 'lateral strategy' for transferred innovation requires four strategic components:

1. It must become clear what is meant by 'good' and 'best' practice among teachers.
2. There needs to be a method of locating good practice and sound innovations.
3. Innovations must be ones that bring real advantages to teachers (and students).
4. Methods of transferring innovation effectively must be devised.

My own suggestion was initially directed at the most common middle tier organisation currently in England – multi-academy trusts (MATs) (Hopkins 2016e). This proposal however can apply to any grouping of schools, networks or middle tier organisations. In outstanding MATs, capacity is built at the local level to ensure that all those in a trust's family of schools progress as rapidly as possible towards excellence. Figure 6.6 illustrates how this works:

• Central to local capacity building is the regional director or executive principal who provides leadership, develops the narrative and acts as the trust's champion in that geographic area for a network of schools.

- One of their key tasks is to build local capacity by training a group of lead practitioners in a MAT's ways of working, materials and strategies.
- The training design used to develop trainers is Joyce and Showers' peer coaching model.
- These trainers then work with the school improvement teams in each school to build within-school capacity and consistency.
- Inter-school networking allows for authentic innovation and the transfer of outstanding practice, thus building the capacity of the network as a whole.

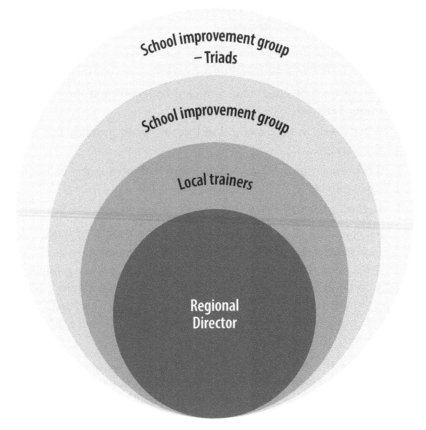

Figure 6.6 Building capacity for school improvement within MATs

To summarise, networks have the potential to support educational innovation and change and enhance student learning by:

- Keeping the focus on the core purposes of schooling, in particular on student learning.

- Enhancing the skill of teachers, leaders and other educators in change agent skills, managing the change process and creating and sustaining a discourse on teaching and learning.

- Providing a focal point for the dissemination of good practice, the generalisability of innovation and the creation of 'action oriented' knowledge about effective educational practices.

- Building capacity for continuous improvement at a local level, and in particular in creating professional learning networks, within and between schools.

- Ensuring that systems of pressure and support are integrated not segmented. For example, professional learning networks incorporate pressure and support in a seamless way.

- Acting as a link between the centralised and decentralised schism resulting from many contemporary policy initiatives; in particular, in contributing to policy coherence horizontally and vertically.

CODA: BUILDING THE PROFESSIONAL LEARNING INFRASTRUCTURE

In this chapter, we have considered the professional learning infrastructure within the school and between schools necessary for *Unleashing Greatness*. In particular, we have explored the concept of intrinsic motivation, the necessity for coaching in workshop settings and peer coaching in classrooms, as well as the potential for network learning between schools. In helping school leaders and school improvement teams plan for action at this stage of their school improvement journey, the following questions may be helpful.

PEER COACHING TRIADS

- Does every member of your school staff part belong to a peer coaching triad?

- Do the peer coaching groups meet regularly as part of timetabled staff development activity?
- How far do the outcomes of these peer observations contribute to higher standards of learning and teaching in the school?

NETWORKING

- Is your school a member of an established network?
- If so, does the network have a coherent and systematic approach to capacity building and learning from each other?
- Do you feel that as part of being a member of your network that best practice is shared and that the whole 'system' is on an improvement trajectory?

The following two case studies are from schools who are members of the University of Bolton Laboratory School network. Here Pikes Lane Primary School, Bolton and Northgate High School, Dereham, Norfolk share the professional learning structures that they have developed as part of engaging in the *Unleashing Greatness* process.

INTRINSIC MOTIVATION, PEER COACHING TRIADS AND NETWORKING

PIKES LANE PRIMARY SCHOOL, BOLTON

When introducing the theories of action to the staff team, the conversation focused on how this was the next phase of our improvement journey. We wanted to emphasise that these TOA were not the finished article, but we would continue to innovate and build practice from this point forward. We ensured professional agency by promoting joint practice staff development (JPD) as the means of taking the theories of action (TOA) forward.

Staff teams were constructed with a careful balance of subject leadership skills and year group teachers to get a good cross section. We deliberately put staff with colleagues who they might not have worked with so closely before. The focus of the TOA was chosen through SLT conversations using evidence from instructional rounds. We prioritised those TOA that were not sufficiently embedded across the school. Staff were tasked with using research informed practice to trial approaches in their JPD and present findings at the end of the term. When this cycle was completed at the end of each term, we added to our TOA padlet technology, creating a WAGOLL (what a good one looks like) as we started to consider how the TOA would apply in different year groups and different subjects.

Half-termly coaching sessions took place for all teaching staff. This was a process of reflecting on how they were using the TOA consistently, and how they develop it further. Actions were planned to support staff with team teaching and paired lesson observations to see others' practice. Informal lesson observations, where staff invited one another to see practice, were encouraged as a means of establishing a rich improvement culture.

PEER COACHING

NORTHGATE HIGH SCHOOL, DEREHAM, NORFOLK

At Northgate, we had already moved away from top-down, authoritarian, graded lessons and embraced staff efficacy as a central theme. The peer coaching process (see figure 6.7), and its focus on metacognition, was the natural environment for all staff (teaching and non-teaching) to consider their own practice with the help of colleagues whom they 'knew, liked and trusted'. They were able to draw on research to fuel the metacognitive process and be observed in a non-judgmental, supportive environment. Follow-up conversations after these observations enabled personal self-reflection to happen. All participants contributed their learned outcomes to an overarching document, which was shared with all staff, meaning that the community built its own research.

Working with over 130 members of staff meant that we did encounter some initial resistance from a few participants. Conversations with these colleagues revealed that for most of them the root problem was a lack of confidence about what they had to offer to others. It was rewarding at the end of the first year to read the feedback from these colleagues as to the value they found in engaging in the process. They realised they had far more to offer than they initially thought! Our most recent Ofsted inspection in May 2023 commented 'Staff training is a priority and there are a range of opportunities available for staff to progress their career'.

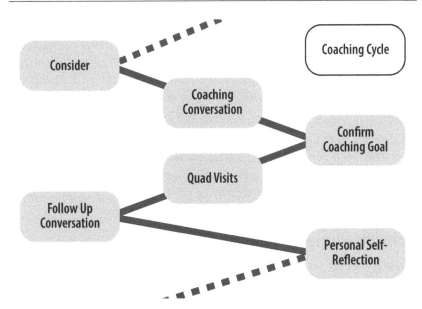

Figure 6.7 The Northgate peer coaching process

PART 3:

MOVING TO SCALE

CHAPTER 7:
LEADERSHIP

INTRODUCTION: PARADOXICAL COMBINATION

One of my favourite studies of leadership is that which Jim Collins published in his book, *From Good to Great* (2001a). The focus of Collins's research was on companies rather than schools, but the comparisons are fascinating. He was curious about what 'great' companies are like, how they became great and how they sustain greatness. This is one of his conclusions (Collins 2001a:195): 'Enduring great companies preserve their core values and purpose while their business strategies and operating practices endlessly adapt to a changing world. This is the magical combination of "preserve the core and stimulate progress".'

The image of schooling conjured up by this quotation is highly consistent with the *Unleashing Greatness* strategy described in this book. It is one of a school and classroom culture of high expectations where students realise their potential as a consequence of the types of pedagogic and curriculum strategies described here. What is more germane for our purposes in this chapter is the type of leadership necessary to enable a school to become great. Collins (2001b) calls this 'Level 5' leadership.

The term 'level 5' refers to a five-level hierarchy of qualities. Level 1 relates to individual capability, level 2 to team skills, level 3 to managerial competence and level 4 to leadership as traditionally conceived. Level 5 leaders possess the skills of levels 1 to 4 but also have an 'extra dimension': a paradoxical blend of personal humility plus professional will. They are somewhat self-effacing individuals who deflect adulation yet who have an almost stoic resolve to do absolutely whatever it takes to make the company great, channelling their ego needs away from themselves and into the larger goal of building a great company.

Collins elaborates: 'It's not that Level 5 leaders have no ego or self-interest. Indeed, they are incredibly ambitious – but their ambition is first and foremost for the institution, not themselves.' As we shall see, these attributes apply well to school leaders and this has recently been validated and confirmed in a range of international research (for example, Hallinger et al 2020). In our own OECD study (Pont, Nusche and Moorman 2008a; Pont, Nusche and Hopkins 2008b), we asked rhetorically 'school leadership: why does it matter?' and answered thus:

- At the **school level**, leadership can improve teaching and learning by setting objectives and influencing classroom practice.
- At the **local level**, school leadership can improve equal opportunities by collaborating with other schools and local communities.
- At the **system level**, school leadership is essential for successful education reform.

In reflecting on the influence of school leadership at the school, local and system levels in the wide range of settings we have been privileged to work in has led me to develop the model of school leadership described in this chapter. In describing the nature of leadership required for unleashing greatness, in this chapter we will:

- First, briefly describe the **field of educational leadership** and our own research on instructional leadership – the style most associated with enhanced student outcomes.
- Then outline our model of school leadership and describe an implementation strategy for **instructional leadership**.
- Then describe the **adaptive** and **strategic** styles of school leadership together with their implementation strategies.
- This leads to a discussion on **system** leadership and its implications for unleashing greatness.
- Finally, in the coda, provide some examples of how schools do this in practice and ask the key *Unleashing Greatness* questions.

THE FIELD OF EDUCATIONAL LEADERSHIP

In exploring the nature of leadership and its application to education as well as the paradox noted already, it is useful to begin with some history. In our review of the research on school and system improvement (Hopkins et al 2014), we noted that although 'principal as instructional leader' was one of Edmonds's (1979) 'five correlates' of school effectiveness, it has taken considerable time for the approach to become accepted and understood.

Murphy (in Hopkins 2013) for example, suggested that the thinking about leadership falls into a number of phases: the focus on trait theories of leadership; the focus on what it is that leaders actually do; developing awareness that task-related and people-centred behaviours may be interpreted quite differently; and, situational approaches to leadership. All these represented a movement towards the notion of leadership as transformational, having the potential to alter the cultural context in which people work and, importantly, the potential for school leaders to 'drive' increases in student achievements.

More recently, it has become clear that the 'transformational' approach to leadership may have been necessary but was an insufficient condition for measurable school improvement. It lacked a specific orientation towards student learning that is the critical feature of the approach to school improvement taken in this book. For this reason, the notion of 'instructional leadership' has become increasingly attractive.

Several research studies support this contention. The meta-analysis conducted by Robinson and her colleagues (Robinson et al 2008) has been remarkably influential in explaining the impact of instructional leadership on student achievement. In a parallel paper, Robinson wrote that (2007:13):

> *Transformational leadership has weak (<.2 ES) indirect effects on student outcomes. While it has moderate effects on teacher attitudes and perceptions of the school climate and organisation, these effects do not, on the whole, flow through to students. Those instructional leadership studies that used similar designs to those used in the transformational leadership group, showed effect sizes that were,*

on average, three times larger than those found in transformational leadership studies.

More recently, Philip Hallinger and colleagues (2020) have produced an authoritative and wide-ranging paper 'Are principals instructional leaders yet?'. This is a science map of the knowledge base on instructional leadership between 1940–2018. They reviewed over 1200 refereed journal articles on instructional leadership published during that time period. They summarise their review like this (Hallinger et al 2020):

The results affirm that the knowledge base on instructional leadership has not only increased in size, but also geographic scope. Contrary to expectations during the 1980s, instructional leadership has demonstrated remarkable staying power, growing into one of the most powerful models guiding research, policy and practice in school leadership. Despite this finding, both author co-citation and co-word analyses revealed the emergence of 'integrated models of school leadership' in which instructional leadership is enacted in concert with dimensions drawn from complementary leadership approaches. Key themes in the recent literature include studies of leadership effects on teachers and students, contexts for leadership practice, and means of developing instructional leaders.

Let us explore some of these points in a little more detail.

The first is the exponential increase in research studies on instructional leadership since the mid 2000s. Hallinger and his colleagues (2020) explain it this way:

While interest in instructional leadership never disappeared, two developments caused scholars to return to this conceptualization of school leadership during the mid-2000s. First, the emergence of a global accountability movement led to renewed calls for 'instructional leadership' capable of bringing about more reliable improvement in student achievement (Leithwood 2001). While this led to a revival of interest in instructional leadership in the USA, it was a completely new trend in most other nations where principals had previously been viewed as 'managers' and 'administrators' of national policies. Second, a complementary series of research reviews presented convincing empirical evidence that supported the efficacy of 'instructional leadership' in efforts to improve student learning (Hallinger and Heck 1996; Leithwood et al 2008; Robinson et al 2008).

The second is the increased global interest in instructional leadership. Hallinger et al (2020) produced a 'heat map' to display the global distribution of the literature on instructional leadership. They wrote:

Consistent with the broader knowledge base in educational administration, 75% of this literature was authored in the USA, the United Kingdom, Australia, continental Europe and Canada. This means that 25% of the studies were authored in Asia, Africa and Latin America. Despite this perceived imbalance in the instructional leadership literature, longitudinal analysis revealed an interesting trend. Specifically, 90% of the articles authored outside of the USA, Europe and Australia were published since 2005. Thus, despite the continuing influence of American scholarship, these trends highlight the increasing global relevance of instructional leadership.

A third comment relates to what Hallinger and colleagues (2020) refer to as the 'intellectual structure' of the knowledge base. This is the self-organised research traditions and lines of inquiry that emerge within a knowledge base over time. Hallinger et al identified a series of clusters that are interpreted as 'schools of thought' and together they comprise a knowledge base. Our own work resides in a cluster of 'school improvement leadership' that Hallinger et al (2020) refer to as:

The green cluster represents a school of thought associated with scholars known for research on school improvement leadership. [...] scholarship within this school has elaborated how school leaders contribute to school improvement and effectiveness. A key contribution of this school has been the elaboration of a longitudinal perspective towards the changing nature of leadership and leadership effects on school improvement over time.

What is reassuring about reviews like this is that a) our work is globally recognised and b) the *Unleashing Greatness* strategy is based on good science.

THE SEVEN STRONG CLAIMS

Our own contribution on instructional leadership was introduced in chapter 2, and it is now appropriate to go into in a little more detail here. In 2008, Ken Leithwood, Alma Harris and I published an article entitled 'Seven Strong Claims about Successful School Leadership' (Leithwood, Harris, and Hopkins 2008). The article was based on a major literature review that was summarised in a paper published by the National College for School Leadership in England (Leithwood et al 2007). Both the National College paper and our subsequent article proved to be far more popular than we anticipated, and both have been extensively cited over the past ten years. Consequently, ten years after the initial publication, we decided to revisit each of the seven claims, summarising what was said about each in the original publications, weighing each of the claims considering recent empirical evidence, and proposing revisions or refinements as warranted (Leithwood, Harris, and Hopkins 2019).

At the outset, the seven claims were introduced with the following caveat (Leithwood, Harris, and Hopkins 2008:27):

> *These claims are not all strong in quite the same way, as we shall explain, but they all find support in varying amounts of quite robust empirical evidence, the first two having attracted the largest amount of such evidence. Those in leadership roles have a tremendous responsibility to get it right. Fortunately, we know a great deal about what getting it right means. The purpose of this article is to provide a synopsis of this knowledge.*

Given that our 'seven strong claims' have stood the test of time, it is worth briefly reviewing them again here and then stress two of the key issues related to *Unleashing Greatness*. Claim 1 is the most widely cited, so that is where we start.

Claim 1: School leadership is second only to classroom teaching as an influence on pupil learning. We considered this claim controversial at the time but have been surprised by its wide acceptance and endorsement within the leadership field. In light of more recent evidence, we revised the claim as follows.

Revised claim 1: School leadership has a significant effect on features of the school organisation, which positively influences the quality of teaching and learning. While moderate in size, this leadership effect is vital to the success of most school improvement efforts.

Claim 2: Almost all successful leaders draw on the same repertoire of basic leadership practices. On reviewing the more recent evidence, we felt that our original claim 2 needs no revision. However, we noted that the number of effective leadership practices, grounded in the available evidence, has grown from 14 to 22 over the past decade. These are seen in table 7.2.

Claim 3: The ways in which leaders apply these basic leadership practices – not the practices themselves – demonstrate responsiveness to, rather than dictation by the contexts in which they work. In the 2008 version of our article, we argued that successful leaders are sensitive to the contexts in which they find themselves but do not enact significantly different leadership practices as contexts change. Rather, they 'apply contextually sensitive combinations of the basic leadership practices' seen in table 7.2. This is a critically important point and central to the wider applicability of the Unleashing Greatness strategy. Having reviewed the more recent research, we felt no need to amend the original claim.

Claim 4: School leaders improve teaching and learning indirectly and most powerfully through their influence on staff motivation, ability and working conditions. This claim is built on the widely endorsed premise that most school leadership effects on students are indirect. Since the original article however, there have been further specification of variables or conditions mediating school leadership effects on students, so we revised the claim as follows.

Revised claim 4: School leadership improves teaching and learning, indirectly and most powerfully, by improving the status of significant key classroom and school conditions and by encouraging parent/child interactions in the home that further enhance student success at school.

Claim 5: School leadership has a greater influence on schools and students when it is widely distributed. We found a broad range of recent evidence that provided considerable support for the original claim 5, which has been revised only slightly.

Revised claim 5: School Leadership can have an especially positive influence on school and student outcomes when it is distributed.

Claim 6: Some patterns of distribution are more effective than others. We found that recent evidence provides further justification for this claim, so saw no need to revise it. Distributed leadership is premised on interactions rather than actions, along with the establishment of new teams, groupings and connections for specific purposes, all of which are highlighted in the Unleashing Greatness strategy.

Claim 7: A small handful of personal traits explains a high proportion of the variation in leadership effectiveness. In the most recent paper, we commented that the 'deep background to this claim is the off-again, on-again interest in leadership traits by the broader leadership research community' (Leithwood, Harris, and Hopkins 2019:11). Since the publication of the original paper, Leithwood (2012) introduced the concept of 'personal leadership resources' (PLRs). This concept was intended to include the non-behavioural, non-practice-related components of leadership, (including traits), which significantly influence the nature of leaders' behaviours or practices. Our original claim 7 referred to 'traits', as they are typically defined, whereas PLRs encompass a much larger proportion of the covert qualities giving rise to especially effective leadership practice, as seen in table 7.1.

Revised claim 7: While further research is required, a well-defined set of cognitive, social and psychological 'personal leadership resources' show promise of explaining a high proportion of variation in the practices enacted by school leaders.

Cognitive resources	• Problem-solving expertise
	• Domain-specific knowledge
	• Systems thinking
Social resources	• Perceiving emotions
	• Managing emotions
	• Acting in emotionally appropriate ways
Psychological resources	• Optimism
	• Self-efficacy
	• Resilience
	• Proactivity

Table 7.1 Personal Leadership Resources (Leithwood, Harris and Hopkins 2019:11)

In concluding the more recent paper, we commented that the field is now in a much stronger empirical position than in 2008' (Leithwood, Harris and Hopkins 2019:13). It supports my claim of earlier that the *Unleashing Greatness* strategy is based on good science. This is pleasing as the leadership model outlined in the following section draws on the same evidence base, particularly the Leithwood, Harris and Hopkins 2019), as seen in table 7.2.

The original four practices – setting directions, building relationships and developing people, redesigning the organisation to support desired practices and improving the instructional programme – have been central to our various school improvement programmes for some time. What is important in the revised version is the increased detail in terms of what each of these components comprise. Table 7.2 gives this detail and we return to a further discussion of instructional leadership in the next section, following the description of our leadership model.

Domains of practice	Specific leadership practices
Set directions	Build a shared vision**
	Identify specific, shared short-term goals
	Create high-performance expectations
	Communicate the vision and goals**
Build relationships and develop people	Stimulate growth in the professional capacities of staff
	Provide support and demonstrate consideration for individual staff members
	Model the school's values and practices**
Develop the organisation to support desired practices	Build trusting relationships with and among staff, students and parents**
	Establish productive working relationships with teacher federation representatives
	Build collaborate culture and distribute leadership**
	Structure the organisation to facilitate collaboration**
Improve the instructional program	Build productive relationships with families and communities**
	Connect the school to its wider environment**
	Allocate resources in support of the school's vision and goals**
	Staff the instructional program**
	Provide instructional support
	Monitor student learning and school improvement progress**
	Buffer staff from distractions to their instructional work

Table 7.2 What successful school leaders do (Leithwood, Harris, and Hopkins 2019:4)

[Note: The practices in table 7.2 with asterisks beside them (**) are close approximations to the labels awarded the ten equity leadership practices by Ishimaru and Galloway 2014]

AN EMERGING MODEL OF LEADERSHIP

Inquiry-focused teaching is fundamental to the *Unleashing Greatness* school improvement strategy because it releases and guides our students' curiosity. By developing their ability to manage their own curiosity, our students extend their capabilities as self-directed, independent learners and their achievement is enhanced. This is our collective moral purpose.

As we know from personal experience and the evidence cited in this chapter, leadership practices and strategies hold the promise of embedding pedagogic practices capable of fulfilling our collective moral purpose.

Working with our principals, heads and school improvement teams over the years, we developed four leadership styles and associated strategies that addressed a range of challenges. How to:

- develop, nurture and embed the reform narrative about student learning – **instructional leadership**.
- create professional learning opportunities relevant to each teachers' development needs and that align with the school's development priorities – **adaptive leadership**.
- ensure consistency and rapid development by precise diagnosis of the school's progress along a well-defined improvement pathway – **strategic leadership**.
- nurture system-wide reform through the adoption of a variety of 'out-of-school' roles and the purposeful use of networks – **system leadership**.

Building on this experience and guided by the research evidence, we developed and deployed the styles of leadership strategies described in *Leadership for Powerful Learning* manual (Hopkins and Craig 2018c). Taken together, they provide a comprehensive set of leadership resources for shaping, embedding and spreading productive professional change.

Before exploring these four forms of leadership in a little more detail, and briefly describing their concomitant implementation strategies, it is important to take a more comprehensive view of school leadership in a framework that includes and links together these various perspectives. This is seen in figure 7.1.

Inner ring:

Moral purpose

Second ring:

- Reflective development
- Strategic acumen

Third ring:

- Managing teaching and learning
- Developing people
- Developing the school as an organisation

Fourth ring:

- Enact network leadership
- Lead and improve a school in difficulty
- Lead in a school improvement project beyond own school

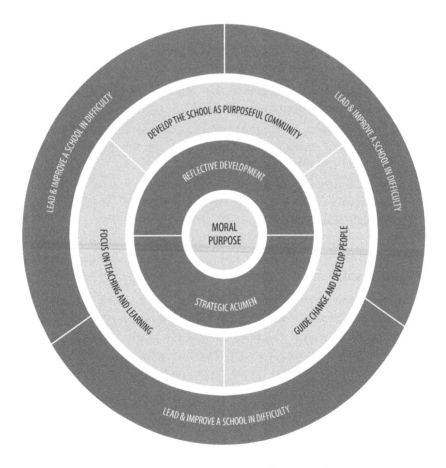

Figure 7.1 The Leadership for Powerful Learning Framework

Moral purpose (inner ring): The model exhibits our inside-out logic. Leaders are driven by a moral purpose about enhancing student learning. Moral purpose activates the passion to reach for the goal and prompts leaders to empower teachers and others to make schools a critical force for improving communities. They create a narrative around the moral purpose that sets the direction of travel.

Reflective development and strategic acumen (second ring): Yet moral purpose is insufficient on its own. As the model shows, the practice of our best system leaders has two characteristic behaviours and skills that bring impact to moral purpose:

• First, they engage in reflective personal development, usually informally. They benchmark themselves against outstanding peers and develop their skill base in response to the context they are working in.

• Second, all the system leaders we have studied have strategic acumen. This means they know how to translate their vision, their moral purpose, into operational principles that have tangible outcomes. They can also think simultaneously in the short and medium term.

Key behaviours of instructional leaders (third ring): The attributes of moral purpose, reflective personal development and strategic acumen are expressed in three key behaviours of instructional leaders (Leithwood et al 2019):

• managing teaching and learning;
• developing people; and,
• developing the school as an organisation.

Working across schools for the benefit of all students (fourth ring): As they make progress on the school improvement journey in their own school, school leaders increasingly assume system leadership roles. They are committed to their own school and to the whole system. Outstanding leaders exemplify the aspirations and commitments embedded in the outer ring of our emerging model of school leadership. They work across schools for the benefit of all students.

The logic behind *Leadership for Powerful Learning* and this chapter is to emphasise the importance of integrating both leadership and implementation in the pursuit of sustainable school improvement. We have therefore begun with presenting both our leadership model, as well as emphasising the importance of implementation.

The leadership model provides both a framework for action and understanding for our school leaders. It helps them appreciate both the purpose of school leadership and how the various leadership strategies complement each other.

In table 7.3, we demonstrate how the leadership style and implementation strategy relates to the various aspect of the overall leadership model. In the left-hand column are the key leadership behaviours identified in the second and third rings of the model. In the left middle column, I have mapped those behaviours onto one of the four leadership styles identified earlier. Then in the right middle column described the implementation strategy related to each of these four styles. There is then in the right-hand column a summary of the research evidence by McREL (Waters, Marzano and McNulty 2003) of the impact of these leadership styles on student achievement.

Leadership model	Leadership style	Implementation strategy	Effect size[6]
Managing teaching and learning	Instructional	Five phase framework	0.22
Developing people	Adaptive	Infrastructure for professional learning	0.21
Developing the organisation	Strategic	Improvement pathway	0.27
Working across schools	System	Networks	0.27

Table 7.3 Leadership for powerful learning

---

6   This is an estimate based on distributing the 21 McREL leadership responsibilities via a content analysis evenly across our four leadership styles.

This analysis allows us in *Leadership for Powerful Learning* to provide a comprehensive approach to school leadership as well as suggesting practical strategies to assist with the various aspects of implementation that we have found in our own work to be of crucial importance.

A FURTHER WORD ON INSTRUCTIONAL LEADERSHIP

We need to continue to remind ourselves that school leaders make a very real difference to student learning and achievement. Because their influence is usually indirect, however, it is often difficult to link their actions directly to student outcomes. Fortunately, the research on the link between leadership and learning as we have already seen in this chapter has developed rapidly in the recent past. Our original definition (Leithwood, Harris and Hopkins 2019) captures the concept well: 'the behaviours of teachers as they engage in activities directly affecting the growth of students'.

Our revised list of the *Seven Strong Claims about Successful School Leadership* (Leithwood, Harris and Hopkins 2019) has already been outlined. Another cut of the repertoire of four basic leadership practices is given in table 7.4. These leadership practices are critically important. They are practices that assemble the scaffolding a school needs for the journey that puts powerful learning in the hands of all students.

Having described the parameters of instructional leadership we now turn to a brief discussion of the Five Phase Implementation Framework, that many of our instructional leaders have found helpful in unleashing greatness.

Core practices	Key instructional leadership behaviours
Setting direction	Total commitment to enable every learner to reach their potential with a strategic vision expressed as a narrative that extends into the future and brings immediacy to the delivery of improvements for students.
	Ability to translate vision into whole school programmes that extend the impact of pedagogic and curricular developments into other classrooms, departments and schools.
Managing teaching and learning	Ensure every child is inspired and challenged through appropriate curriculum and a repertoire of teaching styles and skills amongst staff that underpin personalised learning.
	Develop a high degree of clarity about and consistency of teaching quality to both create the regularities of practice that sustain improvement and to enable sharing of best practice and innovation.
Developing people	Enable students to become more active learners, develop thinking and learning skills and take greater responsibility for their own learning. Involve parents and the community to promote the valuing of positive attitudes to learning and minimise the impact of challenging circumstances on expectations and achievement.
	Develop schools as professional learning communities, with relationships built and fostered across and beyond schools to provide a range of learning experiences and professional development opportunities for staff.
Developing the organisation	Create an evidence-based school, with decisions effectively informed by student data, with self-evaluation and external support used to seek out approaches to school improvement that are most appropriate to specific contextual needs.
	Managing resources, workforce reform and the environment to support learning and wellbeing. Also extend an organisation's vision of learning to involve networks of schools collaborating to build, for instance, curriculum diversity, professional support, extended and welfare services.

Table 7.4 Another cut at the four instructional leadership practices

FIVE CONDITIONS FOR UNLEASHING GREATNESS[7]

The implementation strategy related to instructional leadership is comprised of five interlinking conditions that are in place when schools are on the journey to unleash greatness. The five conditions are shown in the box below. It is useful to note that conditions 1–4 are purposefully directed at changing the work structures in a school. Taken together the first four conditions have a cumulative and positive impact on the fifth condition, the culture of the school. We have developed leadership tools for both enhancing and measuring each of these conditions.

Phase 1	Embed the story of the curiosity journey
Phase 2	Select the key pedagogic strategies that promote inquiry
Phase 3	Place professional learning at the heart of the change process
Phase 4	Achieve consistency in inquiry focused teaching practice
Phase 5	Culture changes and develops to embrace inquiry

When working at scale with many schools we also found that it is most effective to follow a sequenced or phased implementation plan for these conditions – condition 1 is the platform for achieving condition 2, condition 2 is the platform for achieving condition 3, and so on.

We have discussed the detail of some of these conditions earlier and so only comment on those others that require further elaboration here:

- Phase 1: Embed the story of the curiosity journey – see discussion on narrative in chapter 3.
- Phase 2 Select the key pedagogic strategies that promote inquiry – see next page.
- Phase 3: Place professional learning at the heart of the change process – see discussion on coaching in chapter 6.
- Phase 4: Achieve consistency in inquiry focused teaching practice – see page 263.
- Phase 5: Culture changes and develops to embrace inquiry– see page 265.

---

7   Each of these implementation strategies provide practical tools for leaders to use in each of the four domains. They are described in operational detail in *Leadership for Powerful Learning* (Hopkins and Craig 2018c).

PHASE 2: SELECT THE KEY PEDAGOGIC
STRATEGIES THAT PROMOTE INQUIRY

We advise leaders and school improvement teams to initially select high leverage theories of action related to student learning as in the following box.

A high leverage theory of action...	advances learning capabilities and student achievement.
	has almost immediate impact on the school's teaching and learning practices.
	lays the foundation for the next steps in the school improvement journey.

For example, at the start of their school improvement journey many schools select learning intentions as their first theory of action.

Selecting this theory of action at the start of the school improvement journey makes sense for many reasons, including these:

- Harnessing learning intentions impacts on student expectations and engagement in every classroom;

- It lays the basis for differentiated task setting and peer assessment, both of which powerfully enhance student achievement and learning;

- Over time, differentiated task setting and peer assessment influence how the narrative of the curriculum evolves within the school; and,

- The narrative about curriculum moves from simply covering content to encompass sequential, integrated problem-solving activities that deepen both content knowledge and learning skills.

We have also found that learning intentions links well with the co-operative group work theory of action. When these two theories of action are well embedded, that then lays the basis for the progression seen in figure 7.2.

Figure 7.2 Sequencing the theories of action

MONITORING FRAMEWORK: THE THREE-YEAR PLAN

We have also found it helpful to think into the medium term and utilise a three-year school improvement planning framework as seen in figure 7.3 that steers implementation of a theory of action and monitors its impact. The framework provides both guidance and evidence for:

- building the narrative;
- ensuring priorities are selected that produce short-term gains; as well as; and,
- laying the foundations for the next phase of the school improvement journey.

Such a school improvement plan identifies a manageable number of 'priorities for development' that are distributed across three years, pay close attention to sequencing, and come with realistic yet ambitious timeframes. This is a high-level plan that points direction of travel, illustrates the narrative and relates to the school's development as opposed to maintenance structure. The school improvement team is responsible for implementing the school improvement plan.

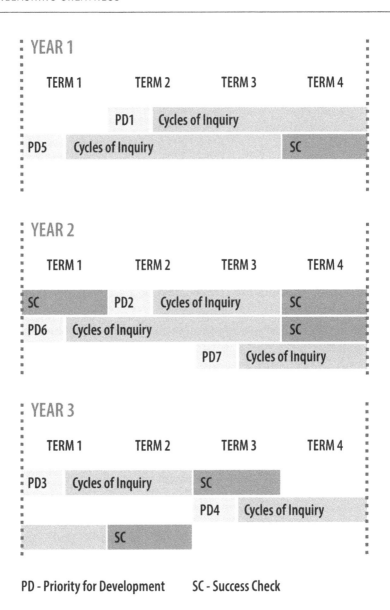

Figure 7.3 A three-year school improvement planning framework

PHASE 4: ACHIEVE CONSISTENCY IN INQUIRY FOCUSED TEACHING PRACTICE

One of the key intentions of *Unleashing Greatness* is to infuse every classroom with the spirit of inquiry. Achieving this fundamentally depends on closely implementing the precise specifications of practice that accompany each priority for development in the school improvement plan. Leaders commonly adopt four deliberate strategies to ensure the specifications of practice are observable in the school as seen below.

LEADERS ENSURE SPECIFICATIONS ARE...	WHAT THIS MEANS IN PRACTICE
Pervasive	They are observable across the whole school and in each classroom.
Precise	They are stated explicitly so that precise implementation is achievable, and is supported as necessary by coaching or other interventions.
Monitored	Close implementation monitoring occurs through Cycles of Inquiry and regular reporting.
Embedded in day to day operations	They are directly and explicitly supported by robust and highly reliable school structures.

Table 7.5

By focusing on consistency, and by tightly aligning activity across the whole school, leaders energise and sustain inside-out school improvement. In particular, leaders establish and defend school structures that reinforce professional accountability *between* teachers. This is ensured when peer coaching is ubiquitous in the school. Vertical accountability 'up the management line' is insufficient for an inside-out approach to school improvement.

MONITORING FRAMEWORK: LEVELS OF USE

We have found Hall and Hord's (1987) 'Levels of Use' framework very useful in assisting school leaders and improvement teams to plan and monitor implementation of high leverage teaching practices that directly and positively influences student learning. The Levels of Use framework describes teacher behaviours that align seven levels of engagement with new practices as seen in figure 7.4.

The framework is used to:

- identify the current relationship between teachers and a selected teaching practice innovation;
- plan implementation of an innovation across the whole school;
- monitor progress and amend implementation plans.

Levels of use	Behaviours associated with the level of use of a teaching practice innovation
0 Non-use	No interest shown in the innovation. No action taken. 'This isn't a priority for me.'
1 Orientation	Begins to gather information about the innovation. 'I'm reading up about it, but not convinced it will work in all my classes.'
2 Preparation	Begins to plan ways to implement the innovation. 'I'm talking about this practice with my colleagues and thinking about how to use it in my science lessons.'
3 Mechanical	Concerned about mechanics of implementation. 'There's a lot of planning involved with this practice. It eats into my time for other important work.'
4A Routine	Comfortable with innovation and implements it as specified. 'I've got this practice working quite well in my junior science classes. I'll introduce it in my other classes now.'
4B Refinement	Begins to explore ways for continuous improvement. 'My students will get more out of this practice now that I've introduced a self-assessment rubric.'
5 Integration	Integrates innovation with other initiatives. See it as adding value. Collaorates with others. 'I've built a good understanding of how this works. I'm coaching two teachers who are new to the school in how to use it.'
6 Renewal	Explores new and different ways to implement innovation. 'We can use cooperative groups more effectively in this practice. We're working on that in my professional learning triad.'

Table 7.6 Hall and Hord's Levels of Use scale

PHASE 5: CULTURE CHANGES AND DEVELOPS TO EMBRACE INQUIRY

Phases 1-4 are purposefully directed at changing the work structures in a school. It matters greatly how we focus, organise, strengthen and monitor the work of teachers and students. Work structures create and sustain an enabling environment. They are the practical expression of a reliable culture underpinned by:

- respect for disciplined action
- a professional ethos that values curiosity and inquiry.

The key message is that a first step in attaining culture change in a school is to establish the structures into which the desired culture grows and is sustained. Existing structures are the product of the existing culture. It is unrealistic to expect that a new culture can take hold if it is grafted on to existing structures. The interactions between the phases 1-4 prepare the ground for phase 5 – a culture of teaching and learning in the school that prizes the spirit of inquiry. It is this cultural attribute that underpins high standards and deeper levels of curiosity and learning. The central point is that one cannot change culture directly, one does so indirectly by changing structures and behaviours first.

MONITORING FRAMEWORK: THE CULTURE GAME

Some years ago, Mel Ainscow, David Hargreaves and I developed a series of new techniques and strategies to *Map the Process of Change in Schools* (Ainscow, Hargreaves and Hopkins 1995). We called one of those techniques the Culture Game which was designed to monitor the development and cohesiveness of the school's culture over time. An illustration of the technique is seen in figure 7.5.

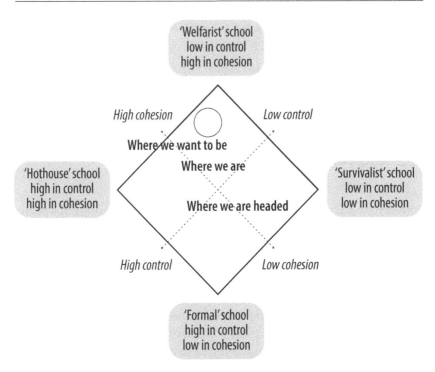

Figure 7.4 The Culture Game (Ainscow, Hargreaves and Hopkins 1995)

ADAPTIVE AND STRATEGIC LEADERSHIP

We have already discussed aspects of adaptive and strategic leadership in previous chapters, so will deal with them more briefly here.

ADAPTIVE LEADERSHIP

Although instructional leadership practices are necessary to ensure pedagogic change, occasionally they are not always sufficient. At times, we have found that there are two other dynamics that leaders must grapple with:

- responding to the resistance caused by the personal and professional challenges faced by educators who engage in pedagogic change.
- creating a work culture or 'infrastructure' that welcomes and sustains change in the repertoire of teaching practice.

To navigate such resistance and social complexity we must look to broader conceptions of leadership, in particular 'adaptive leadership' as a navigation aid for leading school improvement.

It was in 1994 that Ron Heifetz of Harvard University first drew a valuable distinction between adaptive challenges and technical problems (Heifetz 1994). An adaptive challenge is a problem situation for which solutions lie outside current ways of operating. Adaptive leadership is adept at responding to adaptive challenges that require fundamental changes to work organisation, work structures, culture and objectives. Tackling adaptive challenges requires leadership and increasing levels of collaboration.

This is in stark contrast to a technical problem for which the know-how already exists. Resolving a technical problem is simply a management issue. Technical problems are solved by applying existing know-how. Adaptive challenges introduce gaps between where we stand now and where we want to be. To close the gap, as seen in figure 7.6, we will require more than existing know-how.

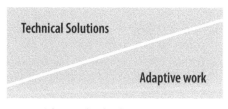

Figure 7.5 Leadership as adaptive work

Among the skills of adaptive work is the ability to discern how old habits detract from our efforts to secure change. Often, we force technical solutions onto adaptive problems and find that the changes we introduce fail to endure and familiar ways of going about our work reassert themselves.

The more demanding challenge is to move from prescription to enduring change in highly competent professional practice. That involves working through the social complexity of change and requires close attention to building teacher capability. Ultimately, adaptive leadership and adaptive work require us to reflect on our shared moral purpose as educators. Drawing again on Heifetz's words (2003):

- Adaptive challenges demand learning, because 'people are the problem' (as well as the solution!) and progress requires new ways of thinking and operating.
- Mobilising people to meet adaptive challenges then is at the heart of leadership practice.
- Ultimately, adaptive work requires us to reflect on the moral purpose by which we seek to thrive and demands diagnostic enquiry into the realities we face that threaten the realisation of those purposes.

We have found that the priority outcome from such 'adaptive reflection' is an honest diagnosis of how well our existing culture and beliefs are suited to making considerable progress towards realising our moral purpose. Having made the diagnosis a deeper level of leadership skill is required to assist colleagues in acquiring 'new ways of thinking and operating' and meeting 'adaptive challenges'.

This is, of course, the territory of adaptive leadership and fostering the 'intrinsic motivation of teachers' is at the heart of it all. Intrinsic motivation is the gift that keeps on giving, because once teachers are in the grip of it, their passion for teaching becomes inexhaustible.

BUILDING AN INFRASTRUCTURE FOR TEACHER LEARNING: THE ACHIEVEMENT OF ADAPTIVE LEADERSHIP

As we have seen in chapter 6, intrinsic motivation is happily a relatively operational concept that is amenable to 'fostering' if adaptive leadership creates the appropriate conditions within the school. We know from Dan Pink's (2009) book *Drive* that intrinsic motivation leads to improved work performance and enhanced job satisfaction, because the individual is enabled to experience higher levels of autonomy, mastery and purpose. These feelings, dispositions and behaviours are self-evidently motivating but do not occur by accident. Adaptive leaders create the conditions in their schools whereby most of their teachers feel this level of job satisfaction, professional pride and personal confidence.

In the schools that we have worked with on our school improvement programmes we have helped school leaders consciously develop structures, processes and ways of working, specifically designed to lead to these feelings of professional and personal self-worth and competence. As part of this implementation strategy, we provide advice and materials for leaders in creating such an infrastructure for teacher learning by:

1. Establishing structures for scaffolding teacher development.
2. Making peer coaching ubiquitous.
3. Creating protocols for both teaching and learning.
4. Incentivising teacher teams.
5. Ensuring that observations are non-judgmental.

All these conditions need to be in place and mutually supportive for intrinsic motivation to flourish. For more detail see the section on adaptive leadership in *Leadership for Powerful Learning* manual (Hopkins and Craig 2018c).

STRATEGIC LEADERSHIP

Our voyage continues. Schools are on an improvement pathway – a journey to excellence. The Five Phase Implementation Framework seen earlier, sets a course for that journey and the 'infrastructure for professional learning' provides a reliable way of ensuring that all teachers can learn. Each school however begins their journey at a different point. A successful school improvement journey commences with an honest appraisal of its starting point. Managing progress towards excellence demands thoughtful and strategic leadership. Progress requires clarity about both the starting point and what is necessary to move from that starting point to higher levels of performance.

To make progress, school leaders need to think of the present and the future at the same time and, of course, the future is less certain and concrete than the present. Making progress in these testing circumstances is best done through the practice of 'strategic leadership'. The concept of strategic leadership is complementary and mutually supportive of the notions of instructional and adaptive leadership already discussed. It just extends the range of skills and perspectives available to those school leaders committed to sustainable school improvement.

Professor Brent Davies and his colleagues have over the years considerably deepened our understanding of the nature of 'strategic leadership'. They define strategy as a 'process of both looking forward to a new way of operating for the school and of developing the means of planning a journey to get there' (Davies 2011). His research points to five critical activities that successful strategic leaders identify as prime activities. These are:

1. Setting the direction of the school.
2. Translating strategy into action.
3. Aligning the people, the organisation and the strategy.
4. Determining effective strategic intervention points.
5. Developing strategic capabilities in the school.

We have already discussed a number of these activities in previous sections. What however adds value to the previous discussion is what Davies (2011) calls 'determining effective strategic intervention points'. Here, the leadership challenge of when to make a significant strategic change is as critical to success as choosing what strategic change to make. Such judgments are manifested in not only knowing what and how but also knowing when and, just as important, knowing what not to do. Unfortunately, there are not many metrics to assist the school leader in making and refining these judgments. That is why we developed the 'school improvement pathway' as a tool to allow school leaders to become more precise in strategic development.

MOVING ALONG THE SCHOOL IMPROVEMENT PATHWAY: THE WORK OF STRATEGIC LEADERSHIP

As we have seen in chapter 3, the school improvement pathway is a performance continuum. It assists a school to determine its starting point, and to navigate its path to excellence from that starting point. The performance continuum describes schools as falling somewhere along the continuum from 'awful to adequate' to 'adequate to good', then 'good to great' and eventually to 'great to excellent'. As a result of the burgeoning school improvement evidence base, much of which is reviewed in this book, we have gained specific knowledge about the combination of strategies needed to move a school and a system.

The school improvement pathway identifies the key issues that emerge at each phase along the school improvement journey and suggest a series of questions to help progress development. These questions assist school leaders and school improvement teams to:

- complete an honest diagnosis of their school's current performance.
- prepare a plan for progress towards excellence.

When systems and schools use this knowledge strategically, they make significant and rapid progress.

SYSTEM LEADERSHIP

We are now able to bring together a number of themes in our review of leadership for powerful learning:

- expressing the moral purpose of enhanced student achievement through **instructional leadership**.
- embracing personal and professional change through **adaptive leadership** that emphasises capacity building and sustainability.
- ensuring the drive towards both sustainability and excellence by progressing on the improvement pathway through **strategic leadership**.

Collectively, these elements lead us to consider system leadership – that is, how school leaders work with schools other than their own to improve the whole system.

System leaders are those heads and senior leaders who are willing to shoulder system wide roles to support the improvement of other schools, as well as their own. As such, system leadership is a new and emerging practice that embraces a variety of responsibilities that are developing either locally or within discrete national, state or regional networks and programmes that when taken together have the potential to contribute to system transformation (Hopkins and Harris 2023). System leadership is increasingly seen as a valuable store of capability and knowledge that can be applied in three ways, as seen in the following box.

SYSTEM LEADERSHIP CAN ACT AS...	
A wider resource for school improvement	Taps successful leaders' capabilities by encouraging and enabling them to: • identify and transfer best practice • lead partnerships that improve and diversify educational pathways for students within and across localities
An authentic response to the needs of low attaining schools	Strong leadership is vital to turn these schools around, but they are often the least able to attract suitable leaders.
A means for resolving, in the longer term, specific systemic challenges	Diverse challenges include: • a limited, or possibly diminishing, supply of well qualified school leaders. • falling student enrolments which increasingly results in non-viable schools.

Table 7.7 System leadership

In *Every School a Great School* (Hopkins 2007:154), I argued that the five striking characteristics of system leaders, through which they realise their moral purpose, are that they deploy their experience, knowledge and skills to:

- actively lead improvements in others schools and measure their success in terms of student learning, achievement and welfare.

- commit staff in their own and other schools to the improvement of teaching and learning.

- lead the development of schools as personal and professional learning communities.

- lead work for equity and inclusion through acting on context and culture.

- manage strategically the impact of the classroom, school and system on one another, understanding that to change the larger system, one has to engage with it in a meaningful way.

Our own research (Higham, Hopkins and Matthews 2009) has pointed to five distinct yet overlapping categories of system leadership and leads to the following taxonomy of roles.

- First, are principals and headteachers who develop and **lead a successful educational improvement partnership** between several schools. These are most usually focused on a set of specific themes that have clear outcomes and reach beyond the capacity of any one single institution.

- Second, are principals who choose to **lead and improve a school in extremely challenging circumstances**. A dual objective of system leadership is to both raise the bar and close the gap(s) in systemic student achievement.

- Third, are headteachers who **partner another school facing difficulties and improve it**. This includes both executive principals and leaders of more informal improvement arrangements who are differentiated from category 1 on the basis that these leaders work from a lead school and support low achieving or underperforming school (or schools) that require intervention.

- Fourth, are headteachers who act as a **community leader** to broker and shape partnerships or networks of wider relationships across local communities to support children's welfare and potential.

- And fifth, are those headteachers who work as a **change agent** or expert leader. The focus is on providing practical knowledge and guidance as well as the transfer of best practice within a formalised school improvement programme.

The skill bases of system leaders comprise a synthesis of those behaviors and approaches previously described under instructional, adaptive and strategic leadership. Effective system leaders have however incorporated this amalgam of skills into a personal repertoire of leadership capabilities as seen in our original leadership model. The additional skill set that they add to this cornucopia is the ability to generate, manage and lead Networks in the pursuit of moral purpose. Networks are the basic unit of change in systemic reform.

ENABLING SCHOOL IMPROVEMENT THROUGH NETWORKS: THE FOCUS OF SYSTEM LEADERSHIP

As we have already seen in chapter 6, networks are the basic organisational unit for system reform. Networks are how a school system becomes a consciously effective learning system. System leaders need to identify which kind of network is best suited to advance their goals. Five types of networks are emerging from practice and research (Hopkins 2022b). These five network types seen in figure 7.5 refer to the roles each type plays in contributing to change within school systems and in wider social systems.

Network type 1	Groups of teachers come together for a common curriculum purpose and to share good practice.
Network type 2	Groups of teachers and schools come together with the explicit aims of: • sharing practice, • pursuing school improvement by enhancing teaching, learning, and student achievement.
Network type 3	System leaders collaborate in knowledge transfer about: • school improvement, • planning and implementing school improvement. Other stakeholders may join with system leaders to implement specific school improvement policies locally or more widely.
Network type 4	Together, groups of networks (within and outside education) pursue system improvement that targets specified objectives such as social justice and inclusion.
Network type 5	Groups of networks collaborate as agents for school system renewal and transformation.

Table 7.8 Five network types

Networks enable school improvement and system leaders enable networks. System leaders empower school networks to invest every school with the capability to deliver high leverage pedagogies that nourish powerful learning.

CODA: REALISING INSTRUCTIONAL LEADERSHIP

This reflection on *Leadership for Powerful Learning* has highlighted the overwhelming importance of instructional leadership in the *Unleashing Greatness* school improvement strategy. It is leadership that realises moral purpose and fuels strategic action. In doing this, we have stepped through four contrasting but complementary styles of leadership each tasked in their different ways with achieving this goal. The underlying proposition being that a synthesis of these styles and skills, but with a predilection for instructional leadership, should overcome both the challenge of 'social complexity' and the paradox of 'change and no-change' so prevalent in many settings.

And so, they should – being as they are based on decades of both accumulated wisdom and the evaluation of best practice. But even this should not lead to hubris.

In helping school leaders and school improvement teams plan for action at this stage of their school improvement journey, the following questions may be found helpful.

- How far are the 'seven strong claims' evident in the leadership behaviours in your school?

- What proportion of their working time are the senior leaders in your school focusing on the four key behaviours? If it is not 75% or above, why not?

- Is there a development or implementation plan in your school that leads coherently and strategically in identifiable phases from narrative to eventual culture change?

The following two case studies are from schools we work with: Wentworth Falls represents the *Curiosity and Powerful Learning* network in New South Wales and the other the University of Bolton Laboratory School network. Here Wentworth Falls and Bolton School share the instructional leadership practices that they have developed as part of engaging in the *Unleashing Greatness* process.

WENTWORTH FALLS PUBLIC SCHOOL, NEW SOUTH WALES

The NSW Department of Education 'School Excellence Framework' states that 'The leadership team maintains a focus on distributed instructional leadership to sustain a culture of effective, evidence-based teaching and ongoing improvement'. At Wentworth Falls PS, we have focused our curiosity and powerful learning journey on achieving excellence in educational leadership. Our school improvement team (SIT) is comprised of the school executive and aspiring school leaders, utilising the skills, knowledge and passion of the entire group to drive towards impactful school improvement.

The pictures included with this case study highlight the specific steps planned by the SIT to ensure that Wentworth Falls remains a 'moving' school striving to achieve excellence through positive progress toward achieving targets outlined in our strategic improvement plan. By utilising the 'school improvement pathway' and the *Unleashing Greatness* framework to guide our planning and analyse our progress, the focus has remained clearly on enhancing student achievement outcomes.

One of the pictures included is a word cloud developed after careful analysis of the 'peer coaching' sessions completed as part of the data collection process to inform future differentiated professional learning for all staff. The word cloud includes the most mentioned words in the lesson observation data. It demonstrates an observable shift in the approach to LI/SC implementation in every classroom.

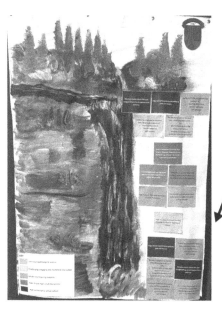

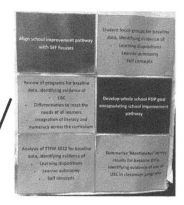

BOLTON SCHOOL, BOLTON

An example of instructional leadership at Bolton School is the scaling up of the teaching and learning groups (TLGs) initiative. This came with its own set of challenges, particularly with the introduction of peer lesson visits, which was a novel concept within the school. Traditionally, staff members were accustomed to occasional observations from senior leadership team or heads of department, but visits from colleagues in other departments were a departure from the norm. To ease this transition, ample lead time was provided for preparation, enabling staff to discuss, adapt and build relationships within their triads. The absence of hierarchical relationships or prior interdepartmental connections within successful triads reduced perceived threats and encouraged an atmosphere of openness.

Throughout this process, staff engagement remained consistently high, owing to the thorough explanation of the initiative's rationale and the steps involved. Staff members came to understand that the heart of this model lies in using lesson visits and conversations to share best practices. Once this became clear, they readily embraced the process and found enjoyment in participating.

Making this approach a central driver for CPD effectively addressed concerns about time constraints. Each division tailored its approach to align with its school's development plan. In the boys' division, the focus was on action research, documented through CPD diaries, with staff emphasising evidence of their progress. In the girls' division, the emphasis was on sharing best practices, and staff received coaching training to facilitate cooperative triad work. A notable distinction from many other CPD initiatives is the significant autonomy granted to individuals in this process. This autonomy has been instrumental in fostering the high levels of intrinsic motivation demonstrated by the staff. Staff members had the freedom to choose which of the three pedagogies to focus on and the flexibility to explore various aspects of their selected pedagogy.

This innovative model has had a profound impact on raising the profile and fostering interest in research-informed pedagogical strategies. Additionally, it has provided the necessary structures and time for staff to work collaboratively, ultimately implementing these strategies in their own teaching practices. The results indicate the beginnings of a transformative journey, as staff members have become more engaged, motivated and empowered in their professional development.

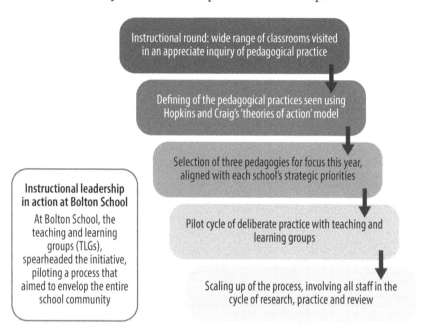

Instructional leadership in action at Bolton School

At Bolton School, the teaching and learning groups (TLGs), spearheaded the initiative, piloting a process that aimed to envelop the entire school community

Instructional round: wide range of classrooms visited in an appreciate inquiry of pedagogical practice

Defining of the pedagogical practices seen using Hopkins and Craig's 'theories of action' model

Selection of three pedagogies for focus this year, aligned with each school's strategic priorities

Pilot cycle of deliberate practice with teaching and learning groups

Scaling up of the process, involving all staff in the cycle of research, practice and review

CHAPTER 8:

SYSTEM REFORM

Hopefully it is clear by now, that the *Unleashing Greatness* strategy is predicated on an understanding a) that schools are on a continuum of development and b) that to fulfil the moral purpose of equity through excellence, then a system view needs to be adopted. This is the perspective taken in this chapter. Three points need to be made at the outset. The first is that the improvement strategy described in this book applies equally to individual schools or groups of schools, as it does to national or local governments and systems. The second point is that unfortunately, most of the time single strategies or policy initiatives tend to be worked on discretely, rather than as a set of complementary and mutually supportive policies as proposed here. Third and critically, the set of strategies that have been selected need to be precisely aligned to the growth-state or performance phase of the school or system. What is needed is a heuristic framework to help systems and schools to reflect on how best to balance these various strategies in a comprehensive approach to educational improvement. Figure 8.1 provides an example of such a framework. It seeks to identify three essential elements of a coherent approach to school and system change. The framework also suggests how these three elements may interact and impact on the learning and achievement of students.

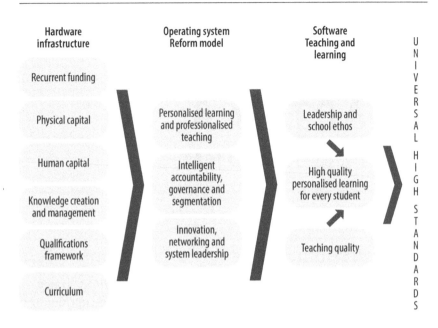

Figure 8.1 Coherent system design

This concept was initially developed by Michael Barber (2005) based on Thomas Friedman's (1999) analogy of a nation's economy being compared to a computer system. There is the hardware – the infrastructure, funding and physical resources as well as human and intellectual capital. There is also the software – the interaction between the school and the student, the process of teaching and learning infused by the leadership of the school. In between the two, there is the operating system, or the strategy for change that the school or system chooses (or not) to employ to develop itself as a whole. The operating system in the diagram refers to that originally proposed in *Every School a Great School* (Hopkins 2007) and reviewed again later here.

Many schools, as well as ministries of education worldwide, assume that there is a direct link between the hardware and the software – as long as the resources are in place then student learning will be satisfactory. This is rarely the case, and the reason is simple. We need an improvement strategy, or in McKinsey's terms, a 'stage-dependent intervention cluster' to link inputs to outputs, as without it, student and school outcomes will remain unpredictable. With it, schools will be more likely to translate their resources more directly into more powerful learning environments and therefore, enhanced learning outcomes for their children (Hopkins 2013; 2017; 2022a).

The same argument goes for local and national governments and systems. The existence of such a framework allows for a more intelligent debate over the policies adopted by different countries in terms of all three elements – the hardware, the software and the operating system and their integrated impact on standards of learning and achievement.

The focus of this chapter is principally on the operating system both at the school and system level. The purpose is to answer the question – how we can put the various elements of the *Unleashing Greatness* strategy into a systemic context and framework? In doing this we:

- First review the PISA related research on stages of development for national systems and then describe a national framework based on *Unleashing Greatness* principles.

- Then, explore the role of middle tier organisations such as local authorities and Multi Academy Trusts in supporting school improvement using the principle that I have termed 'segmentation' (Hopkins 2007).

- Third, champion the role of laboratory schools in leading school improvement at the local level and analyse three case studies from schools in the network.

- Assess the utility of school improvement programmes in supporting system change by examining the *Curiosity and Powerful Learning* (C&PL) and *Unleashing Greatness* programmes at the system level in New South Wales.

- Finally in the coda, consider again Stenhouse's concept of emancipation.

SYSTEM LEVEL REFORM

The evidence base on system change and reform in education has expanded exponentially since the turn of the century. We have learned a great deal about the policy drivers and system reform strategies needed to ensure both equity and excellence in educational systems at a range of phases of development. This expansion of the knowledge base has been fuelled by the advent of international benchmarking studies. Most probably the best known and most influential is the OECD's Programme for International Student Assessment (PISA). Since 2000 when the OECD launched PISA they have been monitoring learning outcomes in the principal industrialised countries on a regular basis. As a result of this work, we have learned a great deal about high performing educational systems over the past two decades. See for example, Andreas Schleicher's (2018) authoritative *World Class – How to Build a 21st Century School System*. Earlier studies such as Fenton Whelan's (2009) *Lessons Learned: how good policies produce better schools* and the McKinsey study (Barber and Mourshed 2007) *How the World's Best Performing School Systems Come Out* on Top, have helped establish the architecture of the knowledge base.

The influential McKinsey studies (e.g. Mourshed et al 2010), have been particularly important in establishing the foundations and pointing the future direction for this work. Mourshed and her colleagues (2010) have drawn lessons from the analysis of PISA results over time to support the idea of stage dependent 'innovation clusters' that follow such a pattern moving progressively from top down to increasingly lateral ways of working (Hopkins 2013). Their analysis builds on our original identification of growth states of schools described in chapter 3, which we then operationalised in the school improvement pathway. In the same ways as schools are at different stages of development, so are educational systems. Four stages of improvement were identified:

- 'Poor to fair': ensuring basic standards.
- 'Fair to good': consolidating system foundations.
- 'Good to great': professionalising teaching and leadership.
- 'Great to excellent': system led innovation.

A brief summary of the progression in these four phases is given in the following sections (for a further discussion see also Hopkins 2016d; 2017; 2022a).

POOR TO FAIR

System improvement journeys in this phase focused on achieving basic literacy and numeracy by emphasising three themes:

1. **Providing scaffolding and motivation for low skill teachers and principals**

   For example: scripted lessons, coaching on curriculum, incentives for high performance, school visits by centre.

2. **Getting all schools to a minimum quality standard**

   For example: targets, data, and assessments, infrastructure, textbooks and learning resources, supporting low performing schools.

3. **Getting students in seats**

   For example: expand seats, fulfil students' basic needs.

FAIR TO GOOD

Improvement journeys in this phase emphasise getting the system foundations in place, focusing on three key strategies that build on those outlined in the previous phase. They are:

1. **Data and accountability foundation**

   For example: transparency and accountability, identify improvement areas.

2. **Financial and organisational foundation**

   For example: organisation structure, financial structure.

3. **Pedagogical foundation**

   For example: establish a learning model.

GOOD TO GREAT

Improvement journeys in this phase emphasise shaping the profession. Systems, to be successful in this phase, need to have the elements of previous phases embedded before progress here can be predicted. The three components of this phase are:

1. **Raising the calibre of entering teachers and principals**

   For example: recruiting, preparation and induction.

2. **Raising the calibre of existing teachers and principals**

   For example: professional development, coaching on practice, career pathways.

3. **School-based decision-making**

   For example: self-evaluation, flexibility.

GREAT TO EXCELLENT

To ensure that there is maximum system capacity at the point of delivery, improvement journeys in this final phase emphasise learning through peers and innovation. In line with the argument of the book, this phase might not be entered into by all systems and certainly not those who espouse top-down or outside-in ways of working. By definition, top-down strategies cannot unleash greatness – they just ensure that all schools regress to the mean. The three broad strategies here are:

1. **Cultivating peer-led learning for teachers and principals**

   For example: learning communities, flexibility, rotations.

2. **Creating additional support mechanisms for professionals**

   For example: provide admin support so that leaders can focus on pedagogy.

3. **System-sponsored innovation across schools**

   For example: stakeholder innovation.

It is also worth noting that at any phase, in its early stages there needs to be a stimulus to 'ignite' the reform programme (Mourshead et al 2010). School systems that have successfully ignited reforms and sustained their momentum have all relied on at least one of three events to get them started: they have taken advantage of a political or economic crisis, they have commissioned a high-profile report critical of the system's performance, or they have appointed a new energetic and visionary political or strategic leader. The role of new leadership is a common and particularly important pattern in igniting school and system reforms. These leaders take advantage of being new but stay a longer time than usual. They also follow a common 'playbook' of practices:

- Deciding what is 'non-negotiable'
- Installing capable and like-minded people in the most critical positions
- Engaging with stakeholders
- Securing the resources for what is non-negotiable
- Getting 'early wins' on the board quickly.

Those countries and schools that utilise this knowledge strategically can make significant progress quite rapidly. This only occurs however when it is realised that:

- Different clusters of policy levers are related to specific phases of system performance.
- This is a sequential process not a la carte.
- Deep implementation is necessary at each phase to ensure a secure foundation for the next.
- Leadership is critical.
- Narrative is crucial.

There are at least two reasons for engaging in this discussion here. The first is that it gives clear examples and some definition as to what an operating system (see figure 8.1), could look like at various stages of system development. The second is to extend the argument initiated in chapter 1 and seen in figure 1.2 about the progression from 'prescription' to 'professionalism'.

As was intimated there, the transition from 'prescription' to 'professionalism' requires strategies that not only continue to raise standards but at the same time, also build capacity within the system. This point is key, one cannot just drive to continue to raise standards in an instrumental way, one also needs to develop social, intellectual and organisational capital. In other words, to unleash greatness.

Building capacity demands that we replace numerous central initiatives with a national consensus on a limited number of educational trends. The four drivers of personalised learning, professionalised teaching, networks and collaboration and intelligent accountability provide the core strategy for systemic improvement in most high performing – 'good to great' educational systems. They are the canvas on which system leadership, so necessary for system transformation, is exercised (Hopkins 2016; 2017; 2022a).

As seen in figure 8.2, the 'diamond of reform', the four trends coalesce and mould to context through the exercise of responsible system leadership. To reiterate the three crucial points:

- First, single reforms do not work, it is only clusters of linked policy initiatives that will provide the necessary traction.
- Second, it is system leadership that drives implementation and adapts policies to context.
- Third, the drivers need to build capacity as well as raising standards.

Figure 8.2 The 'Diamond of Reform', four key drivers for system reform

PERSONALISED LEARNING

The current focus on personalisation, in many systems, is about putting students at the heart of the education process, so as to tailor teaching to individual need, interest and aptitude in order to fulfil every young person's potential. Many schools and teachers have enmeshed curriculum and teaching methods to meet the needs of children and young people with great success for many years. What is new is the drive to make the best practices universal by:

- focusing on curriculum entitlement, STEM and choice;
- systematically inducting students into a range of learning skills;
- making assessment for learning routine; and,
- the promotion of student agency and wellbeing.

A successful system of personalised learning means clear learning pathways through the education system. In this way, it builds capacity through raising standards as well as enabling students to become independent, e-literate, fulfilled, lifelong learners and social beings.

PROFESSIONALISED TEACHING

Significant empirical evidence suggests that teaching quality is the most significant factor influencing student learning that is under the control of the school. The phrase 'professionalised teaching' implies that teachers are on a par with other professions, in terms of diagnosis, the application of evidence-based practices and professional pride. The image here is of teachers who:

- consistently expand their repertoire of pedagogic strategies to personalise learning for all students.
- use data to evaluate the learning needs of their student.
- collectively generate theories of action for teaching and learning through instructional rounds.
- engage in collegial and peer-coaching relationships to embed and extend pedagogic practice.

Professionalised teaching also implies schools that adopt innovative approaches to timetabling and the deployment of increasingly differentiated staffing models, all in the quest for reducing within-school variation. Once again capacity is enhanced because professionalised teaching not only raises student standards but also enhances collaborative professional practice.

INTELLIGENT ACCOUNTABILITY

Because of the resilience and prevalence of external forms of accountability, it is often necessary to compensate by increasing the emphasis on internal forms of accountability. The most common approaches would be:

- The employment of moderated teacher assessment at all levels.
- Bottom-up target setting and use of pupil performance data.
- Value added measures of school performance to help identify strengths/weaknesses.
- The school itself holding itself publicly accountable through publishing its own profile of strengths and weaknesses.
- Benchmarked comparisons giving a more rounded picture of the schools performance, than a single inspection criteria or grade.

It is these forms of accountability that:

- allow a sharper fix on the focus of personalisation.
- develop the professional skill of the teaching staff involved.
- build capacity for internal development.

Consequently, when the balance between external and internal accountability becomes more even, it also becomes more 'intelligent' and appreciative. The assumption also is that over time, as schools increasingly lead reform, internal forms of accountability will become the more important.

NETWORKING AND COLLABORATION

This relates to the various ways in which networks of schools can stimulate and spread innovation, as well as collaborate to provide curriculum diversity, extended services and community support. The prevalence of networking practice supports the contention that there is no contradiction between strong, independent schools and strong networks, rather the reverse. Nor is there a contradiction between collaboration and competition – many sectors of the economy are demonstrating that the combination of competition and collaboration delivers the most rapid improvements. The key features of such an approach are:

- best practice captured and highly specified
- capacity built to transfer and sustain innovation across systems
- keeping the focus on the core purposes of schooling by sustaining a discourse on teaching and learning, and
- ensuring equity, through championing diversity and engaging with and promoting thriving communities.

Although evidence of effectiveness is still accumulating, it is becoming clear that networks build capacity by supporting improvement and innovation by enabling schools to collaborate on building curriculum diversity, extended services and professional support. By doing this, networks help develop a vision of education that is shared and owned well beyond individual school gates (Hopkins 2022b).

The four key drivers provide a core strategy for systemic improvement at the good to great and great to excellent phases described earlier. They also lay the foundation for unleashing greatness at the school level. This is through building capacity whilst also raising standards of learning and achievement. It is system leadership though that adapts them to particular and individual school contexts. This is leadership that enables systemic reform to be both generic, in terms of overall strategy, and specific, in adapting to individual and particular situations. It needs to be made clear, however, that for transformation, system leadership needs to be reflected at the three levels of the school, local and national.

In this section so far, we have focused on system-level frameworks and strategies. This discussion has highlighted the importance of rebalancing top-down and bottom-up change, and focusing on a relatively small number but complementary policy drivers that build capacity, as well as ensuring high standards of student outcomes. These provide the basis for unleashing greatness. In the next section we examine the role of the 'middle tier' or 'mediating level' in sustaining this.

THE ROLE OF THE MIDDLE TIER AND SEGMENTATION

In the last section we looked at system level reform and purposed a framework composed of four drivers linked together through system leadership. The striking feature of this framework is a) that when implemented sensitively, it can build system capacity as well as raising standards; and b) it lays the foundations for unleashing greatness. The focus of this section is on 'middle tier' organisations or what some call the 'mediating level'.

There is currently a myth of autonomy pervading school reform that is reflected in the increasing prevalence of 'right of centre' governments to embrace the trend towards the devolution of school management (Hopkins 2013). The rhetoric that we have already seen in chapter 6 is that if we let schools be free – release them from bureaucratic control and encourage independence, self-governance and making one's own decisions – then they will flourish. This is an attractive and populist image.

However, we know from the evidence of PISA (OECD 2010, Schleicher 2018) that there is no correlation between decentralisation and achievement, and that the world's best performing educational systems sustain improvement by:

- establishing collaborative practices around teaching and learning;
- developing a mediating layer between the schools and the centre; and,
- nurturing tomorrow's leadership.

The McKinsey report on 'Capturing the Leadership Premium' (Barber, Whelan and Clark 2010:8) is unequivocal when it states: 'Finally, differences in what leaders do are not directly related to the level of autonomy they are given. Internationally, there is no relationship between the degree of autonomy enjoyed by a school principal and their relative focus on administrative or instructional leadership.'

This evidence undermines the myth of school autonomy that assumes some inherent value added simply by giving schools freedoms to 'let a thousand flowers bloom', irrespective of their impact on student achievement. This is why we embrace the concept of 'networked autonomy' that was described in chapter 6. The argument being made here is not for any particular form of middle tier organisation, but rather the importance of middle tier organisations in securing systemic reform. The debate should move away from structures, be it a region, district, local authority or multi academy or charter school trust to the functions that the middle tier performs to support systemic improvement.

The 'Capturing the Leadership Premium' report stresses the importance of the middle tier to system reform (Barber et al 2010). It is here where the debate should be located; the discussion of structure is second order as long as it is flexible enough to reflect and support local needs. Barber and colleagues (2010:23) demonstrated that there is a growing body of evidence on the potential for the middle tier to support and drive improvement in schools and student learning. Their review identified five practices that underscore the contributions the middle tier can make.

1. Middle tier leaders can help support weaker school leaders, both improving and supplementing their leadership to raise the overall effectiveness of leadership and management in a school. In the words of one Canadian system leader, 'Many principals cannot be successful without the best possible district leadership'.

2. The middle tier often plays a crucial role in identifying principals' development needs and providing appropriate development support.

3. Managing clusters and lateral learning. For example, in New South Wales, directors of educational leadership, as we shall later in this chapter, are responsible for promoting and managing learning within their network and helping principals in their network put together a plan with specific goals.

4. In systems that go beyond self-identification, the middle tier usually plays a crucial role in helping identify and develop leadership capacity. Frequently this means ensuring that leaders are developing succession plans and identifying talent in their school. In other systems the middle tier also works directly with aspiring leaders.

5. Strengthening and moderating accountability. Despite different performance-evaluation systems and consequences, [effective]

middle tier leaders are all heavily involved in principal reviews and supporting them over the course of the year to achieve their school improvement goals.

If this is the argument for establishing a middle tier within an educational system, it is still important to say a further word about the character of the actual structures involved. This is notwithstanding what was said earlier! In reflecting on the current policy situation in England that favours academisation Schleicher (2018:116), informed by the PISA data, is sceptical about how 'granting greater school autonomy (would) actually lead to better school performance'. He continues: 'The academies show how important it is to combine professional autonomy with a collaborative culture, both among teachers and among schools. The challenge for an academy-style system is to find a way to share knowledge among schools. Knowledge in the field of education is very sticky; it does not spread easily.'

Greany and Higham (2018:12) are even less optimistic about the potential of academies to network effectively: 'With academisation, powers of school oversight are moving from local to national government. This process has been uneven and often fraught. [...] The picture that emerges is of chaotic centralization, characterized by competing claims to authority and legitimacy but diminishing local knowledge about schools.'

In their extensive and well-grounded research *Hierarchy, Markets and Networks*, Toby Greany and Rob Higham (2018) analyse the 'self-improving school-led system' agenda in England and examine the implications for schools. They describe their research as follows (Greany and Higham 2018:10):

This report analyses how schools in England have interpreted and begun to respond to the government's 'self-improving school-led system' (SISS) policy agenda. While largely undefined in official texts, the SISS agenda has become an overarching narrative for schools' policy since 2010, encompassing an ensemble of reforms on academies, the promotion of multi-academy trusts (MATs), the roll back of local authorities (LAs) from school oversight, and the development of new school-to-school support models, such as Teaching School Alliances (TSAs).

As we saw in chapter 6, to Hargreaves the SISS was designed to be radical, empower schools and lead to enhanced equity in student performance. In this respect, his proposals echoed Schleicher's analysis. The irony is that the Department for Education also claimed that their policies introduced using the SISS rhetoric would also lead to a lessening of centralised control and enhanced autonomy.

The reality is that it has done nothing of the sort as these following quotations from Greany and Higham's (2018) book demonstrate:

- *With academization, powers of school oversight are moving from local to national government. This process has been uneven and often fraught. [...] The picture that emerges is of chaotic centralization, characterized by competing claims to authority and legitimacy but diminishing local knowledge about schools.* (p.12)

- *We also show, however, that new local and regional markets in improvement services are particularly incentivizing a focus on the types of knowledge and expertise that can most easily be codified and commoditized (as 'best practices') rather than on the joint-practice development and learning processes advocated by Hargreaves (2012) as essential for a SISS.* (p.14)

- *MATs are commonly referred to as a form of partnership, but we argue that this is inappropriate given a common definition of partnerships as 'legally autonomous organizations that work together'. [...] We argue MATs are best understood in terms of 'mergers and acquisitions', with prescribed models of governance and leadership largely derived from the private and, to a lesser extent, voluntary sectors.* (p.15)

- *MATs have been encouraged to grow or merge by the DfE, in search of efficiencies and "economies of scale". However, our statistical analysis of MAT impact on pupil attainment and progress shows there is no positive impact from MAT status for pupils in either primary or secondary academies when compared to pupils in similar standalone academies.* (p.15)

- *We conclude that rather than 'moving control to the frontline', the SISS agenda has intensified hierarchical governance and the state's powers of intervention, further constraining the professionalism of school staff and steering the system through a model we term 'coercive autonomy'.* (p.16)

- *Our findings are unambiguous in illustrating the importance of Ofsted and the wider accountability framework in influencing the behaviour of schools, suggesting that hierarchical governance is more influential than market or network coordination in England.* (p.16)

These quotes do not do justice to the richness and complexity of Greany and Higham's research and analysis, but they do give a clear understanding of their key conclusions. Their findings are also in line with the conclusions of Schleicher and aspirations of Hargreaves. So let us try to summarise the argument so far about the role of the middle tier in supporting school improvement. To this point, two conclusions can be drawn:

- The evidence from PISA is that forms of collaboration and knowledge transfer are a critical factor in raising standards of student performance in the most successful educational systems.

Yet:

- The design of the middle tier organisation is also critical. Currently in England, the policy framework that emphasises accountability, establishing hierarchies and developing the market militate against this. This of course need not be the case as seen in the New South Wales example presented later.

To ensure the effectiveness of the middle tier, as a means of unleashing greatness and realising both equity and excellence in educational outcomes there are two further features that need emphasizing in the design of any middle tier organisations be they multi-academy trusts, local authorities or regional networks:

- the primacy of teacher development and the reduction of within school variation;
- the embracing of segmentation as a form of networking.

THE PRIMACY OF TEACHER DEVELOPMENT

The argument should be clear by now that any middle tier organisation needs to keep a laser focus on teacher quality. The last two decades of educational research has given us some robust guidelines for action as we have seen in both this and previous chapters. As we have already seen, four stand out (Hopkins 2013; 2017; 2020a):

- It is now clear from all the international comparisons of school systems that 'the quality of a school or system cannot exceed the quality of its teachers'.

- In most western countries the variability between schools is far smaller (34%) than the variability within schools (64%). The implication being that there is a great deal of variance that individual teachers have on student learning.

- The most powerful teacher effects are related to the way teachers establish, implement and monitor the conditions for student learning in the classroom in a precise and reflective way.

- Additionally note the strong leadership effect related to the way a culture of teaching and learning is established within the school.

There is now clear evidence of the characteristics of those schools that have moved along the improvement pathway and that sustain excellence (Ofsted 2009a; 2009b). Peter Matthews' research for Ofsted on schools who excel against the odds has stood the test of time. These are the characteristics that all MAT schools should endeavour to display and be working towards. MATs need to ensure that all their schools:

- have strong values and high expectations that are applied consistently and never relaxed.

- excel at what they do, not just occasionally but for a high proportion of the time.

- prove constantly that disadvantage need not be a barrier to achievement, and that schools really can be learning communities.

- realise that achievements do not happen by chance, but by highly reflective, carefully planned and implemented strategies that serve these schools well in meeting the many challenges that obstruct the path to success.

- gain the trust of parents/carers and the support of the community and are constantly looking for ways to improve further.

SEGMENTATION

To achieve system transformation requires a deeper form of networking that was discussed in chapter 6. I have previously called this approach segmentation (Hopkins 2007). Although I developed this strategy whilst responsible for school standards in the English education system when I was in government, it also applies to the design of MATs and other networks. Segmentation refers to the systematic and strategic collaboration of schools to positively exploit the natural diversity occurring within the system. To be successful this 'segmentation approach' requires a fair degree of boldness in setting system level and middle tier expectations and conditions. There are a number of implications that must be grappled with:

- There is a need to increase the resource of 'system leaders' who are willing and able to shoulder wider system roles. In doing so they are almost as concerned with the success and attainment of students in other schools as they are with their own.

- All failing and underperforming (and potentially low achieving) schools should have a leading school that works with them in either a formal grouping such as a federation (where the leading school [executive] principal assumes overall control and accountability) or in more informal partnership.

- Schools should take greater responsibility for neighbouring schools to build capacity for continuous improvement at the local level. This would be on the condition that these schools provided extended services for all students within a geographic area, but equally on the acceptance that there would be incentives for doing so.

- The incentives for greater system responsibility should include significantly enhanced funding for students most at risk. Beyond incentivising local collaboratives, the potential effects for large-scale long-term reform include:

  □ A more even distribution of 'at risk' students and associated increases in standards, due to more schools seeking to admit a larger proportion of 'at risk' students to increase their overall income.

- A significant reduction of 'sink schools' even where 'at risk' students are concentrated, as there would be much greater potential to respond to social-economic challenges. This could be achieved by paying more to attract the best teachers, or by developing excellent parental involvement and outreach services.
- A rationalisation of national, state and local agency functions and roles to allow the higher degree of regional coordination for this increasingly devolved system. At present there are too many national and local organisations acting in a competitive, uncoordinated and capricious way.

The discussion on the role of the middle tier in this section is intended to highlight its importance in delivering both system level reform on the one hand, as well as securing a strong foundational base for unleashing greatness on the other. The following four statements are directed at multi-academy trusts, but of course have more generalisable applicability:

- Decentralisation by itself increases variation and reduces overall system performance. There is a consequent need for some 'mediating level' within the system to connect the centre to schools and schools to each other – academy chains and MATs can provide this function.
- Leadership is the crucial factor both in school transformation and system renewal, so investment particularly in head/principal and leadership training is essential – hence the use of frameworks such as whole school designs and the school improvement pathway to guide action.
- The quality of teaching is the best determinant of student performance, so that any reform framework must address the professional repertoires of teachers and other adults in the classroom – thus the focus in high-performing trusts on the progress of learners, the specification of theories of action and utilisation of Hattie's (2003) Visible Learning research.
- Outstanding educational systems find ways of learning from its best and strategically uses the diversity within the system to good advantage – this is why capacity needs to be built not only within trusts, but also between them and other middle tier organisations at the system level.

We turn in the following section to the discussion of a particular form of school and/or network that has a long and distinguished tradition – the laboratory school. From the very beginning a century ago, the laboratory school was designed to unleash greatness.

THE LABORATORY SCHOOL AND UNLEASHING GREATNESS

It was in 1896 that John Dewey established an experimental school at the University of Chicago to implement and disseminate his emerging concept of experiential education. The University of Chicago Laboratory School is regarded historically as one of the most distinguished pioneer schools of the progressive education movement. Since then, the concept of the laboratory school that is operated in association with a university, college, or other teacher education institution has achieved an international presence. As should be already clear, there are strong connections between the laboratory school concept and *Unleashing Greatness* strategy. It is these relationships and reciprocity that we explore in this section of the chapter.

From the outset, Dewey envisioned his school as a scientific 'laboratory' staffed with college trained teachers and devoted to research, experiment, and educational innovation. He expected his school – as part of the university's department of education – to perform two functions: firstly, to test and evaluate his theories about schooling and teaching, and secondly, to appraise the findings of these studies and work out subject matters and teaching methods for a curriculum that did not focus on books and recitations but on children and activities. Dewey's aim was laying the foundation for a reform that would revolutionise the educational system and, over time, transform the society into a great democratic community (Durst 2010; Knoll 2014).

The concept has endured and expanded into a global movement (Hopkins 2021). Indeed, Pasi Sahlberg who led the Finnish education reform programme, pointed to Dewey's influence as one of the major reasons for Finland's success (Sahlberg 2021). He maintains that it is understandable that the pragmatic, child-centred educational thinking of John Dewey has been widely accepted among Finnish educators. Dewey's philosophy of education forms a foundation for academic, research-based teacher education in Finland. All primary school teachers read and explore Dewey's and ideas as part of their courses leading to the master's degree. Many Finnish schools have adopted Dewey's view of education for democracy by enhancing students' access to decision-making regarding their own lives and studying in school. Some visitors to Finland, among them the late Seymour Sarason, have observed that the entire Finnish school system looks like John Dewey's laboratory school in the U.S. (Sahlberg 2014).

Bruce Joyce (Joyce and Calhoun 2010), who himself led the laboratory school at Teachers College, University of Columbia, argues that besides the focus on high quality education, the preparation of student teachers, continuing professional development for school staff and continuous inquiry into improving practice, the key function of the laboratory school is as a knowledge producing organisation focused on school improvement. In line with the spirit of collaborative inquiry, Joyce refers to these actions as medium-term relationships characterised by reciprocity and parity, and by commitments to shared beliefs about teaching and learning and issues of equity.

Joyce (see Hopkins 2013:286) has proposed the following four guiding questions as the basis for programme design for the laboratory school:

1. **Clinical skills**: What kinds of knowledge and skill should a new teacher possess?
2. **Programme components**: What are the essential components of teacher education programs?
3. **Teacher learning**: How do teachers learn new teaching and learning strategies?
4. **Alliances**: How will schools work together effectively in a strategic and systemic alliance?

As we began to shape the laboratory school concept at the University of Bolton, we carefully considered Joyce's four questions as is seen in the brief description of the work in the following section. The University of Bolton has developed an ambitious agenda for supporting and contributing to school age education over the past few years. The approach has been informed by four superordinate aims:

1. Ensure continued improvement in the University's University Technical College (UTC), now the University Collegiate School (UCS) and link to local primary schools to provide all through education on the 'knowledge campus'.

2. Develop a sustainable model of multi-academy working that embraces collaborative networks in the local area.

3. Establish the International Centre for Educational Leadership (ICEL) for delivering and researching educational leadership and school improvement programmes, particularly the *Unleashing Greatness* strategy.

4. Then, within the ICEL, create the laboratory school along the lines presaged by John Dewey and Bruce Joyce.

Currently the University of Bolton Laboratory School differs in two significant ways from Dewey and Joyce's original formulation. First, it is not involved in initial Teacher Education but sees this as a prospective medium-term goal. The second is that we have deliberately established a network of some twenty schools around the university rather than just one school. This is to increase local capacity and have impact from the outset. A key element in the capacity building function of laboratory schools is their ability to build alliances and networks on a regional, national and international basis.

All our laboratory schools are part of other networks – be they local authority or multi-academy trusts. As such, they are providing peer support and the dissemination of good practice to their partners. This also aids the development of a vision of education that is shared and owned well beyond individual school gates. And finally, we are also establishing and affiliating with international networks in Australia, China, Sweden and the USA. Constantly looking outside our context and scoping the future must surely be a part of any collaborative reflective journey.

In the early stage of their development, our laboratory schools have identified their expert practice and focus for development through a process of appreciative inquiry, instructional rounds, peer review conversations and visits, and implementing our *Unleashing Greatness* school improvement framework. It is worth briefly highlighting briefly the three structural components that define and scaffold the particular approach that we are taking to implementing the laboratory school concept.

1. We use **instructional rounds**, both symbolically and operationally, as a means of inducting our schools into the laboratory school network. As we have seen in earlier chapters, we use the instructional round to generate a series of theories of action for teaching and learning through non-judgmental observation. The instructional rounds process supports school leadership teams in developing a shared understanding and common language around effective teaching practices. This disciplines and deepen the culture of teaching and learning of all teachers in the school and network and provide the basis of the protocols that ensure precision, consistency and engagement in the classrooms of our schools.

2. We use **peer reviews** between schools as a means of exemplifying, refining and consolidating best practice. Our use of peer reviews is both as part of the induction process and as an ongoing practice that meets Bruce Joyce's *desiderata* for laboratory schools to be 'knowledge producing' organisations. Schools use a similar methodology in the reviews as we do in the instructional rounds. Observations are descriptive rather than judgmental and this data is analysed inductively to generate theories of action and protocols that are then shared across the network.

3. One of the benefits of being a **university laboratory school** is that as teachers go through the process, they can accredit their professional work through a range of post graduate awards for all adults working in the school, be it a diploma, master's degree or the doctorate in educational leadership available through our international centre. As in Finland, we believe that teaching should be a master's level profession. As a matter of course we critically review our work, using action research procedures, to the benefit of our students and the system (Hopkins 2014).

At our current stage of development, we have identified four areas, where the University of Bolton Laboratory School network will demonstrate the principles and best of practice of the concept:

1. The exemplification of research-based classroom practice.

2. As a setting for the professional development teachers.

3. As an example of the practices associated with instructional leadership.

4. Providing a site for the research into educational practice, particularly school improvement and the *Unleashing Greatness* framework.

The following case studies give a flavour of the work.

A CASE STUDY OF THORNLEIGH SALESIAN COLLEGE, BOLTON

CHRIS BINGLEY

Thornleigh Salesian College is a Roman Catholic and state maintained secondary school in Bolton, England. It is a fully comprehensive community of approximately 1600 students, aged 11–18 years old. The staff community consists of approximately 150 teachers and support staff. The school was a founding member of the laboratory school network in December 2020.

Being in the laboratory school network has contributed purposefully to school improvement. This began by reminding us that any system change and whole school design needs to be driven by moral purpose. This helped us to revisit our mission statement and better bring this to life so that it threaded through our school improvement work. We brought staff along in this process by conducting a future search so that we could co-construct improvements to some of our school systems and protocols. Our appraisal model is now based on performance development and professional growth as a result.

The laboratory school network reminds us that development systems which grow a culture of powerful classroom practice are key to school improvement. To achieve this, we have been able to utilise the *Unleashing Greatness* framework. We use a model based on instructional rounds to identify areas of pedagogy that influence deep learning. The identified areas have been organised into a teaching framework and set of teaching protocols that have become the focus of our CPD programme. The programme includes expert workshops, teacher research questions, co-planning in triads and peer coaching. This way of working is seen in figure 8.3.

We also enjoy rising to the challenge of continuing to learn, evolve and improve accepting that school leadership is never 'finished'. We continue to pilot ways in which we can build student agency through how learning is organised and student coaching. We also enjoy collaborating with and building partnerships with other schools so that we can reflect on the quality of education that we provide our students. For example, we have participated in a peer review with other schools in different settings and phases to our own as part of ongoing work within the laboratory school network.

The identified actions from this work contribute to our ongoing school development plan. We are also in a learning network with schools in Sydney, Australia who are part of the Curiosity and Powerful Learning programme that also follows the Unleashing Greatness framework. Together with UK based primary and secondary colleagues, a group of teachers meet three times during an academic year at an international CPD forum. During the forums, teachers reflect on their experiences of implementing the instructional core in their own context. Essentially, each participating teacher presents an exposition of an aspect of teaching and learning that they are trying to improve. It is a powerful collaborative approach to professional learning that offers colleagues a chance to question what they might take for granted, look through a different lens at their own practice and reflect on how they might improve their everyday, but critical, practice. Despite the obvious geographical, phase and contextual differences, it has become clear through the forums that effective teaching and learning is a shared global endeavour.

TSC TEACHING FRAMEWORK

Thornleigh Salesian College

Effective Inclusion Techniques

Done with high expectations, these should help to make learning accessible and challenging to all.

- Use the PSS!
- Chunking learning into small manageable pieces
- Pre-recorded teacher instruction
- Design learning based on real life / local context
- Scaffolding
- Pictures / Diagrams
- Adapt questioning
- Pre-teaching next steps in learning
- Repetition of essential knowledge / task instructions
- Consider amount and size of text

Ready to Learn
Routines, organisation and RUAH expectations

Learning goal and success criteria

'Do now' retrieval task / activity

Teacher Instruction

Literacy: Reading, Vocabulary Instruction

Modelling and worked examples

Independent Practise Tasks
(Individually or collaboratively)

Evaluate
Live feedback and next steps in learning

Formative Assessment Techniques

Frequently checking what students know, understand and can do.

- Retrieval activities
- Questioning
  No hands up to answer
  Hands up to ask
  Cold call - pose, pause, pounce
- Think, pair, share
- Live marking
- Show calling
- Mini white boards

A framework for effective peer coaching

1. Issue ★ What is the challenge for you with your students? ★ What is the barrier to learning that you are trying to overcome? ★ What are your students finding difficult/tricky?	**3. Realities** (during professional inquiry or the lesson visit) ★ What happened when you used the technique? ★ What was is proving most useful for you? ★ What has been the impact? ★ Score your execution out of 10. ★ What would the students view of the technique be? How do you know? ★ Tell me about…X, Y or Z.
2. Goal ★ What technique or intervention have you been using to help? ★ What do you want the students to be able to do? ★ Describe what would success look like?	
4. Options ★ What could you do to make your execution a 10? ★ How do you plan to improve this technique? ★ What could you do differently? ★ What else could you try? ★ What other options are there to use?	**5. Will** ★ What will your next steps be? ★ What can you do about it? ★ What do you need to do to make a start? ★ What action(s) will you take? When?

At Thornleigh we...

Share clear Learning Goals with students

Why?
★ If students don't know where they're going, they'll never arrive.
★ Supports students planning, organising and self-directing their thinking.

* Goal should be focused explicitly on the essential knowledge being learned (not task completion), for example;
  ○ *Specific facts or concepts that students should know and understand and be able to identify, describe, explain, calculate or evaluate.*
  ○ *Procedural knowledge that students should be able to perform/demonstrate independently or with increased fluency.*
* The learning goal should clearly build on prior learning.
* A learning goal is flexible. One goal per period. One goal for more than one period. Multiple goals per period.
* Learning goal should be visible explained and discussed.
* Students do not need to write learning goals into their books robotically.
* Check in regularly on student understanding of learning goals by cold call questioning/using no opt out about learning. Plan hinge moments in lessons to do this. Try and avoid too many questions about task completion such as:
  ○ *Have you finished? Is the table complete? Have you produced enough writing yet?* '*What were/are you learning?*'
* Students should be able to articulate what learning goals are.
* Make it inclusive - a single clear learning goal for everyone (avoid all/most/some)
* To structure a learning goal, use learning conditions, action verbs and successful learning outcomes. *See table adjacent.*

Learning goals: The 3 components	An example...
1: Condition Which learning activity will best allow the student to demonstrate mastery of the essential knowledge? The student will perform the task under these conditions.	By the end of the lesson... After completing the required reading... By the end of the experiment... With the given set of data... During direct competition...
2: Action verb A word that describes what the students will be able to do after the activity. This word makes learning visible: design, construct, solve, analyse, recognise, compare, provide, demonstrate...	You will be able to design... You will be able to construct... You will be able to solve... You will be able to analyse... You will be able to demonstrate...
3: Success What is the essential knowledge that students need to know, remember, or be able to do at the end? This is what you will use to assess and use to judge student performance.	An opening paragraph for a story Addition of integers Controlled and successful dribbling around opponents

Figure 8.3 Thornleigh Salesian College's teaching framework

A CASE STUDY OF BEAUMONT LABORATORY SCHOOL, BOLTON

STACEY POSTLE

In 2019, Beaumont Laboratory Schools embarked on a transformative journey to enhance education by establishing a collective vision of moral purpose in collaboration with all stakeholders. Their approach harnessed the concept of 'everyone' as a catalyst for driving this initiative, with the guidance of the key literature piece *Unleashing Greatness*. This case study explores Beaumont's efforts to align with fellow educators in the University of Bolton Laboratory School Network, engage in rigorous analysis of leadership and pedagogy, cultivate a coaching culture, and establish a robust teaching and learning framework.

THE BEGINNING OF THE JOURNEY

Beaumont Laboratory Schools initiated their journey towards educational excellence in 2019 by forming partnerships with fellow educators who shared common objectives. This collaborative effort was rooted in a commitment to engage in a rigorous analysis of leadership, pedagogy, and the process of enhancing education together.

INSTRUCTIONAL ROUNDS AND THEORIES OF ACTION

As part of their commitment to this endeavour, Beaumont participated in an instructional round. During this process, their laboratory school colleagues collaboratively assisted in the identification of a set of theories of action for the school. This critical step laid the foundation for subsequent professional development and enhancements within the school.

Beaumont Primary School vision statement

The Beaumont family endeavours to create a love of lifelong learning, grow healthy resilient minds and develop aspirational future citizens. Our children will make a difference by leading by example, showing tolerance and compassion within a diverse world and being an active and valuable part of society.

CULTIVATING A COACHING CULTURE

One of the primary goals for Beaumont in this journey was to embed a coaching culture within the school. Throughout the year, they worked diligently on developing more theories of action, using coaching as a vehicle to foster growth in several key areas:

- Vocabulary
- Questioning
- Metacognition
- Collaboration

Furthermore, Beaumont established a valuable international connection with a school in Sydney, Australia, also using the *Unleashing Greatness* framework. This enabled pure pedagogical coaching without bureaucratic constraints. This international collaboration enriched their coaching culture and pedagogical practices.

THEORIES OF ACTION

 1 PRIOR LEARNING

When teachers systematically refers back to prior learning, e.g. last year, last week, yesterday and uses it to scaffold current learning;

Then learner's cognitive load is reduced, their learning is reinforced and they are more confident to proceed.

2 VOCABULARY AQUISITION

When all the adults in the school adopt precise and consistent approach to the acquisition of vocabulary such as subject specific and transferable vocabulary and apply to a variety of contexts;

Then learner's cognitive load is reduced, their learning is reinforced and they are more confident to proceed.

3 COLLABORATION

When teachers consistently utilise paired and group work for discussion and questioning as an expected feature of most lessons;

Then learner's understanding is deepened and they use a range of question strategies and become more confident.

4 HIGH EXPECTATIONS AND PUPIL VOICE

When all adults in the school have high expectations of learners they establish a culture of respect, rapport and value pupil voice;

Then learners themselves feel increasingly valued and they are confidence is enhanced and their learning is increased.

5 ROUTINES AND PACE

When all adults in the school establish routines that are well understood and use this to in-crease the pace of learning ;

Then learners have more time for learning, are increasingly secure in their own progress and work in a calm and purposeful environment.

6 BASIC SKILLS AND TEACHER MODELLING

When teachers take a consistent approach to the acquisition of basic skills through careful modelling, and making the learning steps explicit;

Then learners make more rapid progress and become increasingly confident in the application of these basic skills.

7 SCAFFOLDING

When teachers thoughtfully and explicitly use scaffolding to promote learning in a variety of curricular contexts then learners;

Then learners become more independent in their learning, are able to access the same learning content as their peers and can also use the same scaffolding techniques to teach each other.

8 LEARNING ENVIRONMENT

When the school reflects it's high expectations for its pupils in the learning environment e.g. learning displays of writing and is consistent in it's messaging;

Then learner's learning is continually reinforced and they gain confidence through hav-ing their learning reflected back to them.

9 QUESTIONING

When teachers consistently and self consciously use ques-tioning to probe and deepen learning, to check understand-ing, 'cold call', and are reluc-tant to accept the first answer;

Then learner's understanding deepens and they expand their repertoire of questioning skills to use in their collaborative conversations and situations.

10 METACOGNITION

When the school and it's adults utilize the range of theories of action above in a self conscious and consistent way then a learning culture is established that prizes metacognition;

Then learners become increasingly curious and their passion for learning is ignited.

ACTION RESEARCH AND TEACHER PERFORMANCE MANAGEMENT

Beaumont also integrated action research as a crucial component of their teacher performance management cycle. This strategic move ensured that teachers became lifelong learners, utilising research to develop their own teaching practices and influence school development positively.

LEADERSHIP DEVELOPMENT

Recognizing the importance of leadership development, the Head teacher of Beaumont enrolled in a master's programme in Global Educational Leadership at the University of Bolton. This commitment to ongoing learning and development continuously informs their leadership approach and strategies.

PEER REVIEWS AND COLLABORATIVE PROFESSIONAL DIALOGUES

Beaumont initiated peer reviews with two local laboratory schools – Thornleigh and Bolton College. These reviews provided a platform for collaborative professional dialogues aimed at ensuring alignment with the teaching framework they had developed. This initiative promoted a culture of continuous improvement and shared best practices.

ACHIEVING PROFICIENCY AND SELF-ASSURANCE

Years of dedication and hard work have led to the establishment of solid structures within Beaumont Laboratory School. Elements such as coaching, peer-to-peer reviews, action research, stable networks, and a clearly defined moral purpose have become deeply ingrained and executed with a high degree of proficiency and self-assurance.

FUTURE FOCUS: REFINING PEDAGOGICAL PRACTICES

Having laid a strong foundation, Beaumont Laboratory Schools now find themselves in a position to direct their attention towards the meticulous refinement of pedagogical practices. The upcoming year will centre on refining routines and pacing during the autumn coaching cycle, followed by a transition to scaffolding without suffocation in the spring.

CONCLUSION

Beaumont Laboratory Schools' journey towards unleashing greatness in education is a testament to the power of collective vision, collaboration, and a commitment to continuous improvement. By aligning with fellow educators, cultivating a coaching culture, and embracing action research, they have created a thriving educational community focused on excellence and lifelong learning. This case study serves as an inspiration for educational institutions worldwide seeking to transform and elevate their practices.

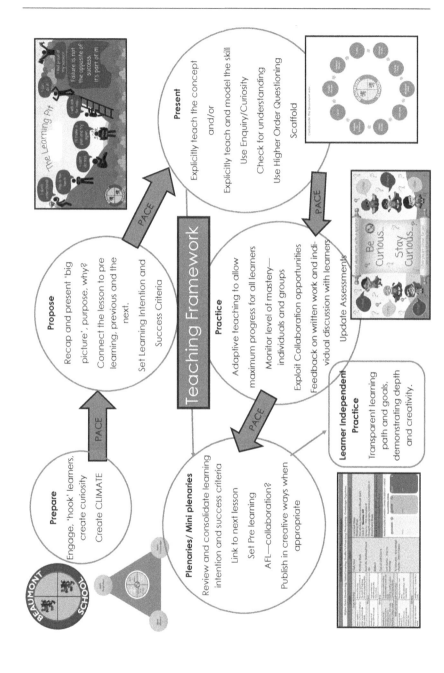

Teaching Framework

Present

Explicitly teach the concept and/or

Explicitly teach and model the skill

Use Enquiry/Curiosity

Check for understanding

Use Higher Order Questioning

Scaffold

Propose

Recap and present 'big picture', purpose, why?

Connect the lesson to pre learning, previous and the next.

Set Learning Intention and Success Criteria

Practice

Adaptive teaching to allow maximum progress for all learners

Monitor level of mastery—individuals and groups

Exploit Collaboration opportunities

Feedback on written work and individual discussion with learners

Update Assessments

Prepare

Engage, 'hook' learners, create curiosity

Create CLIMATE

Plenaries/ Mini plenaries

Review and consolidate learning intention and success criteria

Link to next lesson

Set Pre learning

AFL—collaboration?

Publish in creative ways when appropriate

Learner Independent Practice

Transparent learning path and goals, demonstrating depth and creativity.

PACE

A CASE STUDY OF THE YES TRUST, CONGLETON, CHESHIRE

HELEN PHILLIPS AND NIC BRINDLE

When we as the YES Trust began our journey as a laboratory school, it became immediately apparent that we needed to clarify and unify our moral purpose as a multi-academy trust to ensure that all stakeholders truly understand what it is we believe in and what drives us. Our academies range from primary and secondary alternative provision, to social, emotional and mental health difficulties (SEMH) schools for neurodivergent learners, young people who face mental health challenges and learners who struggle to regulate their emotions.

Our first meeting was with the headteachers of each of our schools to ascertain what they believed was our moral purpose. Each head came up with a similar response but phrased differently. When we, as a group of executive and senior leaders, explored our thoughts more deeply it became readily apparent that what we strive to do is to transform the lives of the young people in our schools and consequently the lives of their families and even whole communities. This was and still is a powerful driving force which defines our moral purpose – The YES Trust ... transforming lives.

We then needed to explore and co-create our core values; what is it that truly defines us and underpins every decision, strategy and action? What is the very essence of who we are? One would imagine that this would take some considerable discussion and deliberation, but in fact, three key strands emerged almost instantaneously as they permeate all that we do as individuals, teams and collectively as a trust. We are:

- Child centred
- Adaptive and sensitive to need
- Authentic in our relationships

These values truly resonate with all our stakeholders and are communicated in every presentation, professional learning session, discussion with other professionals and beyond. This is who we are. Taking this a step further, we were able to establish our aspirational values. It was agreed that we strive for:

- Solution-focused mindsets
- A climate of reflection and feedback
- Intrinsic motivation
- Continual improvement
- A culture of collaboration

We then set out some minimum expectations of everyone in our trust to ensure consistency and clarity, as well as highlighting our commitment to being truly aspirational and ambitious for every learner, regardless of background or individual need. Our aim is to maximise the potential of all, whatever that potential may be.

We see our journey towards achieving excellence as a never-ending progression of self-discovery and awareness, continual improvement and raising the bar. The next stage involved us in developing theories of action through the instructional rounds process, that allowed us to create teaching and learning protocols based upon what is successful with our learners in our contexts. This enabled us to embed a common pedagogy, methodology and terminology across our schools. The result was a celebration of effective and excellent practice that put teachers and support staff at the heart of development. They became the experts in the field, which was not only exciting but transformational! This marked the beginning of our foray into coaching and peer review. These activities generated a culture of appreciative enquiry, feedback and collaboration, centring around the instructional core.

The protocols we co-created have provided a platform from which all teachers and support staff can undertake appreciative enquiry in one another's learning environments, with each individual, regardless of level of experience, having a robust understanding of the meaning of each protocol and how to consider its practical application. Staff now work in triads or quads to discuss practice, research, podcasts and wider reading to ensure that best and next practice is highlighted, celebrated and disseminated. This approach now permeates whole school and whole trust practices.

We, as a trust, are fairly early on in our school and trust improvement journey but, having embraced the Unleashing Greatness framework, we are committed to this exciting, challenging way of working. This strategy engages and inspires our stakeholders and ultimately allow us to do what we already do well even better and in so doing transform lives!

SCHOOL IMPROVEMENT NETWORKS IN NEW SOUTH WALES

We have been supporting school improvement networks in Australia for many years, principally in Victoria and New South Wales, but have had a presence in most of the other states. The initial school improvement design in Victoria built on our original *Improving the Quality of Education for All* (IQEA) programme developed at the Institute of Education, University of Cambridge (Hopkins 2002). With support of the department of education in Victoria and McREL International in Denver, Colorado the programme evolved into the Curiosity and Powerful Learning (C&PL) school improvement programme (Hopkins and Craig 2016a;b;c). More recently under contract with the department of education in New South Wales and with the support of the Australian Council for Educational Leadership (ACEL), C&PL has adopted the *Unleashing Greatness* framework, as is seen in the case study that follows (Hopkins 2020; Kennedy and Exner 2022). As has been seen already, *Unleashing Greatness* has built on the work of both IQEA and C&PL in an organic way.

It is important to stress that neither C&PL nor *Unleashing Greatness* are just another school improvement project, something to be done in addition to what teachers and schools are already doing. It is often said that they are 'not so much a programme, but more a way of life'. Both are successful to the extent that they help teachers and schools achieve their existing educational goals, but more efficiently and with increased depth and precision. There is one pre-condition however that the school and its community is driven by a moral purpose that has the enhancement of student potential as its ultimate goal.

Overall, the programme is designed as an *inside out* approach to school improvement as described in chapter 3. This does not mean that schools ignore the policy context within which they work. Far from it as the programmes align sympathetically with the school development policy agenda of all the states in Australia, the UK and elsewhere. What it does mean however is that the school focuses unrelentingly on the learning needs of all students and builds the learning environment and curriculum outwards from that starting point. In so doing, the school adapts external change for internal purpose.

The programme is built on the belief that successful reform is neither singularly system-led nor led by individual schools – it is best achieved by one supporting the other in an actively interdependent, mutually beneficial relationship. As a consequence, schools involved in the programme network together to share knowledge, skills and transferable practice. These school leaders clearly understand what Aristotle meant when he said, 'We are what we repeatedly do. Excellence, therefore, is not an act but a habit'.

The real strength of the programme in New South Wales is that it is supported by the education department and is facilitated by the Directors Educational Leadership who are responsible for the networks of public schools throughout the state. Directors discuss with their schools whether they wish to join the programme and then support them through it.

The C&PL programme extends over a 15-month period and consists of a series of phases and a culminating conference:

1. Induction to curiosity and powerful learning
2. Establishing the C&PL process
3. Instructional rounds and deepening teaching and learning
4. Instructional leadership
5. Sustaining momentum and conference

Central to the success of C&PL is the ongoing support provided to schools by the Director Educational Leadership, between the face-to-face workshop sessions. There are two main aspects to this:

1. Facilitating network meetings
2. Monitoring the in-school activities led by the school improvement teams

The role of the director is key. They have a critical role in strengthening and moderating accountability to ensure that this is more than just a bolt on programme. The director is the professional advocate and the middle tier capacity that ensures the success of school improvement within the NSW public school system. It is through the director and their partnership with their networks and schools that powerful professional practice is nurtured. Their leadership enables schools and networks to enhance their capacity for positive change, accept the authority to work with and on behalf of the system and embrace accountability within and beyond the school. Above all, the director demonstrates that the school improvement process makes the significant difference to every student in every participating school in the network.

> In the following extract from their paper 'Leading to influence as an instructional leader: A reflection on the Curiosity and Powerful Learning program', Julie Kennedy and Stacey Exner (2022) give a practical example of how the process works.

In the past, there were pockets of excellence across our Metropolitan North School Performance Directorate (MNSPD) but with many networks still working in isolation. There were limited shared beliefs and understandings about quality teaching and learning and limited responsibility and accountability for improved student outcomes.

Then in 2017 when analysing the international tests for PISA (Program for International Student Assessment), TIMSS (Trends in International Mathematics and Science Study) and the national results in NAPLAN (National Assessment Program – Literacy and Numeracy), it was evident that New South Wales's (NSW) student outcomes were declining, and the equity gap was widening. There was recognition that something had to change and change quickly.

So now with the introduction of the school excellence model, the MNSPD has a sharper focus on driving improvement, with the DEL playing a pivotal role in this change. Research now informs our team to drive effective teaching and learning through an enquiry model. This research is directly linked to high impact professional learning to improve teacher quality and student outcomes regardless of their location and circumstances.

In the future, we will amplify our collaborative work and share our expertise to build the Director Educational Leadership (DEL) team's capacity. Students will continue to be the centre of our decision-making, so that every student, every teacher and every school will improve every year.

It is this narrative that has enabled us to proceed with purpose and precision in our leadership of *Curiosity and Powerful Learning* (C&PL) across The Beaches Network.

As participants of the C&PL program, we realised its potential for supporting schools in creating the conditions necessary for continuing the journey of school excellence. Following information sessions we ran with schools in our directorate, five schools indicated their intention to participate. These included four primary schools (small and large) and one secondary school (large, selective, comprehensive) involving over thirty-five school leaders and teachers. Each principal involved in the programme showed strong commitment to build the capacity of their leadership team to drive student improvement and each worked with their teams to create conditions for this to occur.

Our reflection, then, is based upon David Hopkins' school improvement strategy – *Unleashing Greatness: A Strategy for School Improvement* and the eight steps that need to interact purposefully to achieve improvement. In the discussion that follows we discuss these steps with illustrations provided by the principals who underwent the programme and introduced the programme's teachings to their school communities.

CLARIFY MORAL PURPOSE

A first key step which we facilitated was clarifying moral purpose. This was generally something new for our schools to consider and through our professional learning sessions, all of us acknowledged the power of taking the time as a school community, inclusive of students, parents and staff, to articulate this. The Principal of Manly Village Public School, Philippa Becker, provided this insight:

> *When we were developing our school's moral purpose, members of our school improvement team reflected deeply about what they wanted our students to be able to do or to be capable of doing. It gave them a voice as valued contributors and defined a collective purpose on what matters most for our learners.*

The power of establishing this leadership action is linked to determining what the activities will be to achieve the intent. A key leadership action of the school improvement team was to use this not only as a springboard for the next steps but also to ensure it remained central to their school improvement journey.

FOCUS ON CLASSROOM PRACTICE

We believe one of the strengths of the programme is that it gives schools permission to spend quality time focusing on what is happening in classrooms, a sentiment shared by participants in the program. Julie Organ, Principal of Manly West Public School, shared their journey:

Each grade presented regularly at K-6 professional learning sessions with the gradual development of explicit teaching examples particularly in literacy and numeracy using the rubric from intermediate practice to expert practice developing a clear narrative, the pace of the lesson and co-constructed success criteria. We increased skills, by using student, teacher and peer feedback. We then used a novice to master approach, particularly with writing (such as composing texts) and then mathematics (such as learning to use skip counting and representing this on a number line). This model displayed incremental skill development which allowed students to articulate their level of learning and discover what steps to do next. On this journey, teachers developed deeper knowledge and systematic implementation of the most effective strategies to improve student outcomes and to enable our students to become assessment capable learners.'

DECIDE ON THE NON-NEGOTIABLES

As a school leader, it can be overwhelming sometimes being across the policies and procedures required to effectively and efficiently operate a school. As the leading learners, principals are often conflicted about the time required to operationalise these policies to ensure key accountabilities are met. During our workshops, the principals often talked about unlocking quality time to be in the classroom to see and hear the teaching and learning occurring.

Kathy O'Sullivan, Principal of Northern Beaches Secondary College, Manly Campus commented that 'non-negotiables, once articulated and negotiated as essential parts of teaching and learning culture, enable a school to progress along a trajectory of certainty, shared values, and academic success'.

As the principal of an academically selective school, Kathy is acutely aware of the expectations placed upon staff and students to perform at a high level and clarifying the non-negotiables assisted in developing a focused pathway, free of other distractions.

ARTICULATE THE NARRATIVE

We worked with our schools to articulate their strategic narrative and schools found this essential in gaining traction with their school community. When the principal, executive and teachers could tell their strategy and connect with emotion, their enthusiasm and energy for school improvement increased. Just knowing the reasons for a decision made it easier for the entire team to accept the decision for change. Philippa Becker commented that:

Historically our teachers have worked hard to improve student achievement in targeted curriculum areas, resulting in short-term, unsustainable gains. A big shift in our school's narrative has been to focus on a consistent approach to the improvement of pedagogical practice. The theories of action allow our school improvement team to drive this approach, providing opportunities for teachers to really think about their practice and their impact on student learning.

UTILISE INSTRUCTIONAL ROUNDS AND THEORIES OF ACTION

Schools are busy places and principals and their teams can feel like they are rushing from one issue to the other, we know this as both of us have been principals. By the end of the term and sometimes at the beginning, schools find it challenging to maintain a sustained focus on school improvement. We did not achieve our instructional rounds as anticipated due to the coronavirus lockdown with this cohort, although Beacon Hill Public School was able to harness the classroom observations internally.

Peta Hanson, Principal of Beacon Hill Public School, explained that the first theory of action they explored was 'harnessing learning intentions, narrative and pace'. In triads, staff were actively engaged in professional readings, collaborative inquiry, lesson planning, delivery, and observation, enabling them to analyse (using the rubrics in the manuals) key elements of the theory of action evident in impactful classroom practice.

She said:

Facilitating instructional rounds at our school enabled us to critically reflect on how impactful our actions towards achieving the initial theory of action had been. All staff were involved in the instructional rounds process, demonstrating a school-wide commitment to implementing the most effective teaching practices that enrich the learning experiences and attainment of our students. Instructional rounds, with the support of our network schools, assisted us to identify key strengths from our actions to date as well as areas for improvement. This empowered us to collaboratively develop the next steps in our professional development and school improvement journey.

EMBRACE PEER COACHING AND TRIADS

Our schools embraced peer coaching in supporting the acquisition of their chosen theory of actions. The process developed by Bruce Joyce and his colleagues (2009) was established in all five schools. Peer observations were scheduled regularly and became the schools' primary professional learning focus for the year. The peer coaching sessions focused on the observations of teaching, not evaluation or judgment, and observed the consistent implementation of the theories of action. Schools found peer coaching easier to implement when teachers were able to choose the membership of their triad.

Susan Tickle, Principal of Harbord Public School, commented:

During each of the 3-week triad cycles, each member of the triad team would choose a professional reading based on the feedback given from the previous triad sessions for the group to read for the following cycle. This ensured all members of the triad (leader/experienced teacher/ early career teacher) had equal opportunities to be engaged and lead the process each cycle. All triad members gave modelled lessons within their chosen KLA and the target "theory of action" was discussed once all members had completed their lessons. Feedback from all teams was that this increased engagement lessened the supervisor/mentor/ novice bias, thus allowing for more open and equal professional dialogue in a safe environment through shared best practice.

PRACTICE INSTRUCTIONAL LEADERSHIP

We have found that the director's role is instructional at its core. Our focus is setting direction for our networks, leading our principals and middle leaders with a focus on teaching and learning and keeping the main thing 'the main thing'. This outlook reinforces the argument that enhancing learning and teaching is an essential priority for the role of the DEL, principals and schools. Hattie's (2018:174) definition of instructional leadership really resonated with us:

> *Instructional leadership refers to those principals who have their major focus on creating a learning climate free of disruption, a system of clear teaching objectives, and high teacher expectations for teachers and students. It is school leaders who promote challenging goals, and then establish safe environments for teachers to critique, question and support other teachers to reach these goals together that have the most effect on student outcomes.*

Through the implementation of the C&PL program, effective instructional leadership played an essential role in its success. The work of the DEL, principals and school improvement teams in establishing influential professional learning groups that implement their theories of action with a focus on student improvement and building teacher capacity was essential. This capacity-building played a pivotal role in creating impactful professional learning from the inside out.

Susan Tickle explained that:

> *In order to be 'lead learners', all senior executives were paired into triads with an experienced teacher and an early career teacher in their first five years of teaching. This encouraged teachers to know that we were 'walking the talk', and valued the process as teachers in leadership roles. I cannot emphasise the positive impact this had across all triads, and I myself as a principal gained so much from watching my colleague's lessons, as I hope they also took some learnings from mine. The focus was always on the students' learning and engagement, around 'assessment for learning', which we found led us into amazing conversations and research into formative/summative assessment, student voice and quality teacher feedback. This would never have*

occurred in a 'delivered' professional learning on 'assessment for learning'.

EXPLOIT NETWORKING

We both realised that we were central to building the local capacity building of our networks. The DEL role develops the network's narrative with their team and leads as the network's champion. As a result of the program, we created professional learning opportunities for the individual school improvement teams to show their internal ways of working based on the 'theories of action'. This then built the with-in school capacity and consistent teaching and learning protocols.

Julie Organ commented that:

Many of our local schools with representations of principal and executive staff and two directors regularly shared and reported back on their curiosity and powerful journeys across the network in 2020–2021. This gave opportunities for all of us to gain a deeper understanding of the use of the theories of action and principles of school improvement with varying primary and high school contexts using different and authentic focus areas. Teams gained more confidence by sharing specific examples of using triads and instructional rounds in their schools as well as sharing their student stories and professional learning journeys using the Curiosity and Powerful Learning Model.

CONCLUSION

Our schools have been strategically purposeful in introducing Curiosity and Powerful Learning to develop an inside out approach to school improvement focused on student learning and teaching practice. They have been vulnerable, taken small steps, built an improvement team that has developed expertise and a commitment to action underpinned by a deep understanding that school improvement is ongoing and requires continual reflection to 'unleash greatness'.

One of the key strengths of the Curiosity and Powerful Learning programme is the opportunity for schools to share their knowledge, ideas and expertise through collaboration that explicitly aims to improve teacher practices and student outcomes. It is essential to focus on collaboration in schools as it allows teachers to keep on developing and learning throughout their profession and everyday teaching lives (New South Wales Department of Education 2020). Timperley et al (2020) suggest that this form of internal collaboration and professional learning is the most powerful as most professional learning conducted through courses and workshops, external to the school, do not result in the sustained change needed. As David Hopkins reminds us, *Curiosity and Powerful Learning* is not so much a programme but more a 'way of life'. Our schools have clearly demonstrated their commitment to this.

CODA: TOWARDS EMANCIPATION

The purpose of this chapter has been to adopt a systemic perspective on unleashing greatness. We have discussed reform at the system level, reviewed the role of the middle tier in facilitating and energising school improvement and seen practical examples from two of the networks that we support that utilise the *Unleashing Greatness* framework – The University of Bolton Laboratory School network and the Curiosity and Powerful Learning programme in NSW Australia.

As has been argued throughout the book and seen in these case studies, *Unleashing Greatness* is more than just a school improvement programme. It builds capacity as well as raising standards, and by enhancing individual learning skills and independence, in the lexicon of critical theory as seen in chapter 1, 'sets people free'.

As I move towards a conclusion, let me cite the work of Lawrence Stenhouse. It was he who led the teacher research and curriculum development movements in the UK from the late sixties through to his premature death in 1982 (see Stenhouse 1975; 1980). The following two quotes are taken from *Research as a Basis for Teaching*, the book we edited based on his unpublished work (Rudduck and Hopkins 1985).

Stenhouse's writing was characterised by a deep curiosity about the relationship between authority and knowledge. He described the key problem in this way: 'We produce through education a majority who are ruled by knowledge, not served by it – an intellectual, moral and spiritual proletariat characterized by instrumental competencies rather than autonomous power.'

Stenhouse saw the solution as a process of emancipation: 'My theme is an old-fashioned one – emancipation . . . The essence of emancipation as I conceive it is the intellectual, moral and spiritual autonomy which we recognise when we eschew paternalism and the role of authority and hold ourselves obliged to appeal to judgment.'

There are at least four levels at which this concept of emancipation can operate – at the level of the student, the teacher, the school and the system:

- At the level of the **student**, emancipation refers to the ability to stand outside the teacher's authority on forms of knowledge, and to discover and own it for oneself. In his own work, Stenhouse was moving away from a teacher-dominated classroom to a setting where students, unconstrained by the authority of the teacher, could create meaning for themselves based on evidence and discussion and the development of their learning skills.

- The route to emancipation for the **teacher** is through adopting a research stance. There are two aspects to this: first, that research is linked to the strengthening of professional judgment and to the self-directed improvement of practice through peer coaching (Joyce and Calhoun 2010); second, that the most important focus for research is the curriculum in that it is the medium through which knowledge is communicated in schools.

- The knowledge we teach in **schools** is won through research and such knowledge cannot be taught except through some form of research-based teaching and instructional leadership (Leithwood, Harris and Hopkins 2019). This implies a form of learning based on enquiry rather than didactism, a form of assessment based on problem solving rather than standardised tests, and an approach to leadership that cherishes learning and teaching.

- At the level of the **system**, as we imagine a new educational future so we require a new way of working. We need to follow the advocacy of FED, Salzburg and WISE as well as the technical knowledge generated by PISA (e.g. Barber and Mourshed 2007; Mourshed et al 2010; Schleicher 2018; Whelan 2009). We require a different paradigm – capable of realising a future where excellence and equity are ubiquitous. Through embracing the critical theory paradigm and developing a coherent system reform strategy, re-balancing 'top-down' and 'bottom-up' change, the systems that we work can enhance the life chances of increasing numbers of their students.

Through maximising the power of each of these levels and ensuring their synthesis and the integration between them that will eventually lead towards excellence and equity being commonplace, as well as the 'good society'. This is the theme that underpins the discussion in this chapter.

It is the 'good society' that critical theory, emancipation and the principles of *Unleashing Greatness* which eventually and ineluctably lead us towards. I will expand on this theme a little more in the personal epilogue that follows.

A PERSONAL EPILOGUE:

IT IS NEVER TOO LATE TO HAVE A HAPPY CHILDHOOD

It is always a struggle to know how to conclude a book like this. Although intended to be user friendly, we have traversed some complex terrain in these eight chapters. As I re-read the text for a last time before sending the files to the publisher, I have been asking myself whether I have really outlined a sufficiently practical, pragmatic and conceptual framework that leads to the realisation of moral purpose and unleashing greatness.

As I equivocate and as self-doubt begins to enter, I recall a time well over forty years ago when I was a junior lecturer at Simon Fraser University, Vancouver, the place where I had just completed my PhD. Together with my colleague Peter Norman, we were leading a workshop for our faculty associates and teacher training colleagues. I had just read Tom Robbins' third novel *Still Life with Woodpecker* (Robbins 1980). The novel is a 'sort of a love story that takes place inside a pack of Camel cigarettes', according to its blurb. The narrative is quintessential Robbins – as zany, dazzling, and insightful as that description implies. I based my keynote around the themes of the book and received a rapturous reception which of course was all due to Robbins rather than myself. I recalled that moment the other evening as I was wrestling with how to finish the book whilst looking at the stars when taking Echo, our rescued greyhound for his midnight walk.

The overarching theme of *Still Life with Woodpecker* is how to make love stay. Robbins maintains that it is easy to fall in love, the hard part is making it last. As he leads his reader through his kaleidoscopic and unpredictable narrative, he comments on his quest regularly, but quite frankly without adding much value. In concluding the book, he writes this:

> *The romance of new love, the romance of solitude, the romance of objecthood, the romance of ancient pyramids and distant stars are means of making contact with the mystery (his synonym for love). When it comes to perpetuating it however, I got no advice. But I can and will remind you of two of the most important facts I know:*
>
> 1. ***Everything*** *is part of it.*
> 2. *It's never too late to have a **happy childhood**.*

So, what has this whimsy to do with school improvement and *Unleashing Greatness*? It is simple really, all great educators are lifelong learners themselves and have a love affair with learning. More specifically:

1. **Everything counts**: School improvement strategies need to be comprehensive, mutually supportive and all the drivers need to align. This is what I have tried to argue in the preceding chapters – the second part of this book is entitled 'All the moving parts', because all the drivers need to move synchronously within a coherent framework.

2. **It's never too late to have a happy childhood**: This is the joy, and yes, it is joy, one feels when one knows we are making a positive difference to the learning and lives of the students under our care and the colleagues that we work and collaborate with. This is the energy generated by intrinsic motivation and the fulfilment of moral purpose.

Let me embellish and expand on this a little.

EVERYTHING COUNTS

At the risk of repeating the eight steps, let me emphasise the four features of those schools that in my experience have unleashed greatness. The important point is that it is not just one or two or three of these elements, it is all four in concert. *Unleashing Greatness* is not an a la carte menu.

All the schools that have provided case studies for this book have integrated these elements and adapted them to their particular context. Similarly, earlier in this chapter when describing the 'diamond of reform' framework for educational systems, all four drivers linked together and were adapted to context through system leadership. Importantly, all had the potential to build capacity as well as raise standards. So, these four features are:

- **Moral purpose, narrative and strategic action**. All those schools that have unleashed greatness have a strong and pervasive narrative comprised of both moral purpose and strategic action which, as we have already noted, are the opposite sides of the same coin. One is aware of this immediately one enters the school and it becomes increasingly apparent as one wanders the corridors and read the displays on the walls. On entering the classrooms, which are uniformly calm and orderly, the students are fully engaged with their tasks individually or in groups and seem happy. The narrative is omnipresent and seems to scaffold the behaviour and actions of both students and teachers.

- **Taking the instructional core very seriously**. Look carefully at teacher actions in the classroom. They are coherent and purposeful, and the overarching framework is similar classroom to classroom. The teachers link presentation to activity and task seamlessly. Students learning is clearly scaffolded and consequently their independence grows. Within their professional repertoires, teachers have embedded a variety of specifications of practice that they use, as appropriate. In our terms, the theories of action are widely used and discussed.

- **Professional learning and peer coaching**. It is clear that on talking with teachers that a particular form of professional learning is commonplace in the school. It is regarded as being both an entitlement and expectation of being a member of staff there. It is also apparent that the workshop–workplace distinction is fully observed and implemented. Collaborative workshops are about extending repertoire and developing skill. Peer coaching is ubiquitous but not cumbersome or bureaucratic. These encounters are informed by protocols and the follow up conversations are appreciative rather than judgmental. There is also evidence of teacher's action research projects around the school and in the staffroom, and the learning from the courses that individual colleagues have been on are widely disseminated.

- **Instructional leadership**. None of this of course happens by accident. The influence of leadership is clearly evident and distributed. It is a style of leadership that improves teaching and learning indirectly but powerfully through their influence on staff motivation, by developing the narrative and generating an infrastructure that promotes powerful learning for both students and staff. Leaders are evidently conscious of the importance of supporting both development and maintenance functions, and the focus on the non-negotiables is clearly seen.

This is only a snapshot, but the characterisation is not fanciful; it is pervasive and evidenced. As I have just said, these features are well seen in the schools that have provided case studies for this book. This also supports the contention that in school improvement and *Unleashing Greatness*, everything counts.

A HAPPY CHILDHOOD

I used the word 'joy' earlier to apply Robbin's notion of having a 'happy childhood' to education. Let me try and express it in a different way. Throughout my professional life I have fortunately, and more often than not, had positive feelings when entering the workplace. I was looking forward to the day and the interactions to come. Usually, the workday ended feeling tired but content and satisfied at a job (reasonably) well done. On a few occasions when I have felt the opposite – there was a sinking feeling on arrival with a day of drudgery to follow. These emotions are directly related to the workplace culture of the institutions I was entering. Generating a positive culture is the task of leadership. As Michael Fullan once said to me, 'the only thing of real importance that leaders do is to shape and manage culture'. Where the workplace culture is positive then colleagues feel worthwhile, effective – even joyful.

The problem however is that culture manifests itself experientially rather than conceptually and strategically. It is a slippery construct to define, especially in education. As noted in chapter 7, some time ago, we developed a heuristic research tool to measure culture (Ainscow, Hargreaves and Hopkins 1995). This however only indirectly provided us with a means to change culture.

A more direct way of generating a positive culture is provided by Dan Pink's specification on Intrinsic Motivation, as outlined in his book *Drive* (2011). As we saw in chapter 6, to build an intrinsically motivated culture, you need to focus on three key factors (Mind Tools 2023):

1. **Autonomy**: people are trusted and encouraged to take ownership of their own work and skill development.

2. **Mastery**: people see no limits to their potential and are given the tools that they need to continue to improve their skills.

3. **Purpose**: people are encouraged to use their skills to achieve a 'greater' moral purpose.

When an infrastructure is developed that generates autonomy, mastery and purpose, a positive culture ensues, and colleagues have a 'happy childhood' in the sense of a positive or even joyful work life. Once again this does not happen by accident when the workplace culture is positive it is the consequence of purposeful action, as we have discussed throughout this book.

WHY IS YOUR WORK SO HARD?

Unfortunately, an increasing number of teachers and leaders who I meet or read about are not having a 'happy childhood' in their classrooms or schools. For whatever reason, the schools that they work in have failed to unleash greatness and so their work lives are characterised by pressure, stress and surveillance. A few years ago, I was so concerned about this that I informally researched the phenomena and talked to a range of teachers and leaders about their work lives. The common response was that 'my work is so hard'. So, I talked to more and more teachers asking them initially, 'Why is your work so hard?'. These are the conclusions that I drew from those conversations:

- Political imperatives rarely match accurate system diagnosis.
- History of weak implementation means that system foundations are not uniformly in place nor are being built on.

- The narrative of reform although evident at particular points has not been sustained over time.

- Because of its antecedents, teaching has struggled to establish a professional culture built on diagnosis, specifications of practice, collaboration and research.

- Bureaucratic rather than systemic organisational structures and cultures continue to dominate.

When I test these hypotheses out with teachers and leaders in my seminars or at workshops and conferences, I get an immediate recognition, 'Oh that is why I feel that way'. I have reflected much on this and have concluded that these colleagues feel this way because they work within a macro culture or hegemony that is driven by technical, bureaucratic and instrumental ways of working.

CRITICAL THEORY

This is where the narrative of this book comes full circle. In the coda to the first chapter, I introduced Jurgen Habermas's tri-paradigm framework where he identified, contrasted and elaborated three specific ways of learning: the technical, practical and critical. I told the reader that I would return to this discussion at the end of the book and now is the time.

Colleagues feel that their work is hard because a) it is, and b) they are trapped within the technical/instrumental paradigm to which they see no escape. This is Max Weber's 'dark night of the soul'. The argument of this book is that school and system reform should eschew the technical paradigm that is short term and prizes accountability, top-down bureaucratic policy options and narrow outcome measures. Instead, teachers and leaders should embrace and argue for an approach to education that is informed by the values and actions of the critical paradigm. The emphasis here, as we saw in chapter 1 and continued to argue for throughout the book, is a way of working that is:

Critical – transformation	Emancipatory	Is **authentic**, with an
- Critique and liberation	- Critical knowing that combines reflection and action	emphasis on student learning, intervention and empowerment

I have attempted in the book to outline a school improvement strategy that does just this. As I type these words I am once again reminded of the wisdom of Tom Robbins. In *Still Life with Woodpecker*, he memorably distinguishes between criminals and outlaws. To paraphrase him a little:

The difference between a criminal and an outlaw is that while criminals frequently are victims, outlaws never are. Indeed, the first step toward becoming a true outlaw is the refusal to be victimized. All people who live subject to other people's laws are victims. [...] We outlaws, however, live beyond the law [...] When we succeed, we raise the exhilaration content of the universe. We even raise it a little bit when we fail.

This is not to advocate lawlessness but to define a direction of travel, and a set of action-oriented values that condition our work lives. As I have reread the manuscript, I have become acutely aware that what I am advocating is not the conventional policy wisdom in England at least. I feel very much that I too am an outlaw – and revel in it!

Unleashing Greatness is the antidote to the problem of why our work is so hard. Our work is so hard, simply because we live within and tacitly accept the norms of the instrumental paradigm. The argument of this book is that we 'live beyond the law' by eschewing the instrumental paradigm and its control oriented and technical orthodoxy and embrace the critical paradigm. The values and behaviours that prize critical knowing that combines reflection and action, with an emphasis on student learning, intervention and empowerment will surely unleash greatness.

What are the protocols and strategies that enable us to do this? Unfortunately, the evidence base is still not as strong as it could be, but let me leave you with some quotations from a research study that explored the development of a leadership framework based on Habermas' theory of human interests (Quong 2003):

'Emancipatory school leaders, through self-reflection and critique, transcend any interest in control and mutual understanding

335

respectively and incorporate them within an interest in emancipation. A critical school leader, it is suggested, would empower teachers and join with them in a critique of curricula, to expose power relations, tradition, habit, custom, and political restraints. In school leadership the emancipatory (critical) cognitive interest is characterised by:

- *Critical self-reflective and educative leadership.*
- *A need to question purpose and outcomes in order to demystify a direction or policy.*
- *A concern to discover barriers or constraints that restrict people's attainment or cause inequity.*

Emancipatory, critical learning enables school leaders to identify the assumptions and values that constrain the way they (and their staff) think, feel and act. In this domain school leaders address problem-solving by adopting a form of critical self-reflection which may transform their ways of thinking, feeling and acting. Emancipatory learning is a political act. It helps school leaders to separate out 'truth' from 'ideology', and understand how power in social, cultural and political contexts have shaped their thinking. It helps them to understand how others may try to shape their thinking for them, and reveals hidden domination, restrictions and barriers in schools.'

So, as have said, the argument has come full circle. *Unleashing Greatness* is committed to working in the critical paradigm. This is the only way that *Unleashing Greatness* will be realised. All other approaches may achieve initial success but will inevitably regress to the mean.

THE GOOD SOCIETY

The argument is greater than this. *Unleashing Greatness* is, of course, simply about school improvement, but I suggest it aspires to more. As a young trainee teacher, I read carefully Basil Bernstein's writings that 'education cannot compensate for society' (1970). I appreciated his analysis at the time and still do. Nowadays however, I am more optimistic. If we deliver on the values and actions of *Unleashing Greatness*, then I believe that we are also contributing to realising the good society.

So, I conclude this epilogue to *Unleashing Greatness* by reflecting on Amitai Etzioni's (2000) inspirational exhortation contained in the Third Way:

We aspire to a society that is not merely civil but is good. A good society is one in which people treat one another as ends in themselves. And not merely as instruments; [...].

The good society is an ideal. While we may never quite reach it, it guides our endeavours and we measure our progress by it.

The vision of a good society is a tableau on which we project our aspirations, not a full checklist of all that deserves our dedication. And the vision is often reformulated as the world around us changes, and as we change. Moreover, it points to different steps that different societies best undertake, depending on their place on the Third Way.

The Third Way is a road that leads us toward the good society. However, it should be acknowledged at the outset that the Third Way is indeed fuzzy at the edges, not fully etched. But this is one of the main virtues of this approach: it points to the directions that we ought to follow but is neither doctrinaire nor a rigid ideological system.

BIBLIOGRAPHY

Abell, R. G. (1976). *Own Your Own Life*. Philadelphia: David McKay.

Ainscow, M., Hargreaves, D. H. and Hopkins, D. (1995). 'Mapping the process of change in schools: The development of six new research techniques', *Evaluation & Research in Education*, 9(2), 75-90.

Allen, R., Evans, M. and White, B. (2021). *The Next Big Thing In School Improvement*. Woodbridge: John Catt Educational.

Anderson, L .W. and Krathwohl, D .R. (eds) (2001). *A taxonomy for learning, teaching and assessing: a revision of Bloom's Taxonomy of educational objectives*. New York: Longman.

Assessment Reform Group (2002). *Assessment for learning: 10 principles. Research-based principles to guide classroom practice*. London: AGR.

Buisse, A. (2021). *Mont Blanc Lines*. Sheffield: Vertebrate Publishing.

Barber, M. (2005). 'A 21st century self-evaluation framework. Annex 3 in *Journeys of discovery: the search for success by design*', Keynote speech in the National Center on Education and the Economy Annual Conference, Florida.

Barber, M. (2009). 'From system effectiveness to system improvement', in A. Hargreaves and M. Fullan (eds) *Change Wars*, Indiana: Solution Tree.

Barber, M. and Mourshed, M. (2007). *How the world's best performing school systems come out on top*. London: McKinsey & Company.

Barber, M., Whelan, F. and Clark, M. (2010). *Capturing the leadership premium: how the world's top school systems are building leadership capacity for the future*. London: McKinsey & Company.

Becker, E. (1985). *Escape from Evil*. New York: Simon & Schuster.

Berne, E. (2010). *Games People Play: The Psychology of Human Relationships*. London: Penguin Books.

Berne, E. (2018). *What Do You Say After You Say Hello?* London: Penguin Books.

Bernstein, B. (1970). Education cannot compensate for society, in D. Rubinstein and C. Stoneman (eds) *Education for democracy*. Middlesex: Penguin Education, pp. 104–16

Black, P., Harrison, C., Lee, C., Marshall, B. and Wiliam, D. (2003). *Assessment for Learning: Putting it into practice*. Maidenhead, UK: Open University Press.

Bloom, B. S. (1956). *Taxonomy of Educational Objectives. Handbook I: The Cognitive Domain*. New York: Longmans, Green & Co.

Brown, C., White, R. and Kelly, A. (2021). 'Teachers as educational change agents: what do we currently know? findings from a systematic review', *Emerald Open Research*, 3(26).

Bruner, J. (1960). The Process of Education. Cambridge, MA: Belknap Press.

Bruner, J. (1966). *Towards a Theory of Instruction*. Cambridge, MA: Belknap Press.

Brunner, E. (2021). *Find Your True Voice*. London: Transworld Publishers Ltd.

Carr, W. and Kemmis, S. (1986). *Becoming Critical: Knowing through action research*. London: Falmer Press.

City, E. A., Elmore, R. F., Fiarman, S. E. and Teitel, L. (2009). *Instructional Rounds in Education: A network approach to improving teaching and learning*. Cambridge, MA: Harvard Education Press.

Claxton, G. (2017). *The Learning Power Approach: Teaching Learners to Teach Themselves*. Corwin Teaching Essentials. Thousand Oaks, CA: Corwin Press.

Collins, J. (2001a). *Good to Great: Why some companies make the leap and others don't*. New York: Harper Business.

Collins, J. (2001b). 'Level 5 Leadership: The Triumph of Humility and Fierce Resolve', *Harvard Business Review* [Online] 1 January, www.hbr.org/2001/01/level-5-leadership-the-triumph-of-humility-and-fierce-resolve-2.

Comer, J. (1992). *For Children's Sake: Comer School Development Program*, discussion leaders guide. New Haven, CT: Yale Child Study Center.

Day, C., Sammons, P., Hopkins, D., Harris, A., Leithwood, K., Qing, G., Brown, E. and Ahtaridou, E. (2011). *Successful School Leadership: Linking with learning and achievement*. Maidenhead, UK: Open University Press.

Davies, B. (2011). *Leading the Strategically Focused School* (2nd ed). London: Sage.

Doyle, W. (1987). 'Academic work', *Review of Educational Research*, 53(2), 159–99.

Durst A. (2010). *Women Educators in the Progressive Era*. New York: Palgrave Macmillan.

Dusay, J. M. (1981). 'Eric Berne: Contributions and Limitations', *Transactional Analysis Journal*, 11(1), 41–5.

Earl, L., Torrance, N., Sutherland, S., Fullan, M. and Ali, A. S. (2003). Manitoba school improvement program final evaluation report. Toronto: Ontario Institute for Studies in Education.

Edmonds, R. (1979). 'Effective schools for the urban poor', *Educational Leadership*, 37(1), 15–27.

Eisner, E. W. (2002). *The educational imagination: On the design and evaluation of school programs* (3rd edition). New York: Macmillan.

Etzioni, A. (2000). *The Third way to a Good Society*. London: Demos.

Foundation for Education Development [FED] (2022). *National Education Consultation Report*, July.

Friedman, T. (1999). *The Lexus and the Olive Tree: Understanding globalization*. New York: Anchor Books.

Fullan, M. (2003). *The Moral Imperative of School Leadership*. London: Corwin Press.

Fullan, M. (2004). *Leadership and Sustainability: System thinkers in action*. London: Sage.

Fullan, M. (2011). 'Choosing the wrong drivers for whole system reform', *CSE Seminar Series* paper no. 204, May. East Melbourne: Centre for Strategic Education.

Fullan, M. (2015). *The New Meaning of Educational Change* (5th ed). New York: Teachers College Press.

Fullan, M. (2021). 'The Right Drivers for Whole System Success', *CSE Leading Education*, series no. 1, February. East Melbourne: Centre for Strategic Education.

Gardner, H. (2003). *Frames of Mind*. The Theory of Multiple Intelligences. New York: Basic Books.

Goleman, D. (2005). *Emotional Intelligence: Why It Can Matter More Than IQ*. New York: Bantam Books.

Good, T. and Brophy, J. (2008). *Looking in Classrooms* (10th ed). Boston, MA: Allyn and Bacon.

Good, T. and Lavigne, J. (2017). *Looking in Classrooms* (11th ed). London: Routledge.

Glass, G. V., McGaw, B. and Smith, M.L. (1981). *Meta-analysis in Social Research*. London: Sage Publications.

Gray, J., Hopkins, D., Reynolds, D., Wilcox, B., Farrell, S. and Jesson, D. (1999). *Improving Schools: Performance and potential*. Maidenhead, UK: Open University Press.

Greany, T. and Higham, R. (2018). *Hierarchy, Markets and Networks*. London: UCL Institute of Education Press.

Gibson, R. (1986). *Critical Theory in Education*. London: Hodder and Stoughton.

Glickman, C. (1993). *Renewing America's schools: A guide for school-based action*. San Francisco: Jossey-Bass.

Habermas, J. (1972). *Knowledge and Human Interests*. London: Heineman Educational Books.

Hall, G. E. and Hord, S. M. (1987). *Change in Schools: Facilitating the process*. Albany: State University of New York Press.

Hallinger, P. and Heck, R. H. (1996). 'Reassessing the Principal's Role in School Effectiveness: A Review of Empirical Research, 1980–1995', *Educational Administration Quarterly*, 32(1), 5–44.

Hallinger, P. and Kovačević, J. (2019). 'A Bibliometric Review of Research on Educational Administration: Science Mapping the Literature, 1960 to 2018', Review of Educational Research, June, 89(3), 335–69.

Hallinger, P. Gümüs, S. and Bellibaş, M. (2020). '"Are Principals instructional leaders yet?' A science map of the knowledge base on instructional leadership, 1940–2018', *Scientometrics*, 122, 1629–1650.

Harðarson, A. (2017). 'Aims of Education: How to Resist the Temptation of Technocratic Models', *Journal of Philosophy of Education*, 51(1), 59–72.

Hargreaves, A. and Shirley, D. (2009). *The Fourth Way*. Thousand Oaks, California: Corwin Press.

Hargreaves, D. H. (2003). *Educational Epidemic: Transforming Secondary Schools Through Innovation Networks*. London: Demos.

Hargreaves, D. H. (2010). *Creating a Self-Improving School System*. Nottingham: National College for School Leadership.

Hargreaves, D. H. (2011). *Leading a Self-Improving School System*. Nottingham: National College for School Leadership.

Hargreaves, D. H. (2012). *A Self-Improving School System in International Context*. Nottingham: National College for School Leadership.

Hargreaves, D. H. and Hopkins, D. (1991). *The Empowered School: The Management and Practice of Development Planning*. London: Cassell.

Hargreaves, D. H., Ainscow, M. and Hopkins, D. (1991). 'Mapping the Process of Change in Schools', *Evaluation and Research in Education*, 9(2), 75–90.

Harris, A. and Jones, M. (2017a). 'Leading educational change and improvement at scale: some inconvenient truths about system performance', *International Journal of Leadership in Education*, 20(5), 1–10.

Harris, A. and Jones, M. S. (2017b). 'Professional Learning Communities: A Strategy for School and System Improvement?', *Wales Journal of Education*, 19(1), 16–38.

Hattie, J. (2009). *Visible Learning: A synthesis of over 800 meta-analyses relating to achievement*. Routledge.

Hattie, J. (2015). *What Doesn't Work in Education: The Politics of Distraction*. Cambridge: Pearson.

Hattie, J. (2018). *Visible Learning for Teachers*. Routledge.

Hattie, J. (2019). Implementing, scaling up, and valuing expertise to develop worthwhile outcomes in schools (The William Walker Oration), *ACEL Monograph 58:* NSW 2012, Australia.

Hattie, J. (2023). *Visible Learning: The Sequel*. Routledge.

Heath C. and Heath D. (2011). *Switch: How to change things when change is hard*. New York: Random House.

Heifetz, R. (1994). *Leadership Without Easy Answers*. Cambridge, MA: Belknap Press.

Heifetz, R. (2003). *Adaptive Work in the Adaptive State*. London: Demos.

Higham, R., Hopkins, D. and Matthews, P. (2009). *System Leadership in Practice*. Maidenhead, UK: Open University Press/McGraw Hill.

Hopkins, D. (ed.) (1987). *Improving the Quality of Schooling*. Lewes: Falmer Press.

Hopkins, D. (2001). *School Improvement for Real*. London: Routledge/Falmer.

Hopkins, D. (2002). *Improving the Quality of Education for All: A Handbook of Staff Development Activities* (2nd ed). London: David Fulton Publishers.

Hopkins, D. (2007). *Every School a Great School*. Maidenhead: McGraw-Hill/ Open University Press.

Hopkins, D. (2009). *The Emergence of System Leadership*, Nottingham: National College for School Leadership.

Hopkins, D. (2010). 'Personalized learning in school age education', in P. Peterson, E. Baker & B. McGaw (eds), *International Encyclopedia of Education* (3rd ed). Amsterdam: Elsevier Science, 227–32.

Hopkins, D. (2012). *The Adventure Learning Schools Handbook*. Carlisle, UK: Adventure Learning Schools.

Hopkins, D. (2013). *Exploding the myths of school reform*. Open University Press, McGraw Hill Education.

Hopkins, D. (2014). *A Teacher's Guide to Classroom Research* (5th ed). Buckingham: Open University Press.

Hopkins, D. (2016a). Models of Practice 1 & 2. Sydney: ACEL/McREL.

Hopkins, D. (2016b). Models of Practice 3 & 4. Sydney: ACEL/McREL.

Hopkins, D. (2016c). Models of Practice 5 & 6. Sydney: ACEL/McREL.

Hopkins, D. (2016d). 'School and System Reform – An Agenda for Wales', *Welsh Journal of Education*, 18(1), 87–110.

Hopkins, D. (2016e). 'Building capacity for school improvement in multi-academy trusts – from the inside out', *SSAT Journal 07*, Autumn, 19–29.

Hopkins, D. (2017). The Past, Present and Future of School Improvement and System Reform (The William Walker Oration), *ACEL Monograph 56*. NSW Australia.

Hopkins, D. (2019). 'Leadership of Personalised Learning', *Australian Educational Leader*, 41(1), 18–23.

Hopkins, D. (2020). 'Unleashing Greatness – A Strategy for School Improvement', *Australian Educational Leader*, 42(3), 8–17.

Hopkins, D. (2021). What is a Laboratory School? *Professional Development Today*, Issue 22.2, July.

Hopkins, D. (2022a). *School Improvement: Precedents and prospects. C S E LEADING EDUCATION SERIES*, No 12, Centre for Strategic Education, East Melbourne.

Hopkins, D. (2022b). 'The Role of Networks in Supporting School Improvement', in G. Handscomb and C. Brown (eds), *The Power of Professional Learning Networks*. Woodbridge: John Catt Educational.

Hopkins, D., Harris, A. and Jackson, D. (1997). 'Understanding the school's capacity for development: growth states and strategies', *School Leadership and Management*, 17(3), 401–11.

Hopkins, D. and Stern, D. (1996). 'Quality teachers, quality schools: international perspectives and policy implications', *Teaching and Teacher Education*, 12(5), 501–17.

Hopkins, D. and Reynolds, D. (2001). 'The Past, Present and Future of School Improvement: Towards the Third Age', *British Educational Research Journal*, 27(4), 459–75.

Hopkins, D., Munro, J. and Craig, W. (2011). *Powerful Learning: A strategy for systemic educational improvement*. ACER Press.

Hopkins, D., Stringfield, S., Harris, A., Stoll, L. and Mackay, A. (2014). School And System Improvement: A narrative state of the art review, *School Effectiveness and School Improvement*, 25(2), 257–81.

Hopkins, D. (2016). Building Capacity for School Improvement in Multi Academy Trusts – from the inside out. SSAT Journal 07, Autumn 2016, pp. 19-29.

Hopkins, D. and Craig, W. (2018a). *The System and Powerful Learning*. Sydney: ACEL, McREL/Kindle edition. Cambridge: Pearson.

Hopkins, D. and Craig, W. (2018b). *Curiosity and Powerful Learning*. Sydney: ACEL, McREL McREL/Kindle edition. Cambridge: Pearson.

Hopkins, D. and Craig, W. (2018c). *Leadership for Powerful Learning*. Sydney: ACEL, McREL McREL / Kindle edition. Cambridge: Pearson.

Hopkins, D. and Harris, A. (2023). System leadership – emergence and maturity. In: Tierney, R. J., Rizvi, F. and Erkican, K. (eds), *International Encyclopedia of Education*, vol. 4. Elsevier.

Irwin, R. L. and Reynolds, J. K. (2010). The Educational Imagination revisited. *Journal of Curriculum Inquiry*, 40(1), 155-166.

Ishimaru, A. and M. Galloway. (2014). 'Beyond Individual Effectiveness: Conceptualizing Organizational Leadership for Equity.' *Leadership and Policy in Schools*, 13: 93–146.

Johnson, R. and Johnson, D. (2017). *Joining Together: Group Theory and Group Skills* (12th ed). London: Pearson.

Joyce, B. and Showers, B. (1995). *Student achievement through staff development* (2nd ed). New York: Longman.

Joyce, B. and Showers, B. (2002). Student achievement through staff development (3rd ed). Alexandria, VA: Association for Supervision & Curriculum Development (ASCD).

Joyce, B., Calhoun, E. and Hopkins, D. (2009). *Models of Learning: Tools for Teaching* (3rd ed). Buckingham: Open University Press.

Joyce, B. and Calhoun, E. (2010). *Models of Professional Development. Thousand Oaks*, CA: Corwin Press.

Joyce, B., Calhoun, E. and Hopkins, D. (2014). 'Winning with coaching: Strengthening the links between professional learning, CCSS, and STEM', *Changing Schools* (Fall), pp. 8–10.

Joyce, B. and Calhoun, E. (2024). *Models of Teaching* (10th ed). London: Routledge.

Kagan, S. and Kagan, M. (2015). *Kagan Cooperative Learning*. San Clemente, CA: Kagan Publishing.

Kennedy, J. and Exner, S. (2022). 'Leading to Influence as an Instructional Leader: A reflection on the Curiosity and Powerful Learning Program', *Australian Educational Leader*, 44(2), 18–23.

Kolb, D. A. (1984). *Experiential Learning*. Englewood Cliffs, NJ: Prentice-Hall.

Knight, O. (2014). *The Fertile Question*. Stockport: Bright Bytes.

Knoll, M. (2014). Laboratory School, University of Chicago, in D. C. Phillips (ed) *Encyclopedia of Educational Theory and Philosophy*. Thousand Oaks, CA: Sage.

Kress, J. S. and Elias, M. J. (2006). School-Based Social and Emotional Learning Programs, in K. A. Renninger, I. E. Sigel, W. Damon and R. M. Lerner (eds) *Handbook of Child Psychology: Child psychology in practice*. John Wiley & Sons, Inc, pp. 592–618.

Kuhn, T. (1962). *The Structure of Scientific Revolutions*. Chicago: University of Chicago Press.

Leithwood, K. (2012). Strong Districts and Their Leadership. Toronto, ON: Council of Ontario Directors of Education.

Leithwood, K., Day, C., Sammons, P., Hopkins, D. and Harris, A. (2007). *Seven Strong Claims About Successful School Leadership*. Nottingham: National College for School Leadership.

Leithwood, K., A. Harris, and D. Hopkins. (2008). 'Seven Strong Claims About Successful School Leadership', *School Leadership and Management*, 28(1), 27–42.

Leithwood, K., Harris, A. and Hopkins, D. (2019). 'Seven Strong Claims About Successful School Leadership Revisited', *School Leadership & Management*, 40(1), 5–22.

Levin, H. M. (2005). Accelerated Schools: A Decade of Evolution, in M. Fullan (ed) *Fundamental Change*. Dordrecht: Springer.

MacBeath, J. and Mortimore, P. (2001). *Improving School Effectiveness*. Buckingham: Open University Press.

Marzano, R. (2017). *New Art and Science of Teaching*. Bloomington, IN: Solution Tree.

McKinsey & Company (2020). *School-system priorities in the age of coronavirus*, https://www.mckinsey.com/industries/education/our-insights/school-system-priorities-in-the-age-of-coronavirus.

Miliband, D. (2004). *Personalised learning: building a new relationship with schools*. London: Department for Education and Skills.

Mind Tools (2023) *Pink's Autonomy, Mastery and Purpose Framework*. https://www.mindtools.com/asmdp60/pinks-autonomy-mastery-and-purpose-framework

Mourshed, M., Chijioke, C. and Barber, M. (2010). *How the world's most improved school systems keep getting better*. London: McKinsey and Company.

Miujs, D. and Reynolds, D. (2018) *Effective Teaching, Research and Practice 4th edn*. London: Paul Chapman.

New South Wales Department of Education (2020). https://education.nsw.gov.au/teaching-and-learning/school-excellence-and-accountability/school-excellence-in-action/school-improvement-and-excellence.

Nunnery, J. A. (1998). Reform ideology and the locus of development problem in educational restructuring. *Education and Urban Society*, 30(3), 277–95.

Office for Standards in Education (2009a). *Twelve Outstanding Secondary Schools: Excelling Against the Odds* [Report]. London: Ofsted

Office for Standards in Education (2009b). *Twenty Outstanding Primary Schools: Excelling Against the Odds* [Report]. Manchester: Ofsted.

Organisation for Economic Co-operation and Development (2010). *PISA 2009 Results: What Makes a School Successful? Resources, Policies and Practices*. Paris: OECD.

OECD (2018). *Equity in Education. Breaking Down Barriers to Social Mobility*. Paris: OECD.

Oxford University Department of Education (2021). 'Programme for International Student Assessment (PISA) 2021'. https://www.education.ox.ac.uk/programme-for-international-student-assessment-pisa-2021/.

Pinar, W. and Irwin, R. (2004). *Curriculum in a New Key: The Collected Works of Ted T. Aoki*. London: Routledge.

Pink, D. (2011). *Drive: The Surprising Truth About What Motivates Us*. London: Canongate.

Pollard, A. et al. (2018). *Reflective Teaching in Schools*. London: Bloomsbury.

Pont, B., Nusche, D., Moorman, H. (2008a). Improving school leadership. In: Policy and Practice, vol. 1. OECD Publications, Paris.

Pont, B., Nusche, D., Hopkins, D. (2008b). Improving school leadership. In: Case Studies on System Leadership, vol. 1. OECD Publications, Paris.

Powell, J. (2010). *The new Machiavelli: How to wield power in the modern world*. Vintage Books.

Quong, T. (2003). *School Leadership and Cognitive Interests*. Doctor of Philosophy Dissertation. University of Southern Queensland, Australia.

Reynolds, D., Stringfield, S. and Schaffer, E. (2006). 'The High Reliability Schools Project: Some preliminary results and analyses', in J. Chrispeels and A. Harris (eds.), *School improvement: International perspectives*. London: Routledge, pp. 56–76.

Robbins, T. (1980). *Still Life with Woodpecker*. New York: Bantam Books.

Robinson, V. (2007). *The Impact of Leadership on Student Outcomes: Making Sense of the Evidence*. Australian Council for Educational Research.

Robinson, V., Lloyd, C. and Rowe, K. (2008). 'The Impact of Leadership on Student Outcomes: An Analysis of the Differential Effects of Leadership Types', *Educational Administration Quarterly*, 44(5), 635–74.

Rogers, C. R. (1977). *Carl Rogers on Personal Power*. Delacorte.

Rosenshine, B. (2012). Principles of Instruction: Research-Based Strategies That All Teachers Should Know. *American Educator*, 36(1), pp. 12-19, 39.

Rudduck, J. and Hopkins, D. (1985). *Research as a Basis for Teaching*. London: Heinemann.

Rutter, M., Maughan, B., Mortimore, P. and Ouston, J., with Smith, A. (1979). *Fifteen Thousand Hours*. Open Books.

Ryan, R. and Deci, E. (2000). 'Intrinsic and Extrinsic Motivations: Classic Definitions and New Directions', *Contemporary Educational Psychology*, 25, 54–67.

Sahlberg, P. (2012). *Global Educational Reform Movement is here!* https://pasisahlberg.com/global-educational-reform-movement-is-here/.

Sahlberg, P. (2014). 'Five U.S. innovations that helped Finland's schools improve but that American reformers now ignore', *Washington Post*, 24 July.

Sahlberg, P. (2021). *Finnish Lessons 3.0: What can the world learn from educational change in Finland?* New York: Teachers College Press.

Sahlberg, P. (2022). Does the pandemic help us make education more equitable? *Educational Research for Policy and Practice*, 20, 11–18.

Salzburg Global Seminar. (2022). *The Salzburg Statement for Educational Transformation.* www.salburgglobal.org/go/education.

Schleicher, A. (2018). *World Class – How to build a 21st century school system.* Paris: OECD.

Schmuck, R. A. and Runkel, P. J. (1985). *The handbook of organizational development in schools*, 3rd edn, Palo Alto, California.

Simms, E. (2006). *Deep learning.* London: Specialist Schools and Academies Trust.

Sizer, T. R. (1989) Diverse practice, shared ides. The essential school. In H. Walberg and J. Lane (eds.) *Organizing for Learning: Towards the Twenty First Century.* Reston, VA: NASSP.

Slavin, R. E. (1996). *Education for All.* Lisse, The Netherlands: Swets and Zeitlinger.

Slavin, R. E., Madden, N. A., Dolan, L. J. and Wasik, B. A. (1996). *Every Child, Every School: Success for All.* Thousand Oaks, CA: Corwin.

Slavin, R. E. and Madden, N. (2010). *Two Million Children: Success for All.* Thousand Oaks: Sage.

Slavin, R. E. and Madden, N. A. (2013). 'Taking Success for All to Scale', *Phi Delta Kappan*, 95(3), pp. 51–5.

Spalding, E. and Wilson, A. (2002). Demystifying Reflection: A Study of Pedagogical Strategies that Encourage Reflective Journal Writing. Teachers College Record, 104(7), 1393–1421.

Stenhouse, L. (1975). *An Introduction to Curriculum Research and Development.* London: Heinemann Educational Books.

Stenhouse, L. (ed) (1980). *Curriculum Research and Development in Action.* London: Heinemann Educational Books.

Stewart, I. and Joines, V. (2000). *TA Today*. Nottingham: Lifespace Publishing.

Stringfield, S., Ross, S. and Smith, L. (eds.). (1996). *Bold plans for school restructuring: The New American Schools designs*. Mahwah, NJ: Lawrence Erlbaum Associates.

Stringfield, S., Reynolds, D. and Schaffer, E. (2008). Improving secondary students' academic achievement through a focus on reform reliability: 4- and 9-year findings from the High Reliability Schools project. *School Effectiveness and School Improvement*, 19(4), 409–28.

Stringfield, S., Reynolds, D. and Schaffer, E. (2010). *Toward high reliability, high quality public schools*. Invited paper presented at the Best in the World Education Consortium. Denver: McREL.

Stringfield, S. and Nunnery, J. (2010). 'Whole school designs for enhancing student achievement', in P. Peterson, E. Baker and B. McGaw (eds), *International Encyclopedia of Education* (3rd ed), Amsterdam: Elsevier Science (pp. 303–9).

Structural Learning (2021). *Scaffolding in Education: A Teacher's Guide*. https://www.structural-learning.com/post/scaffolding-in-education-a-teachers-guide.

Timperley, H., Ell, F., Fevre, D. L. and Twyford, K. (2020). *Leading Professinal Learning – Practical strategies for impact in schools*. Camberwell, Victoria: ACER Press.

Turner M. (1998). *The Literary Mind: The Origins of Thought and Language*. Oxford University Press.

Tyler, R. (1949). *Basic Principles of Curriculum and Instruction*. Chicago: University of Chicago Press.

van Velzen, W., Miles, M., Ekholm, M., Hameyer, U., and Robin, D. (1985). *Making School Improvement Work – A Conceptual Guide to Practice*. Leuven, Belgium: ACCO.

Vygotsky, L. S. (1962). *Thought and Language*. Cambridge, MA: MIT Press.

Waters, T., Marzano, R. and McNulty, B. (2003). *Balanced Leadership*. Denver, CO: McREL.

Weick, K. E. (1985). 'Sources of order in underorganized systems: themes in recent organizational theory', in Y. S. Lincoln (ed.), *Organizational Theory and Inquiry*. Sage.

West, M. (2000). 'Leadership for sustained school improvement', in K. Myers and K. Seashore Louis, (eds), *Perspectives on School Leadership*. Open University Press.

WISE (2022). *Education Reimagined: Leadership for a New Era*. East Melbourne, Victoria: Centre for Strategic Education.

Whelan, F. (2009). *Lessons learned: how good policies produce better schools*, Fenton Whelan, London (published privately).

Wiliam, D. (2009). *Assessment for learning: Why, what and how?* London: Institute of Education.

Wood, D. (2007). *How Children Think and Learn (2nd edn.* Oxford: Basil Blackwell.

World Bank (2018). *World Bank Education Overview (English)*. Washington, DC: World Bank Group.